"Congratulations to Sas  retelling of her journey Motivated by her weste tional Mongolian medicine and committed to humanitarian pursuits by her Quaker roots, her search for medical knowledge turns into a spiritual quest when she is confronted by an ancient shamanic ritual, a dream come to life. Sas's fascinating book is a remarkable woman's story of finding perhaps her own mystical connections from past lives to a country and place that could not be more incongruent to her home in the woods of Vermont. Sas's written word is up close and personal; one can almost smell the freshly made reindeer milk tea, recline on reindeer hides, and smell the burning of juniper incense.

I have nothing but the greatest respect for Sas Carey and her acts of great kindness and caring. She is doing God's work and I think she has, in the process, found a little bit of God's country on this earth, and somehow it's taken on a whole different meaning as she tells it. Something that has enriched all of us for the sharing of her story. A great read."

— SANJ ALTAN
President of the Mongol-American Cultural Association

"Sas Carey travels from Vermont to Khovsgol each year to pursue her calling to harmonize modern and traditional medicine. Through her journey she makes contact with the spirit world in a way that brings joy to her life. As a person who grew up in our beautiful Khovsgol province, I deeply share the existence of the two worlds depicted in the book—physical and spiritual—and enjoyed Sas Carey's book very much."

— OYUNGEREL TSEDEVDAMBA
Mongolian Minister of Culture, Tourism, and Sports
Member of Parliament

12/12

Priscilla,
May I introduce you to my other family circle?
Love,
Sas

Reindeer Herders in My Heart

Sas Carey

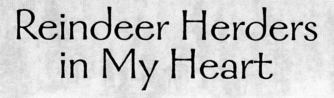

Reindeer Herders in My Heart

Stories of Healing Journeys in Mongolia

Sas Carey

WREN SONG BOOKS
MIDDLEBURY, VERMONT

Reindeer Herders in My Heart
First Edition, November 2012

All rights reserved. No part of this publication may be reproduced, stored in a retrieval system, or transmitted, in any form or by any means, electronic, mechanical, photocopying, recording, or otherwise, without the written prior permission of the author.

Text copyright © 2012 by Sas Carey
Design by Winslow Colwell/WColwell Design

This book was published with a grant from The Shelley & Donald Rubin Foundation. Fifty percent of the proceeds will go to Nomadicare (nomadicare.org).

Front cover: Bayardalai or "Jujigiin", son of Ganbat and Ganbat of the East Taiga, leads one of the family reindeer. Photo © Fred Thodal
Title page: In the East Taiga, a reindeer meets his namesake for the first time—Sas meets Sas. Photo Batbayar Sumkhuu © Nomadicare
Back cover: Elder Punsil of the East Taiga hitches her reindeer to her urts. © Fred Thodal
Author photo © Fred Thodal

Published in the United States by Wren Song Press
PO Box 6
East Middlebury, Vermont 05740
United States of America

The text of this publication was set in Janson Text.

ISBN: 978-0-9753706-6-7
Library of Congress Control Number: 2012953666

1. Sas Carey—Vermont—Memoir. 2. Dukha (Asian people)—Social life and customs. 3. Tsaatan (Asian people)—Religion. 4. Reindeer herding—Mongolia—taiga. 5. Shamanism—Mongolia—taiga. 6. Travel—Mongolia—taiga. I. Title.

Table of Contents

PROLOGUE xi

BEFORE 2003 1

2003 5

2004 17

2005 41

2006 45

2007 89

2008 121

2009 169

2010 187

APPENDICES

GLOSSARY 204   NAMES OF CONTACTS 207
ISSUES THAT AFFECT THE CULTURAL SURVIVAL OF THE DUKHAS 211
REASONS FOR ALCOHOL ABUSE IN MONGOLIA 211
MONGOLIAN SUPPORT AND TRAVEL 211
BIBLIOGRAPHY 212   ACKNOWLEDGMENTS 215
ABOUT THE AUTHOR 216

To my father, Harold F. Carey,
who taught me to love adventure

And my mother, Ann T. Carey,
who taught me to love

Gosta and Sas meet in his urts at Meng Bulag, West Taiga.

photo credit: Dan Plumley

PROLOGUE

> We are sleeping on one ground.
> We need to pray for the mountains,
> the rivers, and the sky.
> – Gosta

Healing the Shaman

At the edge of Siberia, in the *taiga* forest of northern Mongolia, we are camping beside a Siberian tipi called an *urts* belonging to Gosta. He is the elder shaman of the Dukha reindeer herders. Smoke rises from the chimney of the urts, where I imagine Gosta's niece, Khanda, is boiling water on the wood stove for morning milk tea.

Three years ago I interviewed Gosta for the first time. He didn't seem too anxious to talk about the subject I was seeking to learn about: shamanism. In fact, when we turned the video camera off at the end of the interview, he noticeably perked up and asked, "How old are you?"

"Fifty-nine," I said. "How old are you?"

"Fifty-eight," he answered, and proceeded to do a little dance, smirking like a boy meeting a girl his age. Or maybe it was recognition that we were both elder-types. Later during that stay, when I visited his urts with friends, he suggested that we have our picture taken together. His big, flirting smile gave away his thoughts.

Today Gosta requests a healing from me. He is suffering from liver disease. Energy healing, which Mongolians call "bio-energy," is well accepted in Mongolia as a medical treatment to achieve balance. I'm not at my strongest, having just ridden a horse over treacherous terrain for 10 hours to get to this settlement. Both the terrain and the horses make me nervous. And now I feel tired from the 10,000-foot altitude. Usually I am grounded and centered when I begin a healing. Today I am a bit off.

I ask Gosta to lie on the reindeer skins on the ground inside the urts. His brown wool *deel* gives an extra layer of protection from the damp earth. I begin to run my hands six inches above his body, testing his energy field for hot spots. A place of imbalance feels different from the surrounding areas. My hands confirm that the hottest area is just above his liver.

As I start to run energy through me to Gosta, I notice the television, solar storage battery, and sewing machine. Then I am disturbed when I notice that my fingernails are dirty. As I hold my hands above him and he closes his eyes, I begin to go with the energy and everything else disappears. A knowing force guides my hands. I jolt with energy. It is strong energy, coming out or going in—I don't need to know which. Mine is a responsibility to be true to spiritual guidance, not to know or force anything. After a few minutes, Gosta falls asleep.

When I jolt, it is as if a ray of lightning coming through from the spirit gives an extra boost through me to him. I continue moving his energy. It seems more like removing negative energy now. I brush it off him and flick my right wrist to release it from my hand. The fingers of my left hand automatically point to the ground, draining out what I might inadvertently absorb. Again I smooth the field and flick my hand. After 10 or 15 minutes, I close the energy field, making an invisible cocoon around Gosta. In a minute, he sits up and coughs, moves his neck around, nodding, and asks why he went to sleep.

I jolt again. My fingers are not relaxed, they point straight out. As I look at the ground, my fingers begin to relax and I put my glasses on. I burp out energy and put my shoes on. Gosta moves his neck around again, says something about his head and face. I understand his word, *saikhan* (beautiful). I smell the reindeer milk tea before Khanda hands it to Gosta. He lights a cigarette. I hear reindeer sounds through the canvas—the clicking sound the joints of reindeer make when they walk and the calls of fawns that sound like "no-ah, no-ah."

"I feel peaceful," Gosta says.

I lift the tent flap and go out. Aware that I need to gather energy from a deep source, I walk along the river. I swish my hands in it. Although I seldom take on energy from a client, it seems as if I took some from Gosta, probably because I am not as strong as usual. I feel sad and a little nauseated. Perhaps he feels this, too. I take some energy from the river to balance myself. Gosta's energy is still moving through me. I need to come into my own balance again. I walk along the river, jolting and burping until the energy is released.

A week later, Gosta does a shamanic healing for an American boy with autism. (A book and movie have documented this—*The Horse Boy*, by Rupert Isaacson.)

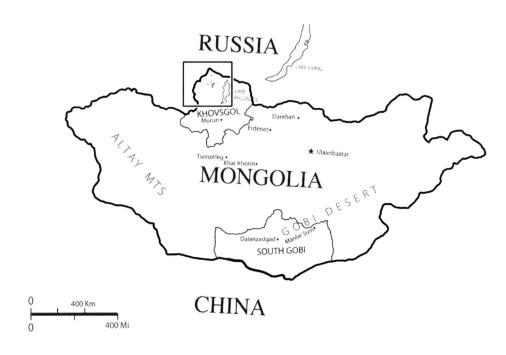

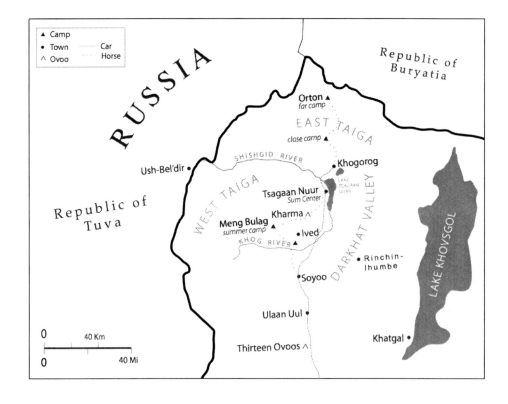

Before 2003

> Let the beauty we love be what we do.
> — Rumi

A client friend gives me $5,000 for my first trip to Mongolia in 1994. In return, I give her seven years of energy healing treatments. The American Holistic Nurses' Association organizes that first trip. I go to learn how Asians practice energy healing in various forms. My heart skips a beat as my feet touch the Mongolian earth and pounds when I ask a traditional Mongolian medicine doctor to be my teacher. Quakers call a strong feeling that spirit is asking you to do something a "leading." When an event allows the leading to fall into place, the Quakers say, "The way opens." I have learned that guidance comes to me from my heart, and going to Mongolia feels like my leading. Knowing from my friend that I need to go to Mongolia, and her handing me the money to do it, feels like the way opening.

I am in Mongolia, thinking about my son making hoop drums in Vermont, when I come across a tiny watercolor of a shaman carrying a drum, riding a reindeer in front of a tipi. The painting is in a vendor's stall at the Natural History Museum, in a room with a huge dinosaur skeleton display. When I look at the painting, I feel a shudder of recognition, of longing—and I buy it for my son.

Traditional Mongolian medicine skills, cultural knowledge, beginning Mongolian language—these I gather for a decade. And then comes a concrete event—an invitation to the Smithsonian Institution to meet with researchers who work in Mongolia. Among those who speak of deer stones, lichen, tree rings, and a Chinggis Khan exhibition, one man, Dan Plumley, speaks about supporting the cultural survival of reindeer herders and shamans who live in tipis on the border of Siberia in northern Mongolia. My whole being is attentive. He explains that the Dukha, Tyvan people from Tyva*, a republic of Russia, say that for their cultural survival they need a healthy reindeer herd, jobs, transportation, education, self-representation in the government, economic opportunities, and health care.

When it is my turn to present on traditional Mongolian medicine, I explain that I am a nurse in the U.S., that I trained in traditional Mongolian medicine in 1995, and that I made a short movie called *Steppe Herbs, Mare's Milk, and Jelly Jars: A Journey to Mongolian Medicine* about the experience. I say that traditional Mongolian medicine is a model of holistic care and that my teacher, Dr. Boldsaikhan, was well received when he taught graduate and undergraduate students at the University of Vermont about it. I discuss the fact that Mongolian medicine has a philosophical base, which folk medicine does not have, and that I would like to learn more about folk medicine, including shamanic healing. All three systems in Mongolia—Western, Mongolian, and folk medicine—have a place in health care. My mission is to harmonize traditional and modern medicine. I believe that everyone in Mongolia needs to have access to Mongolian medicine, which was forbidden during the Soviet period from 1920 to 1990. I end by saying that health care in the U.S. and around the world could benefit from the main concept of traditional Mongolian medicine—balance.

At the next break, Dan Plumley, who founded the Totem Peoples Preservation Project, reiterates the Dukha's need for both modern and traditional medicine. Dan will take veterinary supplies and medicines to the reindeer herders this summer. He asks if I would like to join his team and provide for the herders' health needs. Yes. The time has come for me to experience life inside that little painting.

---

* See the Appendices for a glossary, names, and a list of Dukha cultural survival needs.

Otgon milks her reindeer while interacting with her son, Batbayar. Female reindeer give about a cup of thick milk each day from April until October. Milk is the most precious item in their diet, containing the vitamins and minerals necessary for good health.

photo credit: Fred Thodal

The Furgon van is hung up on a block of ice, even though the driver tested the river ahead of time with an iron pole.

photo credit: Sas Carey

2003

> Mongolia is a land of nomads—everyone is
> eventually on the way to somewhere else.
> — KENT MADIN, HONORARY CONSUL OF MONGOLIA

Delays

First comes SARS (severe acute respiratory syndrome), so we cannot travel through China during the summer. We wait.

Dan and I talk, knowing our goal is cultural survival, knowing we cannot weaken the already endangered Dukhas with an infection. In one of our conversations Dan mentions that the trip will have another delay after we get there. On the way to the taiga (high-altitude boggy forest where the reindeer herders live) we will spend a week in Tsertserleg because he is getting married! His bride is Tsermaa, his Mongolian translator.

When I traveled to Mongolia's countryside during the previous decade, a team—usually Mongolians—traveled with me. The smallest team was made up of three people—interpreter, cameraman, and driver. In 2003, all the team members except for Dan and me are Mongolians. Dan, with his radio announcer voice, has set up the team. Puji, tall, red-faced man full of laughter, and his assistant are drivers. Battulga, petite, heavy-drinking Dukha man, is our guide. Tsermaa, sloe-eyed beauty, is Dan's interpreter. Mende, who dances like he is made of rubber, is my cameraman for the second year. And I have a new interpreter, Zula, a single mother I met at Dan and Tsermaa's wedding. Zula and Tsermaa work together as translators for the Eagle Christian Television Network in Ulaanbaatar. Dan is paying the stipend for his team and I pay for mine. He is supplying transportation, food, and lodging for all of us.

After the weeklong wedding celebration, we all pile into Puji's van. Finally, we are off to the taiga—well, to the top of the hill, where Tsermaa's brothers give us a vodka toast send-off. Then we are off to Murun—the capital of Khovsgol *aimag* (province) and Tsagaan Nuur *soum* (the county center) closest to the herders and the taiga.

Dogs and Wolves

Dan says that we won't have to ride horses this time to meet the Dukha reindeer herders. I sigh with relief. When I took a few riding lessons to prepare for this, I found out I am terrified of riding. So getting there should be pretty easy, I think, as Puji drives the Russian Furgon van over the frozen ground of the steppes. There are eight of us in the van. As the Furgon creaks and bounces along the road, Dan and Battulga tell us that the herders are staying in their winter camp, which is close to the Tsagaan Nuur. Tsagaan Nuur is on the shore of a pristine lake—its name means White Lake. On the third day of jostling and lurching over snowy paths and through rivers, I realize that getting to the taiga to meet the reindeer herders is a big challenge, despite the shorter distance to the winter camp. The mountains are pink from sun and snow as we drive on dirt ruts. Larch trees emit a golden glow. I expect the snow to be fresh, but no—as I look out the window, I realize this is herding country. Human and animal tracks go in every direction.

In the morning we help break river ice and rebuild a ramp for the van, so the driver can get it onto a ferry made of a wooden plank platform on two pontoons. The river has frozen overnight. It is the end of October in Khovsgol aimag, and winter is here already. As we wait for our turn to cross, we watch the boatman move the ferry by grasping a cable and pulling, one hand over the other. We climb out of the van and stand on the ferry with our car, some horses, and their horsemen, who are also crossing. I think I am dressed for winter weather, but the wind cuts through me. Mongolians wear a traditional garment called a deel, a long robe that may be lined with sheepskin or padding for winter. Deels generally have long sleeves, a high collar, and overlapping cloth panels in the front, and are buttoned on the right side and around the neck. The outside of the deel is usually silk, leather, or wool. The traditional deel is belted by wrapping a five-yard length of yellow or orange material around the waist. I am wearing a padded wool deel over my -30° F down coat.

Back in the van, we passengers ride along until we have to get out to walk up a hill so steep that the tough Furgon can't climb it with us inside. Later, we have to get out to walk over a rickety bridge across another river. The ice is already so thick we can walk on it. Generally, though, the van moves through rivers in spite of water up to its axles, and up hills in spite of their steep incline. My Mongolian medicine teacher, Dr. Boldsaikhan, was right when he told us about Russian vehicles. They can go anywhere.

Our driver and assistant carry shoulder-high iron poles to check the depth of the ice and water in each river and stream we come to—to see if we can safely drive through. There are few bridges here. After they measure the depth and the thickness of the ice, they come back to the van and tell us we whether we need to get out or we can ride through this one. Traveling in Mongolia, the driver is the boss.

Further on, the drivers test the depth and survey the muddy ruts leading into the river. We are told to climb out. As the van moves out into deeper water, it gets hung up in the middle of the river on a clump of ice as big as a boulder. We women stand around, slide on the ice, and talk. My clothes are so thick I can barely move, yet I am freezing. When I notice logs scattered on the ground near the river, I realize that we are not the first to have trouble at this crossing. Our drivers and the male passengers try to free the van with chains, logs, and levers. Meanwhile, I imagine sleeping here. Would there be space in the van for all eight of us to sleep? Would we sleep sitting up? Will the van sink into the river? For a while, my imagination plays with these questions, until I give up. This is Mongolia. Something or nothing will happen. *Just be patient*, I tell myself. This is not a place to dramatize life. It already is a drama. Now is a good time to practice calm, let go of expectations, and just BE.

Three hours later, Puji has tried all his tricks and still the van hasn't moved. He finally motions to some nomads herding their sheep off in the distance. Two young men, who have been watching the antics of our team, immediately gallop over on their horses and dismount. One hands me his reins. I swallow. He trusts me with his horse? What do I do now? Zula has caught my raised eyebrows and clenched teeth. We laugh as she reaches for the reins. Quickly, the two herders add their ropes to the logs and chains, pull, push, tug—and free the Furgon.

Now I am sitting on the cloth-covered seat, gripping the handles above the Furgon windows so my head won't smash against them as we navigate the deeply pitted road. Each time we get stuck, Puji opens his door, climbs out, turns his back, and pees. Slowly we all get out. After everyone has peed, the drivers take a look at the car problem.

When we arrive in Murun, we stay with friends of the driver. Zula tells me that Mende is making advances, so we carefully manage the sleeping order—all lined up on the floor. In the morning, by chance or because of the small-town (28,000 people) grapevine, we meet the owners of the guesthouse where we will stay in Tsagaan Nuur. Few cars travel these roads, and they come along with us. Now there are 10 in the van.

At this time of year, nomadic herders all over Mongolia are moving to their winter quarters. On the way from Murun, we catch sight of a train of seven camels crossing the steppes. Some camels carry metal bed frames, bedding, a stove, stools, felt, and a large metal tub. Others are loaded with collapsed wooden walls, a bright orange round *toono* (top), and the roof rafters of the family home or *ger*. A ger is a round, felt-covered yurt or tent, used by most Mongolian nomads, but not by reindeer herders, whose urts is like an American Indian tipi but without the smoke flaps. The toono for a ger is a wooden top ring with eight spokes. The roof rafters attach to the outside of this ring. The center space between the spokes is open to the sky and lets the light in. Dukhas also call the place where the poles meet that is open to the sky a toono. We stop. Dan and Tsermaa have a conversation with the herder, who is clad in a maroon deel. They are wearing deels, too, so they match the herder. Still, talking to someone actually moving with camels to a winter settlement feels like a time warp to me, as if I am witnessing life from thousands of years ago. Then, we see a yak train, the yaks pulling handmade two-wheeled carts with gers and household items, the herders on horses guiding the yaks. Cold weather signals the time of year for nomadic herders to climb the high pass on the way to the Darkhat Valley, where they will spend the winter.

Ovoos (spiritual mounds) break the monotony of the endless steppes. The rock- and branch-filled cone shapes appear at high points along the road. Bright blue *khadaghs* (prayer scarves) tied on the branches match the color of the sky. We stop at the high mountain pass, where we see the Thirteen Ovoos. Twelve ovoos, representing the 12 astrological signs, surround a 15-foot-high ovoo. In the snow, we walk around the mounds three times clockwise and give offerings of small stones and foreign coins in gratitude for our safe passage.

As we travel on, the snow-capped Sayan Mountains under a deep blue sky are stark against the autumn golden steppe land. In this vast space, Puji and Battulga wrestle. Mongolian wrestling involves trying to get your opponent's elbow or knee to touch the ground. Puji, much taller and bigger than Battulga, seems to have the upper hand.

When we arrive in Tsagaan Nuur, Nyama and Ganba, our hosts, prepare the guesthouse for us. We are late for the tourist season, which is why they were in Murun. They make our beds and feed the wood stoves—one for heat and one for cooking. Dan cooks a big meal of spaghetti and feeds us all. Buyantogtokh, more petite than Battulga and walking with a limp, joins us for dinner to learn of our plans. He is the administrator for the *bagh* (the smallest government division) which includes the taiga area. As Dan explains our mission, Buyantogtokh takes notes and says he will come with us. Maybe we will need a border patrol officer, too, since we are traveling into the Tyva and Russian border area; he will check on it. Dan nods his head, compliant with whatever Buyantogtokh needs. The border area is considered dangerous, with cattle rustling back and forth and general lawlessness.

The next morning we are off—this time to the East Taiga winter settlement of Dukha reindeer herders. Byara, a veterinarian who lives in Tsagaan Nuur, joins us. The border patrol decides we will be okay without him as long as Buyantogtokh comes along. He is married and has five or six children, but keeps looking into my eyes.

As we get close to the settlement, we are driving through a larch forest, through invisible paths and around fallen logs. The van winds over hillocks, over ice patches, and between trees. When I look out the window, I see there is an inch between the side of the van and a tree. I quickly glance to the other side. Same. We are squeezing through trees. I am breathless, alive only on driver trust.

We keep going, swaying and bumping. I think I have never felt this far from a human settlement. It feels like we are pushing onward into the unknown. Deeper and deeper.

Then we arrive at the East Taiga winter camp. The taiga here is an alpine forest with sparse trees and wet ground. The tamarack, or larch, trees still hold a few yellow needles. White canvas cones dot the landscape. The urts, home of the Dukha reindeer herders, looks like a tipi, only there are more poles. The urts has no smoke flaps and a round dowel in the door flap is placed in the center of the door, horizontally. In a tipi, the wall canvas comes together above the door and in an urts, the canvas wraps around the poles in a spiral fashion. In a tipi, the canvas continues under the doorway, while in the urts, the door space is open to the ground. I see a stovepipe sticking out among the poles, emitting gentle white smoke. It looks like the fire pit has been replaced with a wood stove.

Smiling women, men, and children come out of their urts and welcome us. I am in awe. Reindeer herders—living nomads—in a magical taiga. We made it! I see the reindeer—white, brown, and grey. I revert to my childhood reference to reindeer and think Santa's must look like these. But there are not seven or eight—here there are many, many more, tied to logs on the ground for the night.

For two nights, an urts becomes our home. Dan cooks in the urts of J. Bat, where I have my first taste of *suutai tsai* (milk tea, in this case reindeer milk). I drink it with trepidation because I am lactose intolerant, yet reindeer milk seems to agree with me. This makes me hopeful that food and drink here might be easier for me than it has been in other areas of Mongolia I have visited. In this country where herders live on meat and dairy, it is not that easy being a lactose-intolerant vegetarian!

When Zula and I ask where to go for nature's toilet, we are directed to a thin larch grove. As we start out, dogs follow us and reindeer hang around like drug dealers waiting to pull off a job. They are ready. In the cold, we squat, do our business as quickly as possible, and walk away, buckling, zipping, and snapping as we go. Turning back, we notice the reindeer licking the ground. "Minerals," explains our host when we question the behavior. The reindeer are seeking minerals that are excreted in urine. Okay. The dogs, though, are alert when the squatting lasts a bit longer. One minute there's a brown mound, then the dogs are walking away licking their jowls. In this land of scarcity, everyone, everything is hungry—all are hunters and gatherers. Herders hunt. Dogs hunt and gather. The dogs have a purpose in this culture—they protect the reindeer from wolves. They are fed flour gruel with some tiny meat scraps or bones that have already been well cleaned by humans, but somehow it is not enough. Something is missing that they get from humans.

With the temperature around 0° Fahrenheit, we move quickly back to the smoky urts. Inside, we set up our sleeping bags on reindeer skins, close to each other. The men are edging their way toward Zula and me. "No," I say. "You sleep on the other side." That settled, we snuggle into our sleeping bags, but can't sleep. The dogs are barking ferociously. "Why?" I call to Buyantogtokh across the urts.

"It's the wolves," he says. "Wolves surround our settlement. The dogs are protecting the reindeer from the wolves."

An early-morning babushka woman is milking her reindeer in the cold, misty quiet. She looks like a postcard, yet life here is no dream. I interview the women about their health issues, and one tells me that a child in the West Taiga died yesterday of an infected dog bite. In our Western world, antibiotics would have saved the boy. I can't believe this could happen today, but there are no antibiotics available in the settlement. This is the place where I am to learn about the herders' health practices and share ours. I feel even more committed to harmonizing various systems of health care at these settlements. What is at risk is the cultural survival of a unique people.

Dan is known and trusted here because he has come to reindeer herders on both the Mongolian and Russian sides of the border 10 times in the past six years to help. He listens, supports the education of veterinary technicians, brings medical supplies for the reindeer, and is an advocate for the Dukhas. Dan introduces me as a nurse and shaman who wants to learn what they need in the area of health care. When I ask later why he called me a shaman, he says, "A shaman is a concept the herders know and respect. With your healing skills, you understand more than basic nurses' concepts—you heal on the spiritual level like shamans do." My way of healing involves opening to let the spirit flow through me. I want to find out and understand how shamans connect to the spirits.

Of the six settlements where 210 Dukha reindeer herders live, four are in the West Taiga and two in the East Taiga. Between the two is the Shishgid River. There is some fluidity between the groups, but mostly just between those on the same side of the river. Mongolians call these taiga people *Tsataan*, which means "reindeer people," but the herders prefer to think of themselves as reindeer herders or Dukhas, not people with antlers coming out of their heads. At least that is what they have told me. Dukha means Tyvan, from Tyva, Autonomous Republic of Russia. Dukhas are a small minority group in Mongolia. Today, in this area, the border from Mongolia to Tyva/Russia is closed. This has a big impact on the Dukhas: it makes their hunting area smaller and shrinks the gene pool for reindeer, and gives people fewer choices for mates, since they are often related. Cattle rustling between the two countries raises the risk of violence, so the area is regulated by the border patrol.

With Dan's introduction, the herders openly answer my questions, which stem from our two main ones: What help in the area of human health do the Dukhas need to maintain their lifestyle? What portion of this health care can our project, Nomadicare, provide?

I meet with the men first. They name their health issues: kidney problems, high blood pressure, hepatitis, gall bladder problems, joint pain, and hearing and sight loss. They ask if I have ways to help them stop smoking and drinking.

"We are worried about the young boys drinking and smoking,"

one man says, his cigarette hanging from his lips. "As for me, after a long trip, I need a strong shot."

I tell them this is very difficult to change and know I will have to learn a lot more of their culture, especially relating to smoking and drinking, before I can make any suggestions.

The women talk of births, contraception, menopause, headaches, and high blood pressure. They speak of long pregnancies and of going back to work three days after delivering a baby, but they say that there are no teen pregnancies here. They are worried about their children's teeth and gums. Could I look at them? Some of the children have bleeding gums. Could it be scurvy? That would indicate vitamin C deficiency.

"Do you go to shamans for healing?" I ask.

"First we use Western medicine," they tell me. "If that doesn't work, we go to a shaman."

The herders tell me what medicines grow in their environment—Vansemberuu (*Saussurea involucrata*) and Wolf's Tongue (*Lonicera altaica*). Vansemberuu is used for lung disease and tuberculosis. They survive by using these medicines. Ulaanbaatar is too far away, so they have no access to high-tech medicine. They usually have their babies in the Tsagaan Nuur soum hospital. Since they are a small minority group and live so far away, supplies get "lost" before they arrive here. I feel inspired to help. A small amount of American money can provide a lot for these people—starting with a first aid kit for dog bites, antibiotics for the hospital, and teaching about infection.

While we are here, Dan keeps the supplies in the car. Everything is frozen. When he tries to break a candy bar, it shatters into small pieces. Dan is cooking beef stew in J. Bat's urts in a large wok-like pan, which fits into a wood stove. When he is done, there will be enough not only for our team, but for the family and everyone who is standing around outside. Dan understands the Dukha culture.

Meanwhile, I am trying to learn everything at once. Because the urts poles are so long and the reindeer are so small, I ask how the poles are transported to the next encampment. I find out that they are left on the ground at the settlement. The herders will return here next year. The canvas, woodstove, tools, and gear are all piled on reindeer. I wonder how the reindeer can transport everything. I wonder how the herders live on reindeer milk and bread. I wonder how people can survive in this cold weather. I want to know this life.

My dream is to meet an authentic shaman who can teach me how they touch the unknown, and I am finally in a place where that might be possible. Battulga takes me to Sanjaa, nephew of Soyan, the 100-year-old shaman in the West Taiga, who tells me that footprints carry a person's individual vibration, recognized by the spirits, and rocks transmit Earth energies. Then he turns to me and asks, "Who is this Jesus? Do you have your god in your house? Who is stronger—Jesus or Buddha?" When our conversation ends, he takes me to Punsil, an elderly woman who, after playing her mouth harp, says to me, "Your work will be good and you will be a success." Hanging from a pole in her urts is her altar, made of khadaghs and strips of white, blue, and green material. Punsil reaches into the cloth strips and pulls out two eagle claws to show us. Neither Sanjaa nor Punsil is a practicing shaman, though.

Maybe meeting them is my first test, because now we are going to visit Tsend, the daughter of Soyan. Tsend, a 68-year-old woman who is blind from cataracts, is a practicing shaman. She welcomes us into her urts with reindeer milk tea and lifts a yellow curtain to reveal her altar of blue khadaghs and cloth strips. The cloth strips represent *ongods* (ancestor spirits). Sitting on the ground inside her urts, Tsend reaches below and behind the wide ribbons of cloth and pulls out a six-inch-deep, round drum with nine sets of three knuckles and a skin on one side. On the inside walls of the drum, Tsend points out *khunkhinguur* (jingle cones), which are pieces of metal that clang against each other so that when the drum moves, it is alive. Tsend smudges with a smoldering juniper branch, accepts a small *tugrik* (Mongolian money) offering from us, and puts her headdress on. It is a navy blue headband with white eyebrows, nose, and lips embroidered on it. Eagle feathers top the headdress and a blue, white, and turquoise fringe hangs over her face. When she takes it off, she begins to unpack a plump reindeer skin bag, first removing her drumbeater. The beater is covered with the white furry hide from a wild sheep's tail, and has a strip of attached metal rings that rattle when the beater moves. Soft boots come out of the bag—made of fur, silk, streamers, and tan corduroy material. The deel costume is cotton with embroidered backbone, muscles, ribs, and breasts and decorated with streamers and silk ropes or cording of various colors, called *manjin*, representing whips or snakes. On the shoulders are feathers representing wings to fly away.

Tsend explains that the first time she put her costume on, she was young and so sick that she nearly died. Her mother told her to wear the costume that was made for her and begin to practice as a shaman. As soon as she started, she became well. Tsend is generous, sharing her sacred shaman objects, telling her story, and explaining how ceremonies should correspond with the phases of the moon. I am grateful to Tsend. She is the first Mongolian-Tyvan shaman to share with me.

Leaving Tsend's urts, Tsogkhuu, one of our hosts, who is riding his reindeer back home, gets off and offers to let me try sitting on it. As the large antlers brush my face, I see the beauty of their lives, the landscape, the simplicity, and the interaction between people, who spend their time going from one urts to another to drink milk tea, hang out, and talk.

"Will you come back?" asks one of the West Taiga women we met with, as we are preparing to leave. "No doctor here would talk to us so personally. We fell in love with you and don't want you to leave. Could we find you a taiga husband?"

We take one photo of the West Taiga *ail* (family group), and I give my deel to Zorig. He can use it all year and it is so thick I can't bend in it. I will have another one made in Ulaanbaatar for another time.

At night, on a back road to Ulaanbaatar, we spot a wolf running from the van. "Now we will have good luck," says our driver. For my part, I have already experienced the good luck of visiting the glowing taiga, connecting with nomadic reindeer herders, and meeting a shaman. I know I will return to the taiga next year.

Tsermaa and her brother prepare for a move from Meng Bulag, West Taiga, to the winter camp by packing all their household items on their reindeer.

photo credit: Sas Carey

# 2004

> Life is either a daring adventure or nothing. Security does not exist in nature, nor do the children of men as a whole experience it. Avoiding danger is no safer in the long run than exposure.
> — HELEN KELLER

Dan's Team

I am in Ulaanbaatar, the capital of Mongolia, back from eight days in the oven-like temperatures of the Gobi. Our project delivered new laboratories to two hospitals and visited hospitals where we delivered laboratories last year—part of meeting our goal of harmonizing all types of medicine in Mongolia's rural areas. It has been a grueling trip, due to the heat and the fact that I broke my foot tripping on a sidewalk here in the city the day before I left.

I am going to the taiga with Dan's team again this year. His goal this time is to bring together various groups and individuals who work with reindeer herders to prevent overlaps in service and help them work together peacefully. While still in the city, Dan sets up meetings for those who work in the taiga. I am not one to thrive on meetings. And with translators, everything takes twice as long—I am impatient to get moving. At the table are three Dukhas from the taiga and the two translators, along with about a dozen people representing a travel company, three international non-profit organizations, and a Mongolian non-governmental organization. A Mongolian state veterinarian and an anthropologist bring their unique views.

In one of our many discussions, J. Bat tells us that 14 taiga herders were hunting and went across the border to Tyva, Russia. Because it is illegal to cross the closed border, they are all in jail for a month. Let's see. There are 50 taiga men. Two are here with us and 14 are in jail. That leaves 34 still herding the reindeer right now. The closed border continues to create problems for the herders.

Dan takes the Dukhas to the Mongolian Parliament to lobby for indigenous rights and the opening of the border, to a radio station where they speak of stereotypes and their needs, and to an interview with *Onoodor*, a well-known newspaper in Mongolia.

After two days of meetings, we prepare to leave for the taiga. In two Furgon vans and a jeep, Dan and I are joined by many others from yesterday's meeting. J. Bat is a Dukha man from the East Taiga who is known for his carvings and hospitality. Zorig is a Dukha man, a young leader in the West Taiga. Oyunbadaam is a Tyvan language teacher and advocate. She brings her six-year-old daughter. Tsermaa, Binde, and Badma are translators. Nansalmaa is a state veterinarian. Tsogtsaikhan works with Taiga Nature and the United Nations. Two National Public Radio reporters join us a couple of days before we leave. One wants sounds and reindeer herder stories, and the other wants shaman stories.

On the Way

Since the reindeer herder's settlements are very close to Russia, we need permission from the border patrol in Murun, capital of Khovsgol, on the way to the taiga. This involves many hours of waiting and, while we are there, some turf issues come up between the team members. We leave at 1:00 PM for the 18-hour ride to Tsagaan Nuur.

Just before midnight, we cross over a rickety bridge and stop at a curve in the river. Along this extremely remote road there are very few gas stations and no restaurants. Traditionally, local herders offer food and a place to sleep along the road. When there is the sign "Guanz" in front of a ger, it is a place to eat and rest. *Guanz* means café. Besides tables for guests, there is a flat wooden platform with a blanket or rug over it. The custom is that the woman of the family seats everyone, brings suutai tsai (sometimes with salt added) to the table in a large thermos, and pours it into a bowl for each person. The driver, after drinking tea, lies on the platform and goes to sleep. The passengers take walks.

Food is made from scratch, so it takes a while. Flour and water are kneaded together, rolled out, and cut into noodles. Mutton is chopped into small pieces. From these ingredients, the family prepares a soup to serve the travelers. When it is done, the driver's nap is over, and the travelers come in and everyone eats.

All this has already happened and we are sitting around the table when the NPR reporters notice that the woman serving us is talking excitedly to the Mongolians with us. They ask for a translation. "My three-year-old niece and four-year-old nephew are unconscious in their ger. No one can bring them to consciousness. They accidentally took some medicine a visitor had left while their parents were out herding. They have no car or phone. They are isolated out there. I don't know if they will survive."

Dan looks at me and says, "Do you want to go check on them?"

"Of course," I answer without thinking about how tired I am or asking how far we will have to drive. I remember my son Kai having a bad fever when he was 14 months old. I was living eight miles from a town, without electricity, phone, or running water, and my husband was away with the car for the day. I imagine the parents are distraught. I remember how scary that day was for me.

The two reporters, Nansalmaa, a translator, the driver, and I climb into the van and ride off into the darkness, through a larch forest, to a ger belonging to the *bagh emch* (the rural bagh doctor). Two women are each holding a child. I am not an emergency room nurse and I don't really know what to do, but I suddenly remember an acupuncture point that a traditional Chinese doctor used when a nurse from our tour group fainted in a hot room during a treatment demonstration in Beijing on my first trip to Asia. When the doctor pressed, it brought the nurse right back. I start with the youngest child, a girl, and press my hardest into the ridge below the bridge of her nose. She wakes up, pees, and cries. The bagh emch and her mother talk excitedly. Then I try the same thing on her brother. Nothing happens. I press really hard. Nothing. I try cold cloths and jarring his body. I consult with Nansalmaa and the NPR reporters to see if they have any ideas. Nothing. With my heart in my throat, I realize there is nothing I can do. We need to go—it is past midnight and we still have eight or nine hours' drive before we reach Tsagaan Nuur.

"Could we come with you?" The mother asks. "Could you drop us off at the Ulaan Uul hospital? We have no other way to get there." Ulaan Uul is on our way. I sigh. There is something we can do—give them a ride. "Of course." They wrap their children in blankets and climb into the back seat of the van.

We drive back to the guanz. The others are sleeping, but everyone gets up and climbs into the cars, and we drive to the Ulaan Uul Hospital. We drop the women and two children off at 3:00 AM. The boy is still unconscious. We will not be able to find out how they are until our return trip, since there is no way to connect by phone. As we continue our way north, I wonder what will happen. All I can do now is what Quakers do—"hold them in the Light," which is similar to praying for them. For me it involves imagining a person in a cocoon of glowing spiritual light, where an abundance of energy surrounds the person so he or she can become healed and whole.

Horseback Ride and West Taiga

During the last visit, I fell in love with the Dukha reindeer herders and their lives. Yet all year I feared the eight-hour horseback ride I would have to make to see them again. I spent a lot of time thinking about going to the taiga, and one night I had a dream where I saw myself stampeded, crushed by horse hooves. Maybe it was another life? How do we know where fears come from? I tried to prepare myself for the ride by taking riding lessons. I rode on a trail in Wyoming. All my friends who ride horses had advice for me—what to wear and what to do.

The special clothes I bring for my ride this time include bike pants with padding, a fall deel made with cotton batting as insulation, leather half chaps from a friend in Ulaanbaatar, and a woolen scarf given to me by the veterinarian, Nansalmaa. All the way from Ulaanbaatar I envision some miracle occurring so I won't have to ride a horse. Maybe a helicopter will appear. Maybe the herders will live close by. I feel extra vulnerable because it was only two weeks ago that I broke my foot. I probably shouldn't be here at all.

I have traded my plaster cast for a plastic splint made by a German-Mongolian joint venture in Ulaanbaatar's trauma hospital. A plaster cast would not work for riding a horse in the wet taiga. The plastic splint is smaller than a cast and I hope to find a boot to fit over it, although I was unable to find any that fit while I was in Ulaanbaatar. When we arrive in Tsagaan Nuur, we stay at the same guesthouse again. Nyama loans me an old pair of her boots that I can just barely pull over the splint. Not waterproof, but good for horseback riding. The fact that I cannot walk on uneven ground adds to my fear of riding a horse. But with the help of ibuprofen, at least I am not feeling pain.

On the day we are ready to meet our horses, we climb back into the cars. It is an hour through a green, rolling steppe to the place where we stop. I see a log building, dung piles, and hitching posts. It is early August; the weather is sunny. I smell sage and horse manure—and the pungent aroma of horse sweat. There are no horse trailers. The horses have already galloped from Tsagaan Nuur while we were driving. *This is it*, I tell myself, but I try to act like this is no big thing. I am about to get on a horse and ride for eight hours—with a broken foot. Sure. Then I see the 20 horses tied up, waiting.

As we step out of the cars, horse wranglers and guides unload our supplies, pack them into plastic or canvas saddlebags, rope pairs together, and heft them to make sure the weight is balanced. Among the supplies are the multivitamins Nomadicare is supplying for the children and the vitamin C for the adults—a year's supply of each—along with all our equipment and camping supplies. Mongolians do not have the habit of introducing everyone right away, so I don't learn the names of the wranglers who will lead the packhorses—and may lead us. My throat is dry as I stand back and watch them saddle the solid Mongolian horses of white, gray, brown, and tan. I notice a variety of saddles on the horses—wooden traditional Mongolian ones painted orange that curve up in front and back, canvas cushion saddles, and leather pad saddles with metal half-rings on the front and back. The wranglers adjust the bridles and the metal bits in the horses' mouths.

All this is happening, yet I can't focus my eyes on it. I am looking through a blurry lens. I have heard the wooden saddle is uncomfortable unless you stand while riding. No chance of me doing that. Dan and his team are giddy, anxious to be off. I sit on the ground behind a fence and burst into tears. The steppes are open, hilly grasslands. There are larch trees on the mountains. I have always felt comfortable in nature. Not today. As I look up, some others are already on their horses, expertly guiding them to the left and right. I can't do that. I will be trampled for sure. Just as I think, *I can't get on a horse, I can't do this*, a white horse with a canvas pad saddle, wet from the night's rain, is led to me. Whatever made me arrange to do this? I say I can't ride on a wet seat, and the wranglers change it for a leather seat. Dan asks Battulga to watch over me. He smells of vodka, and he's not the only one. Yet he knows horses, and helps me up into the saddle.

At first, we move easily along a flat trail. Next, the narrow trail cuts along the side of a steep mountainside. There is a gorge at the bottom. I can't look down. I feel dizzy, but hold onto the reins. My horse plods along. The leather saddle squeaks and creaks. Dan stops and everyone gathers. "Is everyone okay?" he asks, breathless with excitement. "Sure, sure," everyone says. I can't talk. I can't get off. For one thing, I am too scared. For another, I can't walk anyway. The ground is uneven.

As we ride through the woods, horses' hooves clunk against roots, stirrups clang against tree trunks. Battulga turns around in the saddle to watch me. I smell his alcohol breath and at the same time I can't decide if I should go over a log or around it. The horse stands still. Battulga rides to me and takes the reins. I know that when Dukhas or Mongolians are drunk, they can still manage their horses. Riding is like breathing to them. And I really like Battulga, whom I know from last year. Yet having a drunken man as a guide doesn't instill a lot of confidence in me today. I am already petrified and feel terribly vulnerable. Being led by someone compromised doesn't help relieve my fear, no matter what I tell myself.

I think about one of my spiritual principles: "I will not be given more than I can do." If this has ever been tested in my life, now is the time. Friends in Mongolia tell me, "No one over 50—

Mongolian or foreigner—can travel to the taiga like you do." I am in my sixties. I don't question whether I can or not. I am here. Each time I look ahead at Battulga's horse's hooves, I see my dream about being stampeded and trampled. I see the horse smash my neck and smash my head. I will die. I know it with each hoof that snaps a twig and sloshes in water.

Then I get a vision of a time in my early twenties, when I was taking care of children in a family that had horses. The oldest daughter was 17, and on the spur of the moment she saddled up three horses so that she, my husband, and I could ride. I had never been on a horse. It was November, and the horses hadn't been ridden lately. Always ready for adventure, I thought it was a great opportunity to try something new. We had no lessons or even advice. For instance, I didn't know you are supposed to hold on with your legs. The three of us took off on a dirt road, walking along. Then, suddenly, my horse began to gallop. I bounced up and down until I flew off the saddle and down onto the road. I crawled on hands and knees to the house and into bed. I had pinched a vertebra.

That was then. This time I will die. I know it.

The horse snorts, then sneezes, then farts. I laugh. My normally optimistic self appears. I remember I have work to do. I will deliver vitamins. My friends have sent contributions so I can improve the health care of the reindeer herders. How magical—my friends, my work.

A larch tree smashes into my knee. I am not safe. I need to remember to breathe deeply. There is a gorge below the narrow trail. Branches snap in my face. My horse steps into wet ground up to his hocks. He jolts me as he pulls his feet out and sloshes along through a muddy area. He drops his head to look as we go down a steep hill and the short reins fly from my hands. I know I am supposed to lean back; I can't reach the reins. The path goes at an angle of 45 degrees down, then 45 degrees up. Over a shallow river, up over boulders, and then through roaring rivers. I am holding tightly to the metal loop on the saddle. My fingers hurt, but my goal is to stay on the horse and not die today.

I hear a scream. Someone from our group has fallen off her horse as we climb a steep hill through a former stream. She falls onto some boulders and hurts her wrist. Her partner is ahead with the others. I knew something like this would happen—this is too dangerous. I can—and then my mind flies—*break my neck, break my back, and become a vegetable, and there are no doctors here. And no one cares. Would they leave me here to die?*

I need to check on the hurt rider. I am a nurse, after all. With help and great difficulty, I carefully climb off my horse and gently and slowly walk down the steep rocks to look at her wrist. I am the only medical person in the group. Dan is ahead with the first aid kit. The rider is moaning. There is nothing I can do at the moment.

Battulga rides to her, helps me get on my horse, and decides that she needs him more than I do. He tells a wrangler leading a packhorse to lead me and let the packhorse go on its own. Now a person who is so drunk he can't focus his eyes is leading me. He is one of the wranglers I have never really met. He can still ride, of course. The packhorse bumps along by itself. There goes my luggage, the vitamins, and the backpack a friend loaned me. The bags bump from one tree to the next. But the herding instinct of horses is strong, and the horse keeps walking with us. Every time a branch is at a level to hit my face and perhaps blind me, my guide turns and gives a drunken wave in warning. The small confidence I had when Battulga was leading me is gone. I am hyperventilating. Most likely I will die here. No one will hear from me again.

Suddenly I hear voices, Dan's and then the others'. As we climb one last rise, we are at the top of a mountain and see our team resting. As we approach them, it begins to hail and the horse's hooves slip on the wet, smooth boulders. Dan waits, sitting in the saddle.

"Is there any food?" I ask.

"I have a candy bar," Dan says. *Oh, great.*

Since we are the last to arrive at the resting place, the others are ready to go again. Dan and I wrap the injured wrist of the woman who fell. I hope it's not broken or permanently hurt. She plays the flute. She needs to be whole.

I have a moment to lie on the grass and think about the horse I'm riding. He belongs to Buyantogtokh, the government administrator who traveled with us last year. The horse is calm and strong, keeps plodding along, doesn't stop to urinate or defecate, doesn't tug his head down for food or water, and doesn't hold back at roaring rivers or steep boulders. He farts as he walks, that's all. This is how Chinggis Khan (Genghis Khan) must have conquered the world. With horses. They just keep going and going—no food, no water. They just keep walking.

"Four more hours and we will be at the settlement at Meng Bulag," says Dan, cheerfully. I need to focus on staying on the horse and staying alive. That's my goal. When we get started, I practice mind control. I tell myself this is my chance to meet a 100-year-old shaman. She might not be here another year. I remind myself of my women friends. I see their faces one by one. I think about how they have always supported and loved me. I think of the Mongol-American Cultural Association, which gave me a contribution to buy and distribute vitamins. I think of our Quaker meeting holding me in the Light. I picture the donors who helped me get here. This makes me feel better. But when I visualize my family, I get shaky. Will my son, Kai, have to come here to claim my body?

I smell horse, leather, wet earth, vodka, and tamarack resin. Mud splatters me. The trail goes down. "Lean back," motions my guide. The reins slip out of my hand. Lean forward when going uphill. My mind flashes back to my Wyoming friend's words: "Don't look down into the water when crossing a river," she said. "Otherwise you will be drawn into the water." I lean back, lean forward, look ahead, and don't let my eyes wander to the water.

Dan trots over to talk. "Oh, isn't it beautiful? All this nature? All this land? The flowers, the mountains, the green?"

What? What? I am on a minute-to-minute survival mission here. Beauty? Nature? Does he like riding? Am I the only one who's terrified? What have I missed? I take a quick glance around. I see green hills, wet ground, and some larch trees—no roads, cars, or telephone poles. I smell earth, mud. See a snowcapped mountain in the west. Hear a river's small bubbling sounds beside us. I see it but can't fully feel it. I just want to get to the encampment.

"Only a short distance more," says Dan. It's a flat area. We ride over a boggy field. "See those tiny specks? Those are reindeer!" Fifteen minutes more and white cones appear as specks before they become urts. This is Meng Bulag, summer camp of the herders of the West Taiga. We are here!

It is getting dark as the Dukhas and guides unload the packhorses. Chuluu G., an older woman, walks to my horse, welcomes me. Others help me off the horse. She guides me into an urts. I can barely walk, not only because of my foot, but also because of my tense muscles. A young woman named Otgonbayar gives me reindeer milk tea in a bowl. I shiver. My hand shakes. The milk spills before I can put the bowl on the ground. I burst into tears. My whole body begins to shake.

"Lie down here," says Otgonbayar, pointing with her chin to a low platform made of logs. I can't stop shaking. Shock? Cold? Hunger? Thirst? Post-traumatic stress? Dan brings a space blanket. I put my sleeping bag over me and shake for an hour and a half before I fall asleep.

Life in the Settlement

Now it is morning. I am here and alive. My eyes aren't open and already I can hear the creak of the tin stove as it warms the urts with the morning fire. Otgonbayar has returned from milking her reindeer and is quietly moving about. She dips water from a metal jug behind her and with a splash pours it into the dishpan-sized pot that fits into her wood stove. She crosses to the back of the urts where her daughters are sleeping and, lifting a curtain, removes a jar of reindeer milk. She pours it into the dipper and mixes it with the heating water. I hear a steady thud, a pounding, as she crushes tea leaves and stems in her wooden mortar and pestle.

By the time my eyes are open to the blurry interior of the urts, my hostess is handing me a bowl of hot reindeer milk tea. I take it with steady hands. Her baby cries and she sits beside the stove nursing him. As I sip the tea, I have a feeling of relief. We will be here for a week, thank goodness. I don't have to think about the ride back right now—not yet.

I see movement under bedding and Otgonbayar's oldest daughter, 15 years old, gets up and makes a trip outside—the stick on the canvas flap rustles and claps shut. Back inside, she touches her two sisters, who are 10 and 11, telling them to get up. She folds the bedding and mats used for sleeping on the ground and piles them around the base of the urts, where they are out of the way and also act as insulation. Now Zorig, Otgonbayar's husband, is up and she hands him reindeer milk tea.

Otgonbayar scoops flour into a bowl for making sourdough bread. After kneading the dough and letting it rise, she places it in a pan and cooks it on top of the wood stove. Everyone is up now and she is making cheese from reindeer milk. This is our breakfast—milk tea, bread, and cheese—all are delicious.

I step outside and see that we are above the tree line. Snow-capped mountains, a long way off and close by, surround us. The ground looks even and brown, but when I step out I find it is wet and uneven with tussocks of brown grass. I have to move carefully to keep from tripping or stepping in water that might seep through my boots. I walk to the river and break the skin of ice to wash my face. The water shocks me awake. My nightmare is gone and a dream has come true. I am living with a family of reindeer herders.

I walk to a blue and white two-room tent, our headquarters. In one room we have food supplies. In the other Dan and his wife, the one-year honeymooners, are sleeping. We have a gas hot plate for heating water for pasta, ramen, potato flakes, and tea. We have chocolate nut butter for a quick sugar fix. Dan cooks one filling and nourishing meal a day—spaghetti, reindeer meat stew, or fish soup. We buy *khungun*, sourdough bread unique to the taiga, from Otgonbayar for our other meals.

Everything in the camp seems peaceful. Battulga and Tsogsaikhan are fishing in the stream and smoking the fish in a stovepipe they rigged up. Dan meets with the men to teach and demonstrate safe antler carving and distribute carving-tool sets. This is an important part of his work. The herders used to cut off the antlers when they were "in the velvet"—that is, when they were alive. They were sold for Chinese medicine. But cutting live antlers, his team discovered, lowered the reindeer's immunity to disease and increased the risk of parasites. In the past few years, since the herders have stopped this practice, their herds have increased and grown stronger. Sensitive to the income loss that resulted from stopping this practice, Dan encourages antler carving as a substitute. The carvings are sold to tourists.

We have packed the multivitamins for the children in clean, recycled water bottles—one bottle for each family. I check the names on the bottles against those of the herders living here and make sure the number of family members is accurate, since they change groups often. I repack some of the vitamins. In the afternoon, the mothers and children gather to receive their year's supply of multivitamins and vitamin C. Our goal is to boost the health of the children and prevent scurvy in all the herders. Last year we found children with bleeding gums, a symptom of vitamin C deficiency. Since vitamin C is water soluble, our bodies need it every day, and since the herders do not eat vegetables and are unable to get it from reindeer milk in the winter when the animals are not providing milk, they need to take supplements.

Some of the mothers and children who come for vitamins request energy healing. Shaman Soyan walks from her urts with two crooked walking sticks to get her vitamins. She is the elder 100-year-old shaman, mother of them all. Her head reaches my shoulder when we stand, and I am only five feet, three inches tall. Her hat of reindeer fur and silk sits above her round cheeks, one of which has a large black cancer spot on it.

I met Soyan yesterday when I visited her urts. One of the reporters was also there. He and I were asking questions. I asked something about shamanism, and the reporter turned to me and said angrily, "Don't talk about that." Soyan couldn't understand the words, but everyone could understand his tone. I found him abrasive and rude and felt embarrassed to be there with him.

I take the camcorder into her urts. She allows a short interview and then says she's too old to answer my questions and I need to meet Gosta, the next-oldest shaman. "You'll understand why when you are my age," she says. When I leave, she gives me reindeer milk cheese and incense made from juniper. "Make a small silk pouch for the incense, put it around your neck, and you will always have something good to smell."

Dan is beginning a meeting. There are special customs about who sits where in an urts. Normally a foreigner my age would be across from the door, but I am sitting near the door so I can videotape the meeting. I don't have a cameraperson on this trip. An older man arrives with a baby tucked into his deel. He motions me closer to the fire so he can fit in. I move back and motion him closer to the fire. It's a little dance. He eventually moves closer with the baby. Even though it's the beginning of August, the fire feels good. I discover this man is the shaman, Gosta.

Gosta and I go to Soyan's tent for an interview. The NPR reporters want to tape my interview. I say no, because I don't find them respectful and sensitive to the people and culture.

I set up the camera and borrow one of Dan's interpreters. This is the first time Gosta, elder Dukha shaman, and I talk about various aspects of spirit and beliefs.

Although he is restrained about shamanism, I think we make a good connection and I am hopeful that another time he might feel comfortable enough to invite me to a ceremony. I want to learn from him how shaman ceremonies work.

"Just came for the vitamins," he says, as he mounts a reindeer to ride to his encampment an hour away.

Chuluu G. Talks

I am sitting beside Chuluu G., the elderly woman who helped me off my horse after the long ride here. She is a delicately boned woman with prominent rosy cheeks and long, gray hair in a bun. She wears a quilted blue silk deel and a fuchsia headscarf. We are in her urts at Meng Bulag in the West Taiga, with the camcorder on a tripod and Badma translating. Chuluu G. has agreed to tell about her life and the changes that have occurred since she began as a reindeer herder 61 years ago. I am anxious to hear from her because, although I thought she was an elderly woman, she is actually only two years older than I am—and I don't consider myself elderly. Knowing this, though, gives me pause and a feeling of connection.

While I was living nearly the same number of years in houses and riding in cars in the U.S., Chuluu G. was here in the high mountains of Mongolia, riding reindeer. I want to understand her life.

"You are two years older than I am and you have lived this very difficult life all this time. My life is pretty easy. I don't have to move. I don't have animals. My children are grown up."

"Things are changing for us. When I was a child, my father would say it was too long if we stayed in one place 20 days. We moved around a lot. Today we stay for two months at the summer pasture."

Chuluu G. rolls a three-inch strip of birch bark in her hands as she speaks in her melodic yet straightforward voice. Behind her are little birch baskets she has probably made. She follows my eyes and nods.

"The cover of the urts was birch bark when I was young. We sewed the pieces together. First we took birch bark from a tree and boiled it in water. After we boiled it, it got softer. Then we made thread from the wool of sheep or another animal. The rain never got into the urts. It just flowed outside from the top to the bottom. We have birch trees around here now whose trunks are thin, but when I was a child I went to the places where there were a lot of birch trees with broad trunks. My father climbed the tree and cut the bark from the top down, so it was the length of the tree."

Chuluu G. moves her hands in a vertical motion.

"It seems to me the pieces of birch bark were very wide, from big trees, because for one urts cover we used only three or four pieces of bark. Birch bark was light, which made it easy for us to carry those items we made from it when we moved to the next pasture. We made a lot of things from birch bark—for instance, the pail for milking our reindeer and the pot for cooking meat."

She picks up a plastic bag, folds it as if making a French seam on top of the birch bark. I understand that when they soaked the bark and folded it this way, the pot or pail did not leak. Native Americans sealed birch bark for containers by overlapping it, too. The urts I am sitting in today has a canvas cover, similar to those used by the Lakota Sioux.

"In the taiga, it is quite cold in the winter. Sometimes we live in the urts. Sometimes we make a little cabin to live in. In the winter, when I was a child, we used reindeer skin for the winter urts covering. We rubbed it to make it soft, took all the hair off, and covered the urts poles with it. When it rained in summer, it made the leather hard, and that's why we used it only in winter. Reindeer skin covering was actually very warm."

A young girl comes in, singing, and feeds the fire. I hear the ping of the metal as the stove expands. The heat of the stove feels cozy right now. It is a raw day.

"When I was a child, we used to live far from central places, so flour and rice were very rare. We ate a lot of meat. My father was a hunter and I have grown up eating meat. I think they used to hunt squirrels. They used to even make deels out of squirrel skin or reindeer skin. They took the hair off. When I was young, they made a skin deel for me, but I didn't know what was nice and what was not nice. I didn't like it that when it rained the leather got dry and hard and I had to rub it again. When I got older, my teenage years, we had the material we have now and things got more modern. When I started at school, I was competing with the other children to have the nicest clothes and I made my father buy me a new deel. My father used to buy a lot for me. At the time, boys used to wear green deels. It was quite rare to have a deel of silk, but he got me one."

Chuluu G. looks at the birch bark in her hands and pauses before continuing.

"Generally, we didn't have any toys to play with. My father cut down a plant that grew beside the river, put holes in it, and made a musical instrument for me. It had a beautiful sound. Children ran to my father because it was nice to hear him play that instrument. It was a flute. My mother used to make a long instrument from wood and put a string on the side. It became a mouth harp. A lot of children came into the urts to see the musical instruments that my parents made to keep me happy and to have fun."

I understand why children would come to a flute. My son makes and plays flutes and drums; I am always drawn to the sound. A baby reindeer says, "no-ah, no-ah," close to the urts.

"When I was a child, we didn't have a stove like this." Chuluu G. nods toward the wood stove in the center of her urts. "We had an open fire. The fire would make my eyes sore and red, so I thought that if I could go to school, I would be separated from this open fire."

We laugh. We hear singing from outside.

"I wished I could go to school. I was the only child of my parents and there were very few people who had reindeer around here. I wanted to study. We reindeer herders are Dukhas, from Tyva, a country north of here in Russia. At home, we spoke Tyvan, but I had learned Mongolian, too. I kept asking my parents if I could go to school so I could get away from the open fire. Instead of school, my father came home one day with a little tiny silver stove, which had a narrow pipe to take the smoke out. He wanted me to stay home. With that new stove, other children used to come to my home and play with me."

I nod. We hold eye contact. A teenage boy brings in an armload of wood, drops it inside the door, and leaves.

"My parents spoiled me. I liked it then, but now I think a spoiled child is not a very good thing."

"Why not?"

"A spoiled child will do what she wants all the time. I made my father get that stove and it was heavy to pack it on the reindeer when we moved. I feel bad about it now."

Chuluu G. motions with her hands as she talks. The wind moves the canvas closer, then sucks it out, like a bellows.

"In those days, children went to school when they were eight years old. I was 10 when I finally went to Ulaan Uul to school and graduated from the fourth grade. After that, I was sent to Khatgal for secondary school. Khatgal is near Lake Khovsgol, far away. I was homesick. Once when my father came to visit, I was crying, so he brought me home to live in Ulaan Uul. My father then figured that I was alone and lonely because I was an only child, so he adopted a son from another family living in Ulaan Uul.

"I have an adopted daughter and a son. Do you have any children?" I ask.

"Actually, I have 13 children. Seven are my children and the others are the children of my husband's two brothers, who have died. I had eight births. Four girls and four sons. One of our sons has died."

"I have twin grandsons who are five years old now," I say.

"Oh, twin grandsons!"

"How many grandchildren do you have?"

"If I count all the grandchildren, my adopted children and my own children," says Chuluu G., "I have more than 20."

"You are way ahead of me. Two years older and way ahead." We laugh.

"I got married 39 years ago. My oldest is 38. My youngest is 24." We talk about our parents and families. Then I say, "I don't want to tire you. Is there anything else you want to say about your childhood?"

She pauses, thinking. "Do you have any other questions?"

"I have one. I am wondering, do shamans have a role in your life?"

"My father was a shaman, so I know shamans exist. But I always ask myself if it is true."

"What would make it true?"

"He used to wear strange clothes and play a drum. People came from Ulaanbaatar and Darkhan to see my father."

My eyes widen. "Did he heal people? What did he do?"

"He would do a ceremony for them. He told them, 'You need to do this and this.' He used to give them things, a little bit of a plant, a little water from the river—to heal them. My father's father was a shaman, too. My grandfather had five sons—my father was the youngest, so my grandfather trained him."

"I heard it was illegal to be a shaman during the Soviet period from 1920–1990. Was that true here, too?" I asked.

"Yes. During the socialist time, government people used to take the instruments and tools of shamans away from them. There were only two shamans left during the socialist time. My father was one of them. My father was doing something to stop them from taking his tools away from him."

"What did he do?"

"I think he performed ceremonies—talked to the spirits to ask for protection."

"I see." I remember reading about this.

"Right after my father died, I moved his tools and clothes to a special place. When something goes wrong for me, I go to that place, but I don't get a response. I use the place for praying.

"My father died for no reason. He visited my home one day and seven days later somebody came and said, 'Your father has died.' I was thinking, 'No, he has not died, he is okay.' I went to my father's home. I remembered that he used to wear his socks all the time, even when he slept, but when I got there, he was naked. He was just lying down like someone who died in the hospital. I was thinking maybe he was just knocked out or something, but he had died. He had given instructions about what to do with his shaman clothes and instrument. 'Put these things in a place close to here that my daughter can reach.' I looked for that special place—it was a place with a tree. I put them against the tree. I go there when I pray."

"Are there still pieces there?"

"For 13 years, they stayed there and nothing happened to them, but last year, the lower part of the clothing was torn off. When I go to that place, it is very strange. In winter, around the lunar New Year, I visit, and sometimes it snows, but around the clothes and the tree there is no snow. In summer, when it rains, there is an area around the tree where it stays dry. There is a circle around those clothes where no snow or rain falls."

Finished with her story, Chuluu G. smiles, stands up, leaves the urts, and walks with the other herders to meet their reindeer coming back from the pasture. She leads five reindeer to a spot near her urts and ties them to stakes for the night. The wind blows the skirt of her deel in circles, loose canvas from her urts flaps in the breeze, and the reindeer grunt.

I am still thinking about a circle where no rain or snow falls.

Visiting Gosta

The day before we leave, Dan and his wife need to pay for some reindeer meat they got from Gosta. I will go, too, because it is a perfect opportunity to connect with Gosta and Khanda, his niece, who lives with him. Also, I want to practice riding over flatter land so I might have a better time on the horse when we go back down the mountains. I am determined not to fall off, not to hurt myself, and, most of all, not to be scared.

We start on a path. From where we are in a settlement of seven urts, we cross a river and are immediately riding through the next settlement, welcomed by families and barking dogs. Nansalmaa, the state veterinarian who came with us, is cleaning a sore on a reindeer. All four urts in this settlement are alive with activity. The path takes us across a wild river again and again. It seems easier with a sober wrangler leading me. Tsermaa's horse shies at the noisy water each time we have to cross. My horse plods on through, no problem. By the time we see Gosta's urts, I feel calmer about riding. It could be because I've now had a little experience or that my foot has had a week to heal, but I am not feeling so vulnerable.

I want to ask Gosta if he will show me his drum and costume, but I don't. I know these things can't be rushed. I feel honored that he even spoke with me in front of the camera a couple of days ago. We have a quick visit, drink reindeer milk tea, look at photos, and have our picture taken together. Then Dan, Tsermaa, and I climb back on our horses. They ride fast, since they are having another meeting with some people in the other settlement. I am being led at slow speed, but that is fine with me.

As I cross the river for the third time, I notice that where there was a settlement of four urts, three are gone, and the canvas is off the fourth one. Only the poles stand. The herders are moving! I stop and take out my camcorder, thinking, *This is perfect. What do nomadic reindeer herders do? Move. How do they do it? Now I can find out.* What could be better? I see a woman kicking the ashes out of her stove, children playing volleyball without a net, and older children playing a keyboard. I guess it would be relaxed like this if you moved five or more times a year, but still, there is no tension, as there always was when my family packed up to go somewhere.

A nomad named Tsermaa tries to decide whether to take a couch seat to the next encampment. No, it doesn't fit on the reindeer. They leave it on the ground. They tie thermos bottles alongside stovepipes and stoves. A five-year-old boy sits on a reindeer saddle with piles of clothes around him. He tries on different hats while waiting. Urts poles are stacked and left for next summer, when the herders will return here. Couples tie reindeer together so they will walk single file, the pack animals as well as those ridden by the family. It is August 7. "We are leaving for the fall camp," they tell me.

"The weather will soon turn," Tsermaa says as she rides off on her reindeer.

At night, the wind is so loud it sounds like a freight train is plowing into our urts. The storm is so strong that an NPR reporter's tent blows down. He is not a humble person. Both reporters annoy me by asking the herders questions over and over again if they don't get the answers they want. With his tent down, he appears at 3:00 in the morning, like a dog with his tail between his legs, in Zorig's urts, where I am sleeping, along with Zorig's wife and kids and two others. Now there are 11 sleeping here. Zorig gets up and checks to see if my bedding is wet from touching the canvas. Last night, just like every night, after I climbed into my -15° F sleeping bag, he piled two quilts on top of me. Satisfied that the bedding is dry, he goes back to bed on the other side of the urts.

The day dawns cloudy and rainy. The reporter moves back to his tent. As evening falls, on August 8, it begins to snow. Everyone is happy. Reindeer love snow. Children and couples want their photos taken with the reindeer. They choose the ones with the biggest antlers and smile broadly, as more snow falls.

When we wake up the next morning, it is winter, with snow a few inches deep. The weather indeed has turned, as, of course, the herders knew it would. Whiteness is everywhere, perfect for photos, which we take.

It is time for us to leave. The snow melts as we take off down the mountain. The horses need to walk carefully, as they can't see rocks and don't wear shoes, as horses do in the U.S. As we get to a lower altitude, we are back in the green world. The snow is gone.

We stop at an ovoo, one of the sacred cairns, give thanks by walking around it three times, and leave an offering of stones. This time a completely sober Battulga and I are in the lead. He motions for me to get off and walk over some steep boulders while he leads the horses. I am grateful that I can walk now. Battulga checks my horse and saddle. I have insisted on longer reins so they don't slip out of my hands every time the horse puts his head down. Now we have been riding for six hours and I am still not terrified. In fact, the only sign of my former self is a broken blister on my index finger from gripping the metal loop on the front of the saddle. I am determined to make it without falling.

Battulga leads me past the others when they stop to check their horses. They have gotten ahead, and he wants to be in the lead. We are going down a hill lined with reindeer moss, passing the others on the rocky trail. Suddenly, I realize something is wrong. I lean back and farther back, but I keep slipping forward, and then my saddle slides off the side of the horse. I land on some moss, but the camera pack on my side smashes into my ribs. My ribs feel crunchy.

Battulga is horrified. He says it is his fault. He didn't check the saddle cinches the last time everyone stopped, and the back one on my saddle has broken. These are not wide American cinches, but two one-inch leather straps. From the high level of my pain, I wonder, *Do I have broken ribs? Broken blood vessels? Damaged spleen? Punctured lung?* The fall has knocked the wind out of me. Battulga says, "Chud, chud," holding his thumb and index finger an inch apart. I know this means "short, short" or "little, little"—referring to the distance still to ride—but for all I know it could be three hours or five minutes. He hoists me onto his horse and climbs on mine, broken saddle and all, and we are off again. I am impressed that he is completely balanced going down a steep hill with a loose saddle. In 45 minutes we reach the cars. I am hurting and lie on the ground. Battulga gives me a back massage. The team doesn't mention my fall or ask how I am, but on the drive to Tsagaan Nuur, every jounce causes pain in my side.

It is hard to sleep. I can't figure out what's wrong. I don't know if I broke anything and I have no way to find out. It just hurts. Sometimes being a nurse and knowing what it could be is a disadvantage. I run through the same litany—broken ribs, punctured lung, broken blood vessel, damaged pancreas. In any case, I wake up the next morning still in pain, but without specific symptoms. I know I can't go to the East Taiga to deliver vitamins, as I had planned. I need to leave the taiga and get medical help. Veterinarian Nansalmaa will take the vitamins to the East Taiga.

There are other reasons to leave. It is snowing and I know the way would be too hard. With bad weather, there is no guarantee I would make it out for my flight back to Vermont in five days. I ride in the Russian jeep to Ulaan Uul, feeling a stab of pain with every bump. It is here that we left the sick children, so we stop at the Ulaan Uul hospital and ask about them. The girl is okay but the boy's kidneys had shut down, so they sent him to the Murun hospital and have not heard anything since. Without infrastructure, there is no way to get answers. I wonder if I will ever hear how the boy is. Again, I hold him in the Light.

We stay in Ulaan Uul with Yura—a nurse-midwife, pharmacist, and shaman. She unpacks her shaman costume and presses some sacred objects against my side for healing. After she gives me a massage, I fall asleep on her couch for the night. In the morning when we are ready to leave, Yura says, "Sorry I couldn't do a healing ceremony for you this time. My husband is my assistant and I can't do it without him. He is away. Maybe next time."

No problem. My plan is to manage the pain with ibuprofen until I get home—and I do.

United States

On my first back day in Vermont, I go to my doctor. In the waiting room I focus on staying awake. I am jet-lagged. It would be embarrassing to fall over sideways out of the chair in the doctor's office. When I get into her office, she tells me the pain from falling on the camera is only a bruise and it will get better. For my foot, she orders x-rays, which show that there is a fracture, but it is healing well.

A few weeks later, I am safely in my bed in Vermont reading a book when I come across a line about a man who gets angry at his horse and shoots him. My heart races. My stomach feels queasy. My foot twinges. My ribs ache. I slam the book shut and throw it under my bed with shaky hands. No more reading that book. I realize what it must be like to have post-traumatic stress disorder. I calm myself by saying that that level of adventure happens once in a lifetime. I may go again, but next time it will be by helicopter or some easier method. So I think.

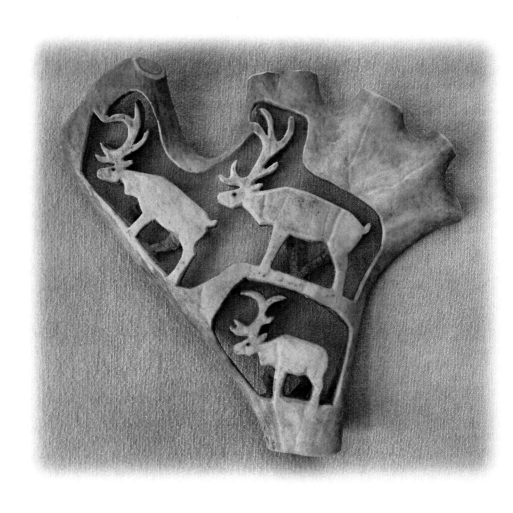

Baasankhuu, of the West Taiga, used hand tools to make this carving from a reindeer antler.

photo credit: Winslow Colwell

2005

> You must not change one thing, one pebble, one grain
> of sand, until you know what good and evil will follow on
> that act. The world is in balance, in Equilibrium. A wizard's
> power of Changing and Summoning can shake the balance
> of the world. It is dangerous, that power. It is most perilous.
> It must follow knowledge, and serve need. To light a candle
> is to cast a shadow.
> — Ursula K. Le Guin, *A Wizard of Earthsea*

A Year Off

The next year I stay home and edit my movie, *Gobi Women's Song*. I appreciate every minute of the soft gentleness of Vermont. In February the following year, though, a yearning begins. I want to see Khanda and Gosta and the others. I check on the cost for a helicopter: $10,000 for a ride from Ulaanbaatar to the taiga and back. That's out—I can only go by car and horse. I need to go back, but I keep telling myself I shouldn't. It would be irresponsible, because I could die or become disabled riding that path to the settlement.

Around the same time I have a conversation with Barbara, whom I call my co-grandmother, because we share twin grandsons. I find myself telling her I shouldn't go because I hate the thought of my son—her son-in-law—having to go to Mongolia to pick up the pieces if I don't make it. She shakes her head. "I don't know about that. You can't stop doing your work for fear of dying. You will die when you die. There is a movie called *Appointment in Samara*, about a man who travels continually to avoid meeting his death and ends up in the place at which he has been appointed to die."

I think about this a lot. We all die eventually. I could die, yet I need to go. I know that I have to conquer this fear. I don't want a lot of unfinished karma left over from this life. To prepare, I take more riding lessons. Riding around a ring is so easy compared to riding the trail to Meng Bulag, where the West Taiga herders are. It's like preparing to take a rowboat across the ocean by sitting in a bathtub.

I have a dream about riding. I wake up knowing I am afraid of heights. My neighbor gives me a hypnotherapy session in which I am encouraged to turn down the volume of the fear. She plants the idea that it will be pleasant riding. I may even find myself humming or singing along the way. I decide that, wimpy as it once seemed, I am going to use a riding helmet this time. And I still have my padded bike shorts and fitted riding pants, as well as a new, thinner, but padded deel. I feel as prepared as I can be.

This farthest settlement of the East Taiga, close to the Russian border and Siberia, is the home of 11 families living in urts. The herders stake their reindeer to keep them close by.

photo credit: Fred Thodal

Khanda sits on a bearskin to protect her from the wet ground of Meng Bulag, West Taiga, and sews saddlebags with her hand-driven sewing machine.

photo credit: Sas Carey

2006

> You gain strength, courage, and confidence by every experience in which you really stop to look fear in the face. You must do the thing which you think cannot do.
> — Eleanor Roosevelt

To the Taiga

Now that I know I am going, I discuss the trip with my friend Roger Desautels, who suggests that I stay longer in the taiga with the reindeer herders this year. My first thought is, *All that time without fresh food? Fruit? Vegetables? Bathrooms? Safe water?* On the other hand—well, it's the same scary horseback ride no matter how long I stay. I can stay as long as I want, take whomever I want, and organize it so it fits my work schedule, because I will be the leader of the trip this time. I learned from Dan, and now it will be my responsibility to gather a team when I get there.

"The advantage," Roger continues, "would be that you could catch the fine points of their life. Think about how we behave with guests. It can last just so long. There are probably certain ways reindeer herders act when tourists visit and other ways when they leave. It all amounts to details for your shaman film."

Sure, it makes sense. Forget about the luxuries of American life. Plan a longer trip. Forget about a tent. How will we experience every detail if we aren't living in the urts with the herders?

Just before I leave Vermont, a friend tells me that The Shelley & Donald Rubin Foundation wants to learn about the health of the Dukha reindeer herders. They are interested in supporting a project to create a Dukha Health Database. Since my purpose is to find out what the herders need for health care, our goals match perfectly. I make a proposal and a budget, but we are unable to talk before

I leave because Bruce Payne, the foundation's executive director, is out of the country. My plan is to begin the database with basic information, like vital signs, and continue it in future years, adding other data as we go along.

Traveling alone halfway around the world requires trust. While driving me to the Burlington Airport, my friend Jon says, "You have a place to sleep tonight, right? An apartment? Someone meeting you?"

"Yes, Enkhe, the country director of the American Center for Mongolian Studies, is on top of it. He has found me an apartment. It is all set."

The plane from Beijing to Ulaanbaatar is delayed three hours. I have already been traveling for 30 hours when I get this news. Instead of leaving at 9:00 PM, it will leave at midnight, arriving in Ulaanbaatar at around 2:00 AM. Still, Enkhe is at the airport with a taxi when I arrive and we drive to the apartment. On the way, though, he tells me that the owner has changed her mind about the price and instead of $400 a month, she wants $30 a day. I have nowhere else to go, so he drops me off there. The bed doesn't even have covers. At 3:00 AM, I lie down, cover myself with my deel, and try to sleep for a few hours.

At 9:00 AM, I call Munkhjin, whom I call my Mongolian daughter. She graduated from Middlebury College, in my town. Munkhjin says, "Come stay with my family, Sas. You can live here this year." Relieved, I hold the door while the taxi driver lugs the bags back downstairs and up the three flights to Munkhjin's. My bags are not light, since I carry 20 pounds of vitamin C crystals, gifts, and video and camping equipment.

I love being with Munkhjin. She is a kind, enthusiastic person who believes I am doing important work for Mongolians. Munkhjin lives in the Sansar district of Ulaanbaatar with her parents, who are my age. A bustling neighborhood, it is full of busy stores and apartment buildings with families. Everything is easy. I can shop close by, get a taxi right out in front, and cook what I want or eat what the family offers. Since Munkhjin's mother is a diplomat and the family has lived around the world, my lactose intolerance and vegetarianism don't seem as weird as they do to other Mongolians. They won't take any rent and will help in any way they can. Not being able to keep the other apartment is a slight deviation in the plan, but it is perfect—it pays to trust.

Now for a team. I start with those on Dan's and my past teams and invite them to meet at a sidewalk café in Ulaanbaatar. I have been in touch with Tsogtsaikhan, who has offered to guide me in this "hiring" process. Besides being the director of Taiga Nature, he works with the United Nations. He has good English and is a high-level person whose judgment I trust. Guide Battulga, translator Zula, veterinarian Nansalmaa (who will be on her own in the taiga, but will ride with us as a representative of the Totem Peoples Project), and cameraman Mende are here. New people are Zula's sister, Davaa, a potential translator, since Zula can't come this time; driver Puji's younger relative, who is called Little Puji, since Big Puji can't come; and Batar, another driver vying for the job. Puji has a Mitsubishi Delica SUV. Batar has a Russian Furgon. How do I decide? Battulga suggests I check out the two cars to see which will be better. I choose the smaller and more comfortable Mitsubishi. Tsogtsaikhan will not come this time—he is just helping today. I am making all the decisions.

When interviewing Davaa for the interpreter job, I tell her that she will need to cook in addition to interpreting, and she says, "Oh, I need to cook, too?"

"Only if you want to eat," I say.

She laughs. "Oh, I get it." This tells me a lot: she can understand humor in English. I hire her. Our taiga team consists of Battulga, Mende, and Davaa, with Little Puji driving and Nansalmaa along for the ride.

As we pack the car, Nansalmaa has her own agenda—she brings her son and then, later, her niece. I am not too happy about this, because I chose the smaller, more comfortable car in consideration of the number of passengers and amount of luggage I thought we would have. Now it is crowded, since we have medical supplies in addition to the camping gear, video equipment, vitamins, and everyone's personal luggage. When the extra passengers slip into the car,

I remind myself that in Mongolia I am not actually in charge. The culture trumps anything I could decide. The Mongolian custom is to never leave an inch of space in the car when going on a long trip. Pack in as many as you can.

We are on our way! I notice changes as we leave the city. Colorful signboards announce gas stations. Concrete pads and digital pumps replace last year's rusty tanks and hoses. Rich sights greet us along the road. The steppes are endless, with mountains and rolling hills. Puji blows his horn to clear herds of horses or flocks of sheep and cashmere goats from the road. Some sheep hesitate, not knowing whether to follow the others across the road or turn back to avoid the car. The land is bright green with gashes of reddish-brown tracks cutting through the land, as many as 20 tracks side by side, going up a hill. If a track is too bumpy, a driver makes a new one. That's why there are so many. A mushroom-shaped ger is visible ahead. Foals are tied to pegs in a line beside the ger, while the mares are out to pasture. When the mares come back to their babies, the woman of the family will milk them. A windmill and solar panel, along with a satellite dish, stand beside the ger to provide electricity and reception for television. We pass wooden electric poles cabled to concrete poles, which are sunk into the ground. Permafrost and severe winter weather necessitate the extensions. Electricity goes to a soum center, but it is unreliable. Under a red, white, and blue plastic cover over a truck bed, two people are playing cards, seemingly impossible along this pitted track. The thought of reading a book in a car makes me laugh. This is impossible on a Mongolian road. We pass a truck that has flipped on its side. A big pile of sacks containing flour or rice lies beside it on the ground. The bone-crunching ride gives our faces a green cast, although our Delica SUV is much more comfortable than the Furgon. I am wearing a seatbelt and there is air conditioning, which is great, because the temperature is 95° F, and there are shock absorbers.

Then we stop at a guanz. The team members eat meat, rice, and potatoes. When I pay the bill for everyone, it totals $8.20. Being in charge means paying for everything.

Demoiselle cranes swoop in front of our car and land beside us.

The land blushes with low purple irises. Then yellow flowers tint the landscape. Brooms can be made from the bush they grow on, Puji tells me. The mountains are tinged with blue from sages of various hues. The sky is deep blue with a few puffy clouds. I am in love with this landscape.

The team is good. Other people go on vacation with friends and family. This feels like family—Puji's brother, Zula's sister—people I have traveled with before. We see a big yak herd. Then we see dead cows along the roadside. Green, green, green land. Every time the car overheats, the driver opens the hood to let the engine cool at the top of a windy hill. The temperature? 97° Fahrenheit. More open land. If we take the wrong track, no problem, just drive over the grass to another one. Then rocky outcroppings. We pass eagles, condors, and magpies. Brown squirrels with thin tails dart in front of our car.

After 18 hours of traveling, we arrive at our goal for today—Murun. When we check into a guesthouse, we find there is an on-demand water heater with a shower! We take showers before the tub gets black from Battulga and Mende scrubbing out some oil that spilled onto Mende's sleeping bag in the car. I appreciate the fact that Mende doesn't complain, but I would have, if it were my problem.

I am suffocating in this heat with my long, thick tee shirt. Thinking of last year, I packed warm clothes for cold weather. But that was October and this is early August. When I mention this to Ganaa, a very nice friend of the guesthouse's owner, she lends me a sleeveless cotton blouse, and immediately I feel more comfortable.

Ganaa offers to help us get border permission for our travel to the taiga, as Dan did last year. Since I am a foreigner, I am told to wait outside the border patrol building while Ganaa goes inside for permission.

It takes so long, I begin to make a plan for what we'll do if we don't get permission and can't go to the taiga. Maybe we can go to Yura's and tape a shaman ceremony. At that point, Ganaa comes out to say that we were supposed to get this permission signed in Ulaanbaatar, and disappears back inside. The next time she comes out, she tells us they don't want foreigners in the taiga. They don't want anyone to get hurt up there, what with livestock rustlers at the border and the challenging terrain. Also, they want to make sure people are good riders. I figure they probably don't want any older people there, either. Finally, the bureaucrats are leaving for lunch, so I walk to a store for food supplies and buy a big bag of pasta, tomato paste, a few onions, and ramen noodles. We also have a watermelon from Ulaanbaatar to eat on the way. We need a lot more food, but there isn't anything else to buy—and no space in the car. Too bad Murun is the last place to buy a variety of foods. North of here, our food choices will run from mutton, yak, and milk to tea, soda, candy, and cookies—no vegetables or fruit.

After lunch, Ganaa walks out waving the paper. It is signed and stamped. I fold it carefully and place it in my passport. Later, I realize that the rigmarole was all about a $10 donation to Ganaa for her help. Maybe the border patrol officer got a cut, too. The paper was supposed to be free, but this is Mongolia, and I am slowly learning the ropes.

Now it is time to leave on the last leg of our trip to the taiga. Puji pushes his Mongolian pop-music tape into the cassette player and we are off. We travel though rocky ridges and over more rivers. For the first time we see trees. Green larches adorn the northern side of the mountains here. Flowers turn a mile of steppe purple. Winter nomadic camps are tucked into the hills, noticeable because of permanent fences and dung piles, but the herders have moved to their spring pastures.

We cross a rickety bridge and stop at a guanz. To me, this is a special place—it's the one where we stopped with Dan and visited two sick children in a remote ger two years ago. I have never heard if the boy lived or not. Today I ask the hostess what happened to those children.

"Oh, you are the one!" she says. Her face lights up and she runs to the next building. The children's mother and father and a round-faced boy come in, beaming. The father says, "If it weren't for you, I wouldn't have any children. They are five and six now."

The mother says, "The hospital said if it had been five minutes more, they would have died." I can't stop smiling when I think about it. I'd been wondering about them and holding them in the Light for two years.

The road we are on now is one of the worst in Mongolia. Sand flats, mountains, tree roots on steep hills, streambeds. I am enjoying the shock absorbers, which are superior to the ones in the Furgon. Yet the Delica ride is still far from being smooth. Beside the road, all the way, are two deep tracks about 15 inches wide. Nothing is growing there. What are these? I want to know. Battulga and Puji explain that a huge Russian bulldozer drove all the way to a gold mine in the taiga. Then the Mongolian government increased the tax on mining and the bulldozer drove all the way back without doing anything except destroying this strip of land for miles and miles.

We stop at Thirteen Ovoos, at the top of the long pass. I feel I am getting close when we stop here. We give thanks for safe passage and take advantage of a photo op, sitting in front of the bright blue khadaghs blowing in the wind while Bayara clicks the shutter. The next stop is the ovoo above the valley where Tsagaan Nuur is. Then the treacherous downhill, the last muddy lowlands ready to suck the car in, around a lake, up a hill, and there below us are the low wooden buildings of Tsagaan Nuur. It has taken 20 hours of driving to get here.

Nyama and Ganba come out to meet our car, smiling, looking me in the eye. "Sas! You have come again. We are happy to have you. How is your foot? Are you hungry? What would you like to eat?"

I am happy to see my friends. They took good care of me last time when I wasn't feeling so well. "Fish," I answer. "I have been looking forward to it." There are whitefish in the lake that Tsagaan Nuur is named after, and when Nyama cooks them they are unimaginably delicious.

It is cold here, about 40° F, so I know it will be very cold in the taiga. We have arranged for eight horses—four for us to ride and two packhorses for each of the wranglers to lead. I am anxious to go to the West Taiga first, to get the riding challenge over with, but word comes to Battulga that the West Taiga Dukhas are still in their spring quarters and will be moving to their summer quarters in a day or two. This means they will be busy and that it is not a good time to visit. Before I left the United States, Dan advised me to visit both the East Taiga and the West Taiga—otherwise the people we didn't visit would feel left out.

After a peaceful sleep at Nyama and Ganba's, we ride horses for four hours to the East Taiga. I won't say I am completely confident, but I enjoy the sounds: splash, clonk, the hollow clunk of the bit in the horse's mouth, and the neighing of the horses. The wind and the gurgling river feel welcoming. Battulga promises that he will not let me fall off. I take his word for it. The smell of horses, the rhythm of my swaying horse, and the pristine air become a meditation. The ground is still a bog. This area of Mongolia has permafrost, so there is nowhere for the water to go. It sits on the ground making mud. Deep mud. Sometimes I wish there were a stronger word that means deep, thick, sticky, hoof-sinking, sucking mud. But there is only the word "mud."

Some rivers still have patches of snow and ice. We are climbing to an altitude of 10,000 feet. It is June, but it is cold enough to wear gloves, a fall deel, and layers. As we ride, our feet swish past miles and miles of wild rhododendron bushes. A purple mist covers the ground. Occasionally the high bushes push my foot out of the stirrup, even though Mongolian stirrups are large and round on the bottom. On my last trip this would have sent terror through me. This time, I calmly stick my foot back in. I see fields of yellow flowers, then pink, then blue as we gain altitude. More mud—so moist it smells fresh, as if I've been digging in my garden. The tamarack trees are sprouting their needles. The view stretches from the top of the mountain we are climbing to the Sayan Mountains on the Russian border. There are no roads, no vehicles, and no electric lines. This is the pure nature of Mongolia, the largest pristine wilderness in the world. This is what Dan saw and I missed the last time we were here.

The East Taiga Dukha are still in their spring camps. The closest group lives in an open field with no trees, beside a river. They have been here a while, and the land close to each urts is getting muddy. We are invited to stay in the urts of Ulzii and Tsogkhuu, two young bachelors. In the morning it is so quiet, I want to sleep all day. Ulzii makes a fire and gives us milk tea. We stayed here last time, and now he and

Tunga, his girlfriend, feel comfortable enough to tell their story.

Ulzii and Tunga, a Story

Ulzii lives in this bachelor urts. Tunga lives with her family of origin. In the taiga, it is hard to find a mate, create a family, and find a way to survive. As for creating a family, most of the reindeer herders here are related. As for survival, the herders do not live on a money economy. Ulzii tells us their story:

"Tunga and I have a one-year-old daughter, Ehkhbayar, and plan to get married in August. At that time, we will get a new urts. Our neighbors will give us animals—maybe two or three reindeer each. They will go hunting and give us meat, reindeer milk, money for clothes, and other things. We have no steady income. In autumn we pick berries and sell them. Two to three hundred kilos (450–650 pounds) of wild cranberries bring 100,000 tugrik ($100). The money from the berries will last two or three months. This buys us basic food—rice and flour."

Davaa and I are sitting on the ground in the urts across the wood stove from Ulzii. As Ulzii continues, I notice his teeth are missing.

"In the spring we collect reindeer antlers. One kilogram (2.2 pounds) brings 15,000 tugrik ($15). We can collect two or three kilos. People come to get antlers to make money. We used to cut live antlers, but we noticed the reindeer became ill, so we stopped cutting live antlers and are not doing that as a business now.

"We don't pick herbs to sell, as there is no one to buy them. We used to pick pine nuts for money. They went to China, and we were making good money on them. They aren't going to China now, so we stopped that business. We are not making any steady money now. We get a total of one liter (.9 quart) of milk a day from our five reindeer. That's what we live on."

Indeed, they do get married, and three years later when we visit to collect data for the health database, they have a healthy 10-day-old baby. Now they live in their own urts with their two children. Tunga's mother lives next door. Unlike many others their age, Ulzii and Tunga are committed to continuing the nomadic way of life.

Herders share stories like this as we go from urts to urts, visiting each family. Our job is to collect health data on every herder: name, age, and any health problems. But the Dukha often tell us much more. Kidney problems, leg and arm cramps, tonsil pain, losing teeth, high blood pressure, anemia, and toothaches are just the beginning.

We are riding horses to the farthest East Taiga settlement, only a few hours away. The land we pass over is varied. We ride from a settlement along a river in open land, through the wet, boggy forest of the taiga, through brush and muddy hills to the next settlement. When we arrive at the camp, which is in a field of high grass bordered by two rivers and tamarack trees, the needles on the trees are just coming out. Nature is soft and quiet here except for the gushing rivers and the grunting of reindeer. Cuckoo birds sing incessantly, sounding just like a cuckoo clock. When the herders come to greet our team, one of the women, Munkhuu, exclaims, "Oh, it's you!" My heart takes a leap. I feel blessed to be known by this ail.

We three—Davaa, Mende, and I—are invited to stay in the urts of a young couple, G. Davaajav and Gantuya, and their two children, Mama, 7, and Batbayar, 4. Battulga stays with relatives. Our family has a television. Whenever it is sunny enough to charge the storage battery with the solar panel, the community gathers here to watch news, weather, or movies dubbed into Mongolian.

We sit outdoors in a circle with the members of the community and explain our goal—to survey them for the health database. At the same time, we ask if they have any problem with our videotaping them and if some would be willing to sing for us. When Battulga's brother starts with very guttural throat singing, I am so moved I feel choked up. Children, teenagers, men, and one elderly woman all give me shivers when they sing songs of mother, reindeer, and nature. The taiga people do not hold back with their voices—they can sing loudly enough to carry to the next mountains, and they do. They sing their hearts out, and I can feel the strong vibrations in mine.

Tsend the Shaman and Local Health Treatments

The families invite our team into their homes to do the health assessments for the database. When we visit one family, the couple's 18-year-old daughter, Sainbayar, is having abdominal pains on the right side. She has had them for a few days and now they are sharp. She is nauseated, can't eat, and has a fever: classic appendicitis symptoms. To say I am alarmed is an understatement. I have no idea what to do out here. We are an eight-hour horseback ride from Tsagaan Nuur. The closest hospital with a surgeon is in Rinchinlhumbe, a three-hour drive from Tsagaan Nuur over the usual washboard tracks. I feel powerless to give any real help.

In my most professional and calm manner, I ask what they will do. The father nonchalantly tells me, "Oh, we have given her a treatment already."

"What kind of treatment?"

"We soak horse manure in water for two hours and she drinks the liquid."

"And what happens?" I ask, never having heard of this folk remedy.

"The appendicitis turns from acute to chronic." I am learning something new, and I don't know what to think about it.

The next day Sainbayar feels better. Her story ends well: not only does she later successfully have her appendix out, but she eventually attends school in Ulaanbaatar.

In another urts, Shaman Tsend is not so lucky. She is 70 years old and has had liver problems since she was a child. In Ulaanbaatar she was diagnosed with liver cancer. Tsend's urts is at the other end of the encampment from where we are staying—to the south and close to the river. I walk there through tall brush to give her a healing. The herders believe that I can miraculously cure Tsend, but when I talk to her I find out that she knows she is beyond curing. I hope I can make her a little more comfortable, and so does she. Tsend understands the difference between curing and healing.

I try to explain this to her daughter the way my traditional Mongolian medicine teacher taught me. Disease is made up of negative ions. Through meditation and attunement, my hands can transmit positive energy. When they move over a sick person's energy field, the positive and negative ions bond, creating neutral energy or balance. This can encourage healing, but curing is up to the spirit. So today, I place my right hand over her midsection for about 15 minutes. Afterwards, she says she feels relaxed and asks me to come back every day that I am here.

Two days later, on the new moon, her family practices a traditional treatment. They kill a reindeer and place its healthy liver on Tsend's diseased one. The belief is that the healthy liver will absorb the disease, leaving her liver disease-free. When I enter the urts, I see blood in the shape of a liver on her blouse. It is the first time I have had a reindeer liver between my patient and me, but the healing work is no different. Energy goes deep—beyond the reindeer liver and beyond the skin. When her energy is balanced, her face relaxes and the wrinkles smooth out.

As I walk back to the urts where I am staying, I think about methods people use to heal. The placebo effect demonstrates that belief in a method increases its effectiveness. Tsend has already been diagnosed and treated in Western-type Ulaanbaatar hospitals. She decided to come home, as a hospice patient in the U.S. would. She wanted her own treatments. And just as families of those dying anywhere do, her family is trying to keep her alive, in this case by using a traditional treatment they believe in. The herders use what they have to help—and I don't judge them.

By evening, the reindeer meat from that reindeer has been distributed. Tsend's family's urts, the one closest to hers, has the most meat hanging in it. As I go further up the rise toward our urts, the amount is progressively less, but each of the nine homes has some new reindeer meat hanging from its poles.

Two months later, Tsend joins the ancestors.

Looking for Shamans in the West Taiga

Back home in Vermont, when Roger suggested I stay longer next time, I knew I wanted to live in Gosta and Khanda's urts. It is still my dream to learn about shamanism from Gosta, one of the oldest shamans among the Dukhas. Since I was in the taiga two years ago, Tsend's mother, Soyan, at 100 the oldest shaman, has joined the ancestors.

Gosta visits us in Tsagaan Nuur while we are packing to go to the West Taiga. He tells us he is on his way to Murun to get health treatments for his liver. Although he says he will be back home in a week, I am resigned to the idea that I will not see him in the taiga this year. Travel takes a long time here and there are many distractions for a reindeer herder.

Just as we climb into the Russian jeep to go to where the horses are and take off for the West Taiga, Nyama slips a yellow plastic shopping bag in my hands. Inside I find eight whitefish, each a foot long, that she smoked yesterday—gourmet food even I can eat. She caught them herself.

The wranglers and horses are already at the take-off spot. We ride up and around the mountains to Meng Bulag. It still takes eight hours and is treacherous, but I don't have the feeling that I will die every minute—just every hour or so. Meng Bulag is high in the Sayan Mountains, above Khovsgol's Darkhat Valley. We are very close to Tyva and the Russian border. At an altitude of 10,000 feet and above the tree line, there are patches of snow even now, at the end of June. At one spot, the snow is nearly two feet deep and Mende, an excellent rider but loaded down with the camera backpack, falls into the snow. In other places, the ground is soggy. We are back in the land of permafrost, with deep mud for our horses to stumble through.

Reindeer thrive here. Cold. Lichens. Reindeer moss. With feet like snowshoes, reindeer easily travel over snow and soggy ground. Battulga tells us reindeer are "the jeeps of the taiga." They can go anywhere.

"Where do you want to sleep?" Battulga asks, as some urts become visible ahead. We can stop at any urts and the family will find space for us. I long to go to Khanda's, but her settlement is another hour away. It looks as if my dream to be near shamans and to see a shaman ceremony won't come true this year, either. This is my third trip to the taiga, and I haven't seen a ceremony here yet. We will have to wait until tomorrow to go to Khanda's. It is a little hard to wait because I have already come so far, but on the other hand, eight hours of riding in a day are enough.

We choose to stay with Dalai and Bolortsetseg and their two-year-old daughter, Sara. Inside their urts, earthy smells of larch wood, horse, bread, damp ground, and leather greet us. Bolortsetseg sits in front of the wood stove, making shavings from a log with a knife and placing them in the stove at the center of the living space. She squats in front of the stove and feeds it with split logs after the splinters catch fire. The canvas cover of the urts holds the smell of wood smoke and a gray cloud trails out of the stovepipe through the cluster of poles overhead.

I watch as Bolortsetseg repeats the ritual that I saw Otgonbayar perform the last time I was here. She removes the cover from the stove, sets a large, wok-like pan in the hole, ladles water from the five-gallon jug beside the door, pounds tea in a mortar and pestle, and adds it to the water in the pan. Daily chores do not let up here. Nomadic women don't get downtime. As the water boils, she uncovers the milk that is stored on the north side of the urts and adds it by the ladleful, then puts the cover back on the pan so the milk tea will heat. This same ritual happens many times each day in all the urts and gers in Mongolia.

Bolortsetseg cuts fresh sourdough bread and places it in a pan in front of us. My stomach reminds me that I haven't eaten all day. Before our luggage is piled inside the urts door, Bolortsetseg has ladled the fresh milk tea into a teakettle and is pouring it into porcelain bowls for us. With the sweet, creamy smell and the warmth of the bowl in my hands, I can feel my shoulders relaxing. Riding a horse to Meng Bulag is the most stressful and challenging part of the trip.

I am still drinking Bolortsetseg's morning tea when Battulga arrives. He has already met someone from the other settlement.

"Good news, Sas. Ganzorig, Gosta's brother, is also a shaman. He says MAYBE there will be a ceremony while you are here. 'Maybe' is good. He didn't say, 'No.' He also says he will come here and lead you to his and Khanda's ail later today. You can stay in their settlement."

I want to jump up, yelp, and hug Battulga, but since I strive to be culturally appropriate and honor people the way they are, I just nod. Mongolians make contact with each other by shaking hands. No hugs. Battulga knows me well, though. I'll bet he sees the gleam in my eyes.

Ganzorig—a shaman. I don't know him. I remember the first time that I came to Mongolia and found out there are shamans here. Ever since then, my personal goal has been to connect with them. I kept looking for them, but looking is not the way to find shamans; they have to find you. I guess I know that now. Even though Gosta is not here, maybe I can hear the story of a shaman's life. And if I'm lucky, there will be a ceremony.

The urts flap flips open and in comes Ganzorig, a man shorter than I am, with a knit hat pulled over his forehead and a giggle that reminds me of a dear friend of mine back in New York. He looks like some kind of elf. "I'll come pick you up at 10:00 AM," Ganzorig says, leaving as soon as his bowl of tea is empty.

"He won't be here until 4:00 or 5:00 this afternoon," says Dalai, sipping from his bowl of tea. "So you can stay with Sara while we go to get wood. We'll be back in a couple of hours."

I look around at the distant horizon. I cannot see any forest. The land is smooth and treeless. Seems like we will be waiting here a long time. We watch Dalai and his ail pad their reindeer with blankets and old deels. He ties wooden saddle frames on top of the soft cover. Each reindeer is tied to another one, forming a long line. Dalai and Bolortsetseg mount their horses and lead the reindeer and two oxen, which are also saddled up. We watch the reindeer train until it is over the horizon and out of sight.

Mende, Davaa, Sara, and I have the urts to ourselves. Sara busies herself with a ladle, a little pail, and puddle of water. She dips the ladle into the puddle and pours the water into the pail. This is how her mother and all taiga women get water, although it comes from the river, not a puddle. Davaa and I decide to make spaghetti. Not hard, right? First she has to start a fire in the stove. We set the pan in the stovetop and ladle some water into it. When it boils, we add spaghetti. Then we have to drain it somehow. She carries the pan outside. I hold the spaghetti back with the top as she tips the pan.

A few pieces of spaghetti slip around the top and touch the ground. We push them back into the pan before we realize that on the ground just below the pan, like everywhere around a herder's home, is a clod of manure. It is too late to do anything. We are not going to start all over again, so we carry the pan back inside and place it on top of a triangle made of three split logs on the ground. I am horrified, though, as all my nursing training comes rushing back: bacteria. *E. coli.* In a small pan, we heat some sauce we have brought with us. We add it to the spaghetti and eat it. There are times to let things go. This is one.

Sara is asleep when Dalai comes back in three hours with the first load of wood. The taiga forest has to be far away, but it must be there, because they bring wood. Obviously, they have already cut the trees down because every animal is loaded with logs. Family members appear from the other six urts. The logs, some a foot in diameter, are balanced on the two sides of the reindeer, just as our packs were balanced on horses. It takes two people to remove the load from one reindeer. One holds one side as the other unties it from the other side, then slowly and at the same time, they lower the four-foot-long logs. The wood is larch, so it is not as heavy as I think. The reindeer look comfortable, for they are used to this work.

As soon as the logs are unloaded, the reindeer train takes off for a second load. We again watch our hosts ride with the reindeer in a long line and disappear over the horizon. Around 4:00 in the afternoon, after Dalai and Bolortsetseg return from two trips to the forest for wood, Dalai tells us that Ganzorig is coming. Through his binoculars, Dalai sees that Ganzorig is riding toward us on his reindeer, leading a horse and four other reindeer. He is still so far away I can't see him with my naked eyes.

I am a little embarrassed when I realize that the horse is for me, the inept rider. The eight horses we rode in yesterday have gone back down the mountains. Today the men pack our luggage on two reindeer. I watch as Ganzorig helps Mende and Davaa mount the other reindeer. Mende gets on and immediately slides off, which makes Davaa and me laugh. It is a little surprising because of his skill as a horse rider. When she climbs on, Davaa, too, slides over her reindeer and off the other side. Unlike horses' skin, reindeer skin is loose, so it is quite slippery riding a reindeer. However, reindeer are so close to the ground that falling from them doesn't hurt.

Mende and Davaa manage to stay on, but they are a little shaky. They are from Ulaanbaatar, and this is their first reindeer ride. They lead the two reindeer that are carrying our packs. I ride the horse and Ganzorig leads me on his reindeer. He turns often to make sure I am okay, looking at me with an impish smile and twinkling eyes. I'd think he was one of Santa's elves if it weren't for the cigarette hanging from his lips.

"Do you have a tent?" he asks me in Mongolian. Fortunately I understand, because Mende and Davaa have lagged behind and I have no translator.

"No," I respond in Mongolian.

"Will you stay at Khanda's or with my family?" asks Ganzorig.

"Khanda's," I say. "You have a big family." He turns on the reindeer and holds up seven fingers for his seven children and nods. We cross a river, climb a hill, dismount, and enter Khanda's urts. "How long will you stay?" asks Khanda when we are sitting on reindeer skins drinking reindeer milk tea.

"Two weeks." I am still without a translator, but managing.

"Fine."

I think about the casual way Khanda accepts this. I would be tearing my hair out if a foreigner landed in my house—which is much bigger than an urts —and told me that she and her two friends would be staying for two weeks, even though I have running water, a car, a cook stove, access to food, and automatic heat. Mongolian-Tyvan hospitality has a lot to teach me.

Suddenly it begins to rain, pouring rain, and soon after it starts, Mende and Davaa, looking like wet cats, struggle into the urts. The pack reindeer are here and our bags are wet, too. As soon as Mende and Davaa have cups of warm tea in their hands, Khanda continues.

"Fine," says Khanda, again. "But there is one thing I need to request. Don't walk near the altar." She sweeps her arm around the north side of the urts. I see strips of white, blue, green, and gold colored cloth and khadaghs hanging from a tent pole. It is a shaman's altar—the sacred space of her powerful uncle, Gosta. Okay, sure, no problem. Gosta is considered the mightiest shaman among the Dukhas, one of the strongest shamans in Mongolia. We don't want to interfere with that energy in any way.

"Other guests have walked there and very bad things happened," she adds.

"Of course," I say.

Later, when I am outside with Mende and Davaa, they whisper that they are worried that maybe she doesn't want us here. No Mongolian ever gives qualifications when offering hospitality. They feel unwelcome. Maybe we should leave, they suggest.

I have studied about shamanism and the animistic beliefs. I respect this culture. I believe Khanda is asking us to respect her beliefs, which seems like a small thing to ask. She is letting us visit for two weeks. We will respect her request.

"Things will only get better," I tell them, although I don't know for sure.

Evening is coming. We hear the clicking sounds of reindeer's joints and the calves crying "no-ah, no-ah" as they return from the pasture. Reindeer noses press against the canvas as they peek under or look in the door. Khanda leaves, the pole in the canvas door snapping behind her. It's milking time.

I look around her urts, facing out. It is organized like a ger. The door faces south. The woman's area, the area dealing with food and water, is to the east, to the left of the door. Some logs create a slightly raised area on the ground where pans, bowls, silverware, and food are kept. A pink and red curtain hangs from poles and closes off the kitchen. Right near the door is the firewood and next to that the water containers. The husband's, or in this case the uncle's, area is on the west side. It contains saddles, a hunting rifle, horse blankets, and riding boots. Around the perimeter, tucked into the angle where the poles and canvas meet the ground, are the household goods and out-of-season clothing. This serves as insulation and reminds me of the hay bales Vermonters put outside around their foundations for insulation in winter. In the center of her urts is, of course, a metal wood stove with a pipe extending out the toono. Fire is sacred. Garbage is not burned in it. Feet aren't pointed at it. Khanda, like all Dukha women, is the mistress of the fire. And the fire is the source of heat for cooking and warmth.

Sanjim, elder and Chuluu G.'s husband, has ridden from the other settlement. He lies in front of the television waiting to see a lottery someone has told him about. Holding the remote, Khanda cycles through a Korean soap opera, a fashion show, news, an American movie dubbed into Mongolian with Italian subtitles, and the World Soccer Cup. No lottery.

Sanjim turns to me. "You know, with those vitamins you gave us, our children didn't have coughs and colds this past winter. They took them all. The vitamins were helpful for everyone."

Hearing that the vitamins were helpful makes me really happy, but being in this urts is not what I imagined. I am living my dream of staying with Khanda, but what I really have are two men from the border patrol and one elder smoking about two feet from me. I don't even have a television at home, and this one is blasting about three feet away. I smell well-worn boots, smoke from the fire, and sourdough bread baking. Who knows how late it is? Sanjim leaves and Khanda shows us where to sleep—between the stove and the household items. It is a space of four feet. I lie with my knees pulled up. The stove is old and I can see the fire through the cracks. A spark could pop out and ignite my down sleeping bag. Davaa and Mende are beside me. Khanda is sleeping on reindeer skins on the other side of the stove, in front of the altar, with her three-year-old son, Battummur. Just before we go to sleep, Khanda says, "If you hear the dogs barking, wake me up. It means that wolves are here for the reindeer." I am tired and I just can't worry about things that might happen, so I fall asleep.

The next day, a male reindeer is missing. Khanda thinks one of us walked near the altar. I know we haven't. Herders connect events that, to me, may seem unrelated. Close to mid-morning, the reindeer returns. Now she says, "You must be very powerful. He came back." I feel a little uncomfortable, wondering what else I will be held accountable for.

Every day Khanda has a constant rhythm of activities: chop wood, carry water, make fire, heat water, add reindeer milk, milk reindeer, take them to pasture, move the stove outside the urts when the weather is hot, move it inside when it's cold. Chop wood, carry water, mix flour with water and salt. Roll dough into a hoop, flatten it, make it round, bake it in the coals, cook it in a pan or fry it in the wok. Use sourdough starter hanging on the urts pole. Boil rice in reindeer milk. Milk reindeer. When your child has to pee at night and it's too cold, hold out a bowl for him to use. Split kindling with a knife. Don't get close to the altar, move the solar panel as the sun moves, pee on the ground, cover your head with cloth during thunder and lightning so your hair won't be antennae, remember the high altitude and the gold and metals under the ground. Separate matted strands of horse mane, roll into a tube, pull out into a spool, twist into a rope and twist again. Don't get bedding near the fire, pack your things around the base of the urts, put your bedding away every day, have newspaper ready for male visitors to roll a cigarette and hang it on their lips. Chop wood. Carry water.

Visitors. Khanda serves them milk tea and bread. The gold mine 20 kilometers (14 miles) away is uppermost in these travelers' minds. They come back with three or four or five grams of gold. One has his gold in a tiny white plastic bottle. Another has his in a pouch around his neck. I am happy that they are getting something for themselves, but what changes will occur from having a gold mine close by?

I am exhausted just watching Khanda, so I take frequent naps. Mende is splitting and stacking wood, making jokes, and relating to Ganzorig and Khanda's children. One day I decide to help by carrying water. I walk to the river with wild scallions growing along its bank. I start with a lot of energy, ladling the water into the five-gallon pails. *This is really hard*, I am thinking, along with feeling virtuous for finally helping. We have been here a week. When I begin to walk back, my arms go from hurting a little to stabbing pain. I begin to wonder if I can do this at all. Little hillocks cover the ground and between them are pools of water. There is no way to get a walking rhythm. Mine is more like a stumbling gait. My shoulders ache. I don't think I can make it—the urts is so far away. I feel out of breath from the altitude. All the time I am thinking, *Khanda does this many times a day—more because we are here.* Ganzorig's young son comes along, grabs the pails from me, and fairly runs up the slope, hitting a dry hillock with each foot, and delivers the water to Khanda's urts. It's a good thing Khanda calls me "Grandmother" and that Dukhas respect their elders, because my athletic friends in the U.S. would never put up with such softness from me.

Maggots

Khanda's urts door, like all the others, has a dowel the size of a broomstick attached crosswise to a rectangle of canvas. The dowel keeps the material spread so that the door has an overlap of about six inches on the top and sides. If it is cold, you lift the flap and pass through—it will settle back around the opening. If it is hot and stuffy inside the urts, the flap is flipped to the right (facing out) or west side, where it rests on the urts canvas. (In Mongolian there is one word, *baruun*, which means right and west, and *zuun*, which means left and east; directions are always given as if someone is facing south.) Every time someone opens the door, a dog tries to sneak in to scavenge some food. Khanda sharply yells "CHAR!" Sometimes she throws a piece of firewood at the dog as he runs away. People and animals are hungry here.

During the first week we eat spaghetti. I make Spanish rice in the big pan that fits in the opening of the stove. It makes a hit and even the herders eat it. A week later, I make curried rice. Even though I think it is mild, Khanda says it is "too spicy" for her. For breakfast and lunch we eat sourdough bread and drink reindeer milk tea that Khanda gives us. I pick cowslips and scallions at the edge of the river but then can't get water to boil on top of the stove—probably due to the altitude, and also that the stove doesn't get hot on the top. The wok-like pan fits down into the fire and water boils fine in it, but it is constantly used for milk tea and then washed out and used for whatever one-dish food is made for each meal. I would also like to boil water to drink, but it just sits in a little pan and gets a smoky taste. No bubbles.

When we open a jar of jelly or peanut butter and share it with Khanda, she hands the jar and a spoon to Battummur and he finishes it. Our supplies are disappearing pretty fast. There is no refrigeration. The only foods that are okay for a few days are the handmade noodles Khanda makes and a big can of tomato paste, which is open but not spoiling. So far we have eaten five of those special smoked fish. I am nervous that we won't have enough food to last. "No more fish now," I say to Mende and Davaa. "We need to save them. We have seven more days."

The next day, the ration is one fish. Mende is excited. He joyfully pulls one of the long fish from its yellow plastic bag by the tail. He hungrily takes a bite of the fish. Then he glances down. There is a cluster of maggots teeming around inside it. What happens next I can hardly follow, it happens so fast. With a rumbling hiss, Mende spits, drops the fish into the yellow plastic, and hurls the whole bag out the open urts door, and before it even hits the ground, it falls into the open mouth of a dog who races away to a private place with his good fortune. So much for rationing fish.

Meeting Shaman Ganzorig

I am wondering how Ganzorig became a shaman.

"When did it start?" I ask him.

"My father was a famous shaman who had to hide during the forbidden days of the Soviet period. I grew up in a shaman family but never expected to become a shaman. When I was 22, I felt some spirits. At that time, I often left by myself to wander in the mountains. I felt strange things. I didn't think I was a shaman, but my mother asked a fortune teller about me and the woman said I was a shaman. When my father died, my older brother Gosta and my niece Khanda made shaman clothes for me. Gosta was my teacher."

Ganzorig and I share experiences. I tell him that in my practice, when I feel the spirit I sometimes cry. He says he feels that he loses control of himself. I say I can feel my own energy as well as the spirit's energy and that I don't completely surrender. He says it is good to feel both, that he would like to do that so he could have more control. One way does not seem better than another to me. I think they are just different experiences. "Some shamans," he tells me, "can control the spirits. Those are the real shamans. I have to approach the spirits carefully and humbly to convince them to do what I want."

I am not so sure that one way is more real than another.

Ganzorig describes his experience of performing a ritual ceremony. "First I call the ongods. After they are inside of me, I connect with the mountain and nature. Those are my main ongods. They take me to other ongods. Generally, I don't know what happens until it is over and I depart from them."

There is a hush and a bustle in the settlement today. Everyone is charged. The moon is full. Tonight Ganzorig will perform a ritual ceremony.

When the stars are out and the drum creates a rhythm, the ceremony begins. The only way I can tell the story of the ritual ceremony is in this poem that came to me later. I have to imagine the drum beating with the words.

>
> Bread baking
> Smoke saturated canvas
> Insides groaning, knocking
> Head scarf covering
> Offerings. Anticipation
> Lightening, stars, midnight
>
> Incense induced dream state
> Drum skin rolled dry
> Over open flames
> Hit with juniper branch
> Testing timber
> Rattling clinking *khunkhinuur*[*]
> Jingle cones
> Livening drum

---

[*] Khunkhinuur are metal jingle cones.

Lit juniper branch cleansing
Daily boots, felt liners, deel aside
Soft leather boots
And costume on
Streamers, feathers, khunkhinuur

Hat off, headdress on
Feathers and embroidered face
Fringe over eyes
Sacred khadagh tied on costume

Drum new deer skin
Wild sheep tail beater
Dum *dum*
Dum *dum*
Dum *dum*
A soft hypnotizing heartbeat

Spirit calling song
Thick smoke of juniper
Burning candle
Other arms spread
For protection
From danger

Rhythm incense fire smoke
Frenzy ecstasy dance song
Angry soothing powerful
Jumping dancing
Yip! Yip! Yip!

A wave subsides
Ancestor fed cigarette
Milk tea and vodka
Like a baby

New ancestor demanding
Directing, pointing
Blind elder Olzii
Answering back

Eyelids lower
More juniper smoke
Another cigarette
Candle burns

Chu, chu, chu
Jump, sing, drum
Suddenly wild sheep beater
In Olzii's spread deel lap
Message from ancestor

Beater thrown into my lap
Hand back with prompted *"Tuguu"*
Tyvan sacred message
Relayed from ancestors

Like a record running down
The dance becomes calmer
The voice softer
The drum quiet

More incense
Headdress off, hat on
Shaman deel off, usual deel on
Tan leather boots off
Black with liners on

Stoke up the fire
Light another candle
Boil milk tea
Cut sourdough bread

> Early morning circle
> Around the stove
> Sharing bread, tea, smoke
> And talk

Taiga Weather

There is a saying in Vermont, "If you don't like the weather, wait a minute." In the taiga, you can have all the seasons in one day. Today, reindeer are panting from the heat. I need to meditate, be alone. I want to feel the sun, but the ground is too damp to lie on, so I head down toward the river, past the golden Asian Globeflowers, and notice a rocky island. It is actually a tiny rise of gravel and small pebbles, a couple of steps through the frigid water. The islet is barely big enough for me to lie with my knees raised. I have never felt it so warm here—I am wearing that thin cotton top that I borrowed in Murun. The sun pours down and the river runs by me. I feel the small stones—lumpy under me but dry. Breathe.

I close my eyes. Last night for the first time in the taiga, I actually experienced a shaman ceremony! Everything that happened seems like a dream.

During the day, everyone was busy. Even Khanda wasn't in her urts. I found her at Ganzorig's, sewing a new skin onto his drum with her cousin BG. Next they put the drum in the sun to dry. After dinner, Khanda made bread. Usually this happens in the morning. Unusual things were happening. Energy was building.

When the stars came out last night around midnight, we were invited into Ganzorig's urts. The urts was full of people—our team, Ganzorig's big family, and a few from the other settlement, including Dalai's sister and their elder mother, Olzii, who is blind. Someone lit a sprig of juniper from the stove fire, which filled the urts with incense and cleansed the space, the costume, the headdress, and the altar of cloth strips representing the ongods. My eyes felt itchy from the dense smoke. Dressing the shaman was actually the beginning of the ceremony. Khanda and BG unfastened Ganzorig's deel buttons.

Khanda slipped his right arm out and immediately BG put the costume's right sleeve on him. It was like a smooth wave, daily clothes off, shaman costume on. Khanda pulled off the heavy felt-lined boots and pulled up the soft brown suede ones. Ganzorig's costume was a gray deel with white streamers attached in the back and fingers and ribs embroidered above his own. Bits of other materials adorned the deel—khunkhinguur, feathers, and silk.

Lastly, Khanda and BG took Ganzorig's knit cap off his head and tied on a headdress. In the area of his forehead, a face was embroidered, and flowing from that was a fringe that hid his face. Eagle feathers decorated the top. His drum was placed into his hands and he began gently, softly patting the drum with the wild sheep tail beater. He added a soft chant. Mende videotaped. Then the chant and the drumming became louder and more frenzied. At once, the assistants motioned to turn the camera light off. The ancestors came into Ganzorig's body. Ancestors require dark, a smoke, or maybe a drink of milk tea. One after another Ganzorig welcomed seven ancestors—some benign, docile, peaceful, others demanding, disruptive. He jumped into the air, swirled around—all in the small space of the urts. His sons squatted between him and the hot wood stove with their arms spread open so he wouldn't fall or get too close to the fire while he was in the trance. The air was thick with juniper incense. I nodded off and awoke each time a new ongod came. I felt the ancestors, one after another. The drum beat in my heart. Ganzorig was a bird, a wolf, and a spirit. After half the night, he slowed down, threw his beater onto Olzii's deel, and gave her a message, then one to each person. I had a slight panic feeling as he came toward me. I didn't know what to expect, what I needed to do or say. I watched, spread my deel skirt open to catch the beater. I needed to say something, but what? He threw the beater. Khanda prompted me. "*Tuguu*," I repeated as I handed the beater back. He said something to me. Davaa translated.

"Water is very precious. Don't pollute it."

Then he was done and the reverse was happening with his clothes. First his hat and his boots. His own brown deel was placed back on him, one arm at a time. He left the urts. When he returned, he was Ganzorig. We shared milk tea and bread, sitting on reindeer skins around the stove.

He turned to me and asked, "Was that okay?" I was thinking, *Was that okay? You mean seeing, feeling, smelling, experiencing a shaman ceremony here in the taiga? Not just okay, it was the answer to a dream. What I have wanted for 12 years! Only that.*

But I didn't have the right words and maybe there weren't any right words, so I didn't say anything, just nodded. Yes.

Now, the next day, lying on the ground, the soft warmth of the sun reminds me how grateful I feel toward Ganzorig for being so generous as to share his ceremony with an old white foreigner. I am in love with these people. So why am I lying here on this little island, alone?

I jump up. Too American—that feeling that I need to be alone, to think about things. Got to get back to the others, I tell myself, and wade through the icy water to shore. When I get to the urts, Battulga is here.

"Time to go, Sas," he says. "We need to meet with the others, do the health survey, give the vitamins, and visit the other settlements. Today, now."

Glad to have had these few rare, reflective moments, I put on my riding boots, fleece, and shell. The sky has darkened; it's cooler already and we need to leave. Mende and Davaa are mounted on reindeer. I'm still not ready for a "taiga jeep." I tried mounting Ganzorig's reindeer last night and, to the amusement of everyone, kept sliding off. I tell myself that my problem is that the reindeer's loose skin slides over his ribs, but the real problem is that I can't balance on him. Aha, balance. I am not just trying to balance on a reindeer. I am trying to balance spirituality and health, East and West, old and new. Sometimes I am just as shaky in the other areas as I am on the reindeer.

So today, I am on a horse and Battulga is leading us along the riverbank where the ground is more stable. There are no trees here, just brush. Green-brown landscape. If they knew where to go, Mende and Davaa could be taking a direct route, bushwhacking on their reindeer instead of following those of us on horseback.

The sky is getting noticeably darker, and just before we reach the first settlement, it begins to pour. Dripping as we enter Bayandalai's large urts, we catch the smell of fresh-baked bread. We settle in near the wood stove, drink reindeer milk tea and yogurt, and eat the fresh sourdough bread. Bayandalai's daughter is cutting out a deel on the floor and stitching the seams on their hand-powered sewing machine.

The rest of the herders of this settlement come in family groups or one by one to talk about their health. We give out hygiene kits, vitamin C, and first aid kits from Nomadicare. I give Bayandalai's wife, Tsetsegmaa, a book on the medicinal herbs of Mongolia, written by my teacher, Boldsaikhan, which she asked for when I showed her my copy last year. With Davaa translating, we sit together and talk about what herbs grow in the taiga and how they are used. The rain is stronger. It starts running down the tent poles. I watch as one of the older sons reaches up high and makes a notch in the pole with his knife "to keep the water from dripping down," he explains. It works.

After we have assessed the health care of all the herders in the settlement and dispensed vitamins and supplies, there is a lull in the rain, so Battulga and I mount our horses and Davaa and Mende their reindeer. We cross the river to visit the third settlement. The river is higher now, running faster. By the time we have finished meeting with the herders in this settlement, though, the water is white froth, nearly flooding. The sound of gushing water fills the landscape. Battulga tells Mende and Davaa to go home directly over the mountain, since it's shorter. He points in the right direction. We go the long way, along the river. The loud rain beating on my poncho is soft compared to the roar of the river. When we cross it on the horses, my feet nearly touch the water. My heart pounds in my ears along with the rain.

"Come down this bank, Sas, you won't get wet," Battulga urges when he sees me hesitate to cross the raging river.

When we finally get back to Khanda's urts, with its warmth and homey smell of wood smoke, I remember that tiny island of dry rocks I lay on this morning. Those pebbles are now under at least two feet of rushing water.

In the evening, after the wood fire dries us, Ganzorig's son visits. He tips his head back to look out the toono, through the tent poles. "It's going to snow," he says casually, holding his position. Today is July 8, the midsummer day my son was born. It's usually a hot day back in Vermont. I can't believe it could snow today, especially given this morning's weather. Yet in a moment, the pinging sounds on the wood stove change to sizzles as snowflakes drop from the sky. Now it is colder and darker, and the flakes are creating wet patches before they melt. When we go to bed, the snow is still falling.

In the morning, I am the first one out. I lift the tent flap as I always do, but it doesn't move easily. It's heavy. Not an Asian Globeflower in sight. Instead there are 10 inches of snow covering everything.

To Khanda, this weather is normal. She milks her reindeer, gets water, brings in wood, makes a fire, cooks bread, and makes rope from horsehair. She advises us not to put our bedding away. It's too cold today, she says. I sit inside my sleeping bag. When she finishes the rope, she uses this inside day to write me a poem:

> White-haired American grandmother has been with us in our home for 10 days.
> Grandmother's white hair reminds me of my dear mother.
> While Grandmother Sas was here we had heavy snow.
> In spite of it, she didn't complain.
> She didn't once say, "Oh, I'm cold."
> The cold weather of the taiga seemed like a wonder to her.
> Surely, Grandmother Sas will think about me.
> She wasn't with us a month but we became good friends.
> The cool weather of the taiga will remain in her heart.
> Gray-haired Grandmother from far away, have a good trip.
> When you get home, don't forget about our special taiga.

Toilet Issues

With the snow, the landscape changes. I already know that the proper question when you visit a settlement is, "What direction should I walk?"

In other settlements and at other times I didn't know it, but in each settlement, a small, discreet hole is dug to accommodate the daily bowel movements of the people. This "nature toilet" is made of three flat stones, one on each side of the hole for feet and one to screen the person off from the back when squatting. There are no trees here—we are above the tree line. I am relieved when I find the nature toilet—otherwise I wonder if I am using a sacred spot, desecrating something, or using a pathway. One thing is for sure: When I find a nice secluded pee spot and look around to make sure no one is close, I always see someone walking or riding toward me. I act nonchalant, as if I am admiring this particular reindeer moss, until they pass, and I continue.

While we are here with Khanda, we discover the nature toilet just south of the path between Ganzorig's and Gosta's urts. Convenient—if no one is walking the path. Inconvenient because, with visitors here, the hole fills fast—toilet paper, tampons, pads. The taiga people use leaves and stones, not toilet paper. We try collecting our paper products in a plastic bag and tying it tightly, but that doesn't work. The dogs just grab the bags when they sneak into the urts and paper is strewn around the ground. We can't burn it. Fire is sacred. No waste is burned. The latrine hole must be deep enough to prevent the dogs from raiding it, but not too deep, because of the water table just below the ground.

The latrine works fairly well until the storm of July 8, when the river rises two feet from the rain. While still on the horse returning from the other settlement, I catch a glimpse of that handy latrine. The overflowing nature toilet's contents are sliding down the rise. With the rainwater, the paper and other white products have become soggy and are scattered like a herd of sheep in the distance. Seeing this particular sight is enough to make me wish that we, like the nomads, used ecological products like stones or sticks instead of toilet paper.

After the night's 10 inches of snow, I wonder where to pee. Squatting is hard now because, no matter how I clear a square with my feet, my bare butt touches snow. No one mentions the nature toilet. The snow has covered the refuse scattered around it. No one walks in that direction, either, I notice. This could be because Ganzorig has moved his urts to drier ground, so the path leads nowhere. I guess nature will recycle those paper products, but we will not be here to see it.

The next day we leave. Battulga has gone ahead, so Dalai is my guide. He ties my stirrups together under the horse. Now I can't move. What happens if I slide off sideways? I will be dragged under the horse's hooves. I have no idea why Dalai does this, but, as a driver is the boss of the car in Mongolia, the guide is the boss of the horses and riders. As we ride along the flat pasture, a foot of snow hides rocks. Since horses here have no shoes, it is painful if a rock sticks into the soft part of the foot inside the hoof. They stumble when we come to the rocky top of a mountain. No one mentions that this is really dangerous. My fingers are gripping the metal loop on the saddle and my heart is pounding. After a couple of hours, when we are at a lower altitude where the snow is gone and trees appear, Dalai unties my stirrups. Later we stop for tea. He builds a tripod of branches while the wranglers get water and gather wood for the fire. We lie on the ground, resting. When they decide to do the process again, gathering water and wood for more tea, I feel a little edgy, thinking, *shouldn't we be going?* But everyone is relaxed and Dalai is the boss.

I am riding Khanda's white horse, who is a bit friskier than the ones they usually give me, so I am holding him back most of the time. Then he decides to jump over a log and my heart is in my throat, but I keep breathing and stay on.

As we descend the mountain, the land becomes flat, steppe land, so I have a chance to relax a bit and think over the trip. In the last month, I have spent 30 hours on a horse and ridden over the same path I was so fearful of two years ago. I have visited all six settlements. I didn't fall off my horse, even when he fell on his side as we went down a narrow path to a river. "Get off, Sas," said Battulga. Even when my horse stopped abruptly, I didn't fly over his head. Even when my horse got all four feet stuck in mud up to his hocks and refused to move, I followed Battulga's instructions. I got off and walked away.

"Good, Sas," said Battulga each time, and I understood this to mean, "Congratulations, you are still on the horse." And…you are still alive.

All the rivers are swollen. Dalai says this is the last river we have to cross. It is wide, deep, and roaring. Dalai tries to ford at one place but the water is too high and the current too strong. Then he tries another. Finally, the third time, as his horse steps into the raging water, he turns to me and points to his knees. He has lifted his legs to his chest and placed them on his saddle. I take it that I need to do the same and quickly lift my feet. I make it across and am relieved to be where we are to meet Battulga. I learn the name of the place. The place is called "Karma." But of course it is.

Dollar Shower

The first years in Tsagaan Nuur, we had no idea we could get a shower there. Generally, soum centers, county centers like Tsagaan Nuur, lack utilities. There is no electricity, no running water, and only one phone—occasionally working—at the post office (if it hasn't rained lately). A month ago, when we drove into town from Ulaanbaatar, we saw a group of people spilling out of a tiny wooden house. When we asked, Battulga told us it was a shower building. A shower building! Showers, here? You mean Mende, Davaa, and I will have something to look forward to when we get back from our long stay in the taiga? After riding horses and living in an urts, a shower will be heaven. Weekends, Battulga mentioned, are the best time for showers because more locals want them then and all the work of preparation can be used for a number of customers.

I have found that nomads have no way of taking showers. In the taiga, up to nine herders and their children live in one urts. There is no privacy to change clothes or take a bath. The ground is wet and cold, impossible to sit on. And the rivers? Run-off snow. Icy cold.

Good for washing face and hands, that's about it. Herders smell like earth, leather, wood smoke, and horses. Everything is out in the air, so there are no musty, moldy smells.

Today we are back from the taiga, and a strong horse smell adds to larch resin and juniper incense, plus some other, not-so-pleasant odors. We have bits of reindeer hair still clinging to our clothes. By some magic, it is Saturday. Thank goodness. Battulga goes to a house near the shower building, where the owners live, to ask if the shower is working. Yes.

A shower costs 500 tugrik (50 cents) for Mongolians and the equivalent of one dollar for a foreigner like me. Considering the amount of work it takes, you couldn't get it for $100 in the U.S. First, the family who owns it gets water from Tsagaan Nuur (the White Lake). Since the family doesn't have a car, two children have to walk all the way—pulling a handcart with two five-gallon milk jugs on it—over a rutty path, over soft, muddy ground, over a hill and down to the edge of the lake. They scoop the water by the ladleful until the two containers are full. Now I know first hand that this is no easy task. The heavy load must be pulled up the hill, over the soft, muddy ground and through the rutty path back to the shower building.

Inside, there are three small rooms and a hallway with a bench that serves as a waiting room. The room to the left as we enter the door has a large wood stove with a cauldron on it. The heavy jugs are carried into the stove room, and the water is poured into the cauldron. The fire under it is blazing. Of course, trees have been felled and the wood has been cut, split, and transported to create the fire. When the water is hot, the owner, a woman, ladles the water back into the container, carries it to the other end of the hall, and climbs the steep, narrow staircase to the low-ceilinged attic. Crouching down, she lugs the hot water across the floor and pours it into the upstairs cauldrons, which have pipes to the showerheads in the two downstairs rooms.

My interpreter and I sit on the bench, waiting to be invited into the shower rooms. The building has the hot, wet-wood smell of a sauna. I suddenly remember something Sugar, a soum director in the Gobi Desert, said when I interviewed him about health a few years ago: "The reason city people get sick more than countryside people is that they take showers. It's not good for health." I wonder how often soum people here take showers. I wonder if I will get sick from taking a shower. I glance at the mirror across from me. Look at that hair. No one can talk me out of taking one today. I look around me. Between the two shower rooms, there is another wood stove that will be cranked up in the dead of winter, I imagine. Children play in the mud outside the open doorway and inside the fence around the building, which keeps the cows and horses at a distance.

It is time for my dollar shower. The owner opens the door to one little room, pours water on the floor, swishes her mop around the concrete, wipes off the shiny wooden pallet under the showerhead, and swishes the cement gutter, pushing the water outside. I enter the stall, ecstatic. I notice the hooks for clothes on the door in the small dressing area. I haven't taken my clothes off for two weeks. How could I, living in an urts with so many others? Outside, the ground was too wet and the river was too cold. Now I strip out of the ripe clothes and put them into a plastic bag so I won't have to touch them again until they are clean.

With great anticipation, I turn the handle of the shower faucet. Nothing happens. I call out to my interpreter, who is in the other stall with the sound of running water. She tells the owner. The owner tells me to turn it harder. I do. The handle comes off in my hand. No water. After relaying through my interpreter that I have broken the faucet and there's still no water, the owner tells me she will come in to turn it on. This means I have to put my grungy clothes back on. I do. The water works right away for her. She leaves it running, so as soon as she leaves I strip off my clothes as fast as I can. I don't want to miss a drop of water. Good thing I am thinking about drops, too, because there are now three trickles of water coming down on me. And I am grateful. Heaven couldn't offer more.

Khatgal Airplane

After the shower, we are ready to start our return journey over the beautiful and difficult land to Ulaanbaatar. My plan is simple: Drive to Khatgal. Take a plane to Ulaanbaatar. Yet I should know that nothing is simple in Mongolia, especially if it involves driving over non-existent and now flooded roads.

I am looking forward to winding up the trip with the four of us who have spent the past month together—the ride will be a time to smooth out some challenges we have had. Mende and Davaa spent a lot of time off somewhere together, so I had no access to translation. The advantage of this was that I had time alone with Khanda to practice my Mongolian. The disadvantage was that I was missing my team too much of the time. I think the two-day trip to Khatgal could be a nice way to complete our time together. Maybe we can talk about our experiences. Then I learn that we won't be riding alone. I should have remembered that if a car goes anywhere, it is an opportunity for a ride—and our car, empty by Mongolian standards, is free. The rich American is paying.

When the car arrives three hours late because the driver, Tsogoo, has had to work on the brakes, there is an extra person—a heavy man in the passenger seat. Why the brakes this morning? I really don't know. This trip has been planned for a month and we already waited an extra day because of floods. As usual, I don't understand what's going on. No one introduces the extra person or tells me who he is. I figure maybe he's the relief driver, in case we drive around the clock, get stuck in a river or mud, or the car breaks down—things that happened the year I came with Dan.

We pile our luggage in the back of the Russian van. Mine consists of a duffle bag, a stuff sack for my sleeping bag, an L.L. Bean school knapsack, and a large padded knapsack for the professional video camera we have been using for filming. All are bulging. Battulga throws in a small, flat duffle bag, explaining that it's everything he owns. I used to think Mongolians were amazing at restraint—they carry so little with them. Now I know it is the opposite. I am privileged to have a lot of stuff.

Like a bus, we make stops before we leave Tsagaan Nuur. First we stop at the border patrol station, and Battulga runs out to get my permission stamped now that I am leaving the border area. We stop to give vitamins to the bagh chief's family. Next we pick up passengers—a woman my age, an eight-year-old boy, a family—grandmother, daughter, teenage boy, and baby. No introductions are given. I hear fragments: "not going all the way to Khatgal," "stopping at the mineral springs," "going to stay with nomadic grandparents." This is the level of my Mongolian language ability. Davaa doesn't translate. She is in her own world.

Our car now has 11 passengers. As the car leaves Tsagaan Nuur, I settle into the rhythm of the road and the nomadic smell of mutton, wet wool, and wood smoke. I concentrate on tucking my feet under my seat so I won't kick a woman across from me when the van lurches. In Mongolia, if you touch someone's leg with your foot, you are said to steal that person's soul. To make up for this, you shake hands. In these close, bumpy quarters, I could be shaking her hand the whole trip. With the extra people, there is no opportunity for our team to process the trip. Then I notice that Davaa's face is bluish-white from carsickness, and I realize she is in no condition to talk anyway.

To maneuver the road outside Tsagaan Nuur, Tsogoo steers around tree roots and large stones, avoids tree trunks, and slows for deep ruts, all the while gunning the motor in low gear to get up the steep hills. When the land levels off, there is mud. Along the river, the sides are eroded from recent floods. That deep snow we got at Khanda's was rain here, and the water in the river is moving fast. Tsogoo inches his way down one bank, guns the engine through the water, heads toward car tracks on the other side, and guns it up the opposite bank.

Battulga is the only person communicating with me. He points to a mountain to our west. "That's where we were two days ago," he says, pointing to Meng Bulag, way up there where the mountain is still white. The land here is green and hilly, and there is another river bank in sight. At a toll bridge, we stop for our first cigarette/pee break. The women wander away from the car. The men step out of the van, turn their backs to the car and the road, take a step or two, and pee. They roll and light up their cigarettes. Sometimes they light up before they step out of the van, but I complain if they do. After five hours we arrive at a mineral spring, where most of our passengers get off. There are only two drivers, Battulga's aunt, and the team left now.

In Ulaan Uul we visit Yura, whom I met two years ago, and give her some photos that I took back then. We drive into her *khashaa*, a fenced-in home area, right up to her log house. It is Naadam Festival time at Ulaan Uul, and she is all dressed up in a gray silk summer deel, with nylons and high heels. She fans herself as she smiles and welcomes us, asks how my foot has healed, and lights a cigarette. She asks about our trip, and if we can we stay overnight. "Not this time," we answer, drinking the tea she offers. Sitting here with Yura, I remember what it feels like to be a person—which makes me realize that Mende and Davaa do not include me. Yura is my age. When she talks to me, I feel noticed, respected. In the van, I feel like an outsider. I need a translator to make a connection with everyone. Davaa hasn't been available.

Up ahead, a billboard announces Khovsgol Preservation Park. Five thousand tugrik for foreigners. Free for Mongolians. I hand over the five dollars and we have nearly arrived in Khatgal.

"Do you know where the airport in Khatgal is?" I ask Tsogoo when we are nearing the village. "Could you stop there? We need to confirm our flight."

The airport is on the edge of town. As we drive closer, my eyes widen. It is good that I have a sense of humor. What I see is a field with a barbed wire fence around it. Driving closer, we see two gers and a shack. A woman is painting some trim on her door. Tsogoo gets out. He returns. No airport building.

So we go to the post office and phone the airline. Davaa reports, "They say Monday's flight leaves from Ulaanbaatar at 12:30."

I don't think we have confirmed the flight, but I am not sure.

"Where to?" asks Tsogoo. We have to find Tummurtsogt, a friend of a friend, who has a guesthouse. Instead, we find his daughter.

"Well, come in," she says and puts out a spread of warm, freshly made bread, butter, cream, and milk tea. It is late afternoon and we haven't eaten yet. This is the most luxurious thing that has happened in a month. The bread, butter, cream, and milk tea disappear before Battulga and Tsogoo leave. Her home feels like the epitome of modern life. There is a phone. There is fresh food. There is a kitchen. When Battulga leaves, I feel sad that our team has broken up and that the trip is ending.

Tummurtsogt arrives in the evening and offers to help. "We have reservations for Monday on the plane," I say.

"Good," he says. "It is good to get the plane here. They don't really check your luggage, so you don't have to pay for overweight like you do in Murun. It is a lot more relaxed here. Only, if it rains, the plane doesn't come."

On Monday, the day of our flight, I am eager to get to the airport to check in. I don't feel very confident about this barbed wire–fenced runway and our non-reservation. We arrive two hours early in Tummurtsogt's Russian jeep. A young man on the other side of the barbed wire calls, "The plane isn't coming."

We ask, "What do you mean? Why? Today is sunny."

"The field is wet. We told them not to come here. There were only five people boarding."

"What about the other passengers?"

"They have left for Murun already. They will hold the plane for you."

I have my doubts, but I just stay open and flow. There is no other choice.

"I wish I could drive you," says Tummurtsogt when he gets back into the car, "but I have to get to work. You can take my jeep, though, and I will get you a driver." We aren't on the road two minutes with our new driver before the oil light comes on. Our driver stops and opens the hood and checks. "We have enough oil," he says. "It must be the oil pressure." The oil light stays on. We keep driving. We drive 60 km (37 miles) with the light on. The motor begins to clink. Valves, I think. Head gasket. That's it for this car. That's it for the plane ride. We stop. Nothing about this trip is as simple as I thought it might be.

Two vans full of Japanese tourists come along the road and stop. No one has any idea what to do about the oil, the oil light, or the clink of the valves. We can't go any farther in this car. Luckily, the translator speaks Mongolian, Japanese, and English. Our driver asks the tourists if we can ride in their vans to Murun. They agree to take us.

I am invited into the first van, and Mende and Davaa go in the other one. The drivers throw our luggage on the top of the first van. It has a metal railing like a balcony. They don't tie it down. The way the roads are, the luggage can easily bounce off, I think. Yet there is no choice, because the driver is the boss and this driver is already doing us a favor. It is a perfect time to practice the Buddhist teaching of non-attachment. But when they are about to throw the knapsack with the video camera up there, I say, "Ah, could we possibly keep that one inside?" The kind translator puts it on the motor between the front seats. Either the luggage will arrive or it won't. Either we will arrive or we won't. The plane will be there—or not. We will get to Ulaanbaatar today, or another day. Being flexible is the only way to survive here.

The Japanese tourists actually have plenty of space in the van. I notice they are really clean, with starched shirts, neat jackets, and clean hair. I haven't seen anyone so clean for a month. Also, they are my age.

"What is your work?" asks the man facing me.

"I do energy healing."

"Oh," he says, "I am a doctor of massage. Back there is my wife. She and this man beside you are middle school teachers."

I hope I am far enough away that they can't smell me. That dollar shower went only so far. I hope they don't notice how scraggly my hair is, see the black around my fingernails that won't come off. Can they tell I have worn these outer clothes for a month? Can they smell the horses I rode for 30 hours? They seem so gentle, as if their trip is soft, protected, spacious, planned, organized. And even that it is working just as they planned it. I feel gritty, like I am made of smoke, dirt, water, mud, grass, roaring rivers, wet luggage, ground sleeping, and shaman song. And that I have had no clue what would happen at any moment.

What a relief for me to be on my own with people my age! I realize I have had to expand my energy in order to protect myself from my team's unkindness. I realize it is not bad for someone to have a soft experience like these people. This is my first chance to put my experience into any perspective, and I can see that if I had to rate my past month on a scale of 1 to 10 in wildness, I would call it a 10. In spite of the underlying stress of trying to catch a plane, this ride is relaxing in contrast.

After an hour, the translator looks at a dot in the distance and says, "I see the plane. It looks like they are waiting."

Well, that's a relief, I think, *let's just get there before it leaves.*

As we approach the airport, I tell the Japanese tourists how grateful I am to them for giving me a ride. Amidst many smiles and bows, they tell me it was their pleasure. As soon as the van stops, I say goodbye and rush into the terminal, grabbing the bags I can carry. The other van hasn't arrived yet. A tour group of Austrians I met in Khatgal are hanging out under a tree in front of the airport. "They are holding the plane for you," one woman calls to me as I pass. I go immediately to the ticket counter, passing groups of waiting passengers. There is only one plane a day. They are all waiting for the same plane, and that plane is waiting for us. It hasn't boarded yet. The driver and translator bring the rest of the bags in. The air personnel weigh them.

"That will be 67,000 T."

I take out my money. "All I have left is 12,000 T. It's not my fault the plane didn't go to Khatgal. I paid more for the ticket from there. Plus, I just paid for a car to travel from there. Here, you can have everything I have—12,000 T."

"Okay, okay," a heavyset man says from behind his desk. "Give me 7,000 T."

Mende and Davaa arrive just as I have negotiated this. Their driver didn't want to jostle the Japanese tourists, so he drove very slowly. *Oh, my.* As soon as they check their bags and get boarding passes, the flight is announced.

Our seats are in the back of what used to be a cargo plane, so we squeeze into the seats, which do not recline, and there is less than eight inches for our knees. Fine. No problem. It is only a short ride. And as we begin to fly over green mountains, steppes, and the vast expanses, I remember how I love this gorgeous, spacious land. This is a magnificent place—a place where my heart lives. The hardships of the past month fade a little, yet I am relieved to be looking from this height and not experiencing every dip and bump driving to Ulaanbaatar in a car. As I look down, I am overwhelmed by Mongolia's pristine wilderness, which from here is so obvious. I see no agriculture, no people, no houses, and no industry—only steppes of a blue-green color sloping to an occasional river. The hills are smooth, with no trees. Naked, I think. The vastness takes my breath away. Annoyed as I have been at times to have no translator when I needed her and no cameraman when I needed him, I feel my heart full of love for Mongolia all the way back to Ulaanbaatar. At the same time, I pledge to put together a more cohesive group next year.

Monkhtsetseg, of the farthest East Taiga settlement, carries her daughter, Nominzul, from her urts to visit a neighbor.

photo credit: Fred Thodal

Gosta's son, Baasankhuu, and his wife, Narantuya, sit on the family side of the urts while visiting another West Taiga settlement.

photo credit: Sas Carey

2007

If you drink their water, follow their customs.
— MONGOLIAN PROVERB

The Great Team

Now it is July 2007 and, except for Battulga, my team is new. Connections for my team have come in strange ways. When presenting my film in Montana this past year, I met a Mongolian woman whose brother-in-law is a filmmaker in Ulaanbaatar. He and I communicated while I was in the United States, and he had planned to be our cameraman on this trip—until the last minute, when he couldn't make it. His son and nephew join us instead. His son, Bayara, is 25 years old, soft, gentle, slow-moving, and inconspicuous—my dream cameraman—a film-school graduate who works at a television station. A stroke of luck for me. Bayara is thorough. Even when I try to interrupt him, he finishes his shot. This makes for good footage. Augi, Bayara's cousin and assistant cameraman, attended school in Montana, where he learned perfect English and how to be assertive—definitely not a Mongolian trait. At 23, he is tall, slim, and active. I give Bayara and Augi each a video camera to use—Augi a small Sony and Bayara a professional Sony PD 150. And Khongoroo—if ever there was an angel sent to me, it was Khongoroo. She and I got to know each other by e-mail after Enkhe, the Mongolian director of the American Center for Mongolian Studies, introduced her to me. A 21-year-old pharmacy student from the Health and Sciences University who knows the name of every plant and flower, Khongoroo applied for an internship this summer. Enkhe sent me her resume. The internship didn't work out, because my funding came later than the cut-off date for the application. When she found out that she didn't get it, Khongoroo e-mailed me that she was having a very bad week. I wrote back to not worry, because I would need a translator anyway. I would let her know as soon as I found out about the funding for the trip. A week later, The Shelley & Donald Rubin Foundation approved the funds for our proposal to continue the Dukha Health Database. This would cover horses, ferries, cars, trains, and planes to get to the taiga. The Mongol-American Cultural Association donated funds for vitamin C for reindeer herders. And 70 friends generously contributed so that we could supply hygiene kits and pay Mongolian salaries for a driver, a guide, a video cameramen—and a translator.

What impresses me about Khongoroo right from the first moment when she becomes my translator is that I can communicate with her and get answers to questions about Mongolia without being there. Munkhjin interviews Khongoroo and writes, "She is like a Middlebury College student." This means she is competent, efficient, and outgoing. I send Khongoroo an e-mail to ask how much it will cost to get a year's supply of vitamin C for 210 reindeer herders. The next day, I get the answer. Can we get toothbrushes, toothpaste, floss, soap, nail clippers, combs, and flypaper for the herders? The answer is in my e-mail when I get up the next morning. How long will it take us to get the equipment, supplies, and food for the taiga? "I know someone at *zakh* (the black market)," she writes back. "We can do it fast." This makes my planning a lot easier.

In the past, I always had a mixture of excitement and fear when I went to zakh. That was before I went with Khongoroo. She taught me there is an organized and methodical way to shop. Khongoroo knows how. She has friends with a booth inside the big sales building and calls ahead of time to ask if we can leave our purchases there.

When we get to zakh, I hold my breath and try not to look as we go through the meat section. We search the booths until we find #91—her friends' booth—where we can purchase chamois dishcloths, sunscreen, lipstick, hair decorations, thermos bottles, and towels.

Today we are buying food and supplies for four of us to go to the taiga for a month. From past experience, I now know what the families need, so we also buy gifts and hygiene kit contents. Khongoroo paces us. She knows where each section is. Before this, I didn't even know there were sections.

First there is the camping section. After living in Khanda's urts for two weeks and sleeping with my knees bent between the stove and the storage area, I tell Khongoroo we need to buy a tent where we can sleep. The tent we buy has fiberglass poles that snap together with elastic cords inside them. It is a two-person tent with a fly (protective cover) and a vestibule, which can be zipped at night and opened during the day. Unlike the urts, the tent will be a space without television or cigarette smoke where our gear will be accessible to us. Visitors can come when our vestibule is open, not at any hour of the day or night. On the other hand, the tent will not keep us as warm as the urts. It will also get a bit damp with rain. I don't know how it will stand up to the blasting wind, but in any case it will give us our own space. Khongoroo needs a sleeping pad and bag. Finally, we buy a camp stove and fuel.

Next we move to the kitchen section, where we buy pans, dishes, silverware, and a large thermos for tea. Then we go from booth to booth, stocking up on canned meat, fish, and tomato paste, salt, tea, nuts, rice, pasta, cereal, ramen noodles. At the household section we get candles, soap, matches, and toothpaste for the 36 taiga families. When our arms are full of boxes, we walk back to Khongoroo's friends' booth and store them behind the counter.

We want to take a solar panel to the Tsagaan Nuur school dormitory, because the Dukha children live there when they go to school. Khongoroo leads me to the electronic section. A young man says to follow him to a metal shipping container, the kind that can go on a train or an 18-wheeler truck. Piled inside from floor to ceiling are electronic supplies. We need a whole set-up—solar panel, storage battery, wiring, three outlets, and three light bulbs. The young man says, "Sure. Just sit here." He points to a canvas director's chair inside the container, where it is still hot but out of the sun. It feels good to sit. I take a drink of the water I have with me and watch the electrician put the proper ends on the wires and plug them into the solar panel. With a smile, he plugs the other end into a black and white television. It works! He will need more time to get the light sockets connected, so we go looking for hygiene supplies—flypapers and combs for the families. When we return to the container, the wiring is all connected. Khongoroo carries the storage battery. I carry the box of wires. The electrician carries the three-by-four-foot solar panel. Just as we reach the booth where our things are stored, Bayara calls on his cell phone to say he is driving over to help us. When he arrives we rent a flat metal handcart, and a man to pull it, for the equivalent of a couple of dollars and pile the boxes on it. We take them to the parking lot and pack them into Bayara's car. I stay in the hot car while they go back to get the next load. I won't say shopping at zakh is comfortable today, with the temperature at 96° F, but it sure beats all the past years' experiences because of Khongoroo.

Khongoroo packs the bags for the taiga with me, plans with me, finds everything we need, and even helps get the registration stamp for my passport. Then one evening, the day before we leave, she calls me at Munkhjin's apartment. "I will come up and get you," she says. "My father would like to meet you."

Augi arrives in an SUV with Khongoroo. Her father is in the back seat. I am not prepared for what happens next. "Have a seat," Khongoroo says, pointing to the front passenger seat, and she goes around to sit in back. "My father has a few questions for you." When he begins to speak I can feel fear and lack of trust in words I don't understand. Khongoroo translates. "What makes you think you can keep my daughter safe on a trip to the countryside?" he asks. "How are you going to protect her from bears and wolves?"

I feel like the wind has been knocked out of me. I feel ambushed. How *am* I going to do that? For a moment, I see myself as he sees me—an old, gray-haired, foreign woman. I think, *Why, he's right. Why should he let his daughter go with me?* But couldn't she have told me to be prepared for an interrogation? Maybe I would have some good answers. Then I speak. I can't tell you exactly what I say—something like "we have wranglers with us" or "we stay with taiga people who live there." Or maybe that this will be my fourth trip and I haven't seen any bears or wolves. I don't mention the wolves surrounding the camp, the bear tracks I have seen, or the huge black bearskin in Khanda's urts. Maybe I tell him, "Look, I lived through the experience." I am shaking when I leave the car, upset that we are so close to leaving and if I didn't answer the questions right, Khongoroo won't be able to go with us. As soon as Khongoroo gets home, though, she calls me. She doesn't mention my meeting with her father. She is calling to remind me that we need to pick up the dental floss tomorrow. From this, I know she is still in this with me. I take a deep breath and continue packing.

We spend the remaining days in Ulaanbaatar buying a bathroom scale for weighing people for our medical database, the vitamin C, and more contents for the hygiene kits, like dental floss. I study Mongolian every morning for an hour. My comprehension is improving, but it is still hard for me to make sentences. I remember that we are supposed to get border permission to go to the taiga in Ulaanbaatar. This involves driving to a large brown building with columns and a tall black and gold fence around it. At a small opening in the fence, there are three men in uniforms—two in desert fatigues and one in fancy green with stripes. They only let Khongoroo in—no foreigners. I sit across the street on a metal fence to wait. Khongoroo comes out with a list of things we need in order to get the permission. We drive around the city getting pieces of paper, including a letter from the Ministry of Health saying that I am collaborating with them. We make copies of the passports of everyone going with us and write up our goals: to collect health assessment data, to distribute vitamins and health kits to the Dukhas, and to film shamans.

We wait, wait, wait, and ride in taxis. It is over 90° F. Then, when Khongoroo takes the papers to the border patrol, the guard says they are at a meeting and to come back at 6:00 PM. She goes back at 6:00 and no one is there. Typical Mongolian red tape. Since we are leaving tomorrow, we now have to get the paper in Murun, as we did last year—even though the officer warned us then to get it in Ulaanbaatar.

After 18 hours of squeaking shock absorbers, along with the clatter, clang, rattle, and bang of driving in the countryside, we arrive in Murun. Getting the border permission turns out to be easy, because the young border patrol officer takes a liking to Khongoroo and asks for her phone number. He even allows me to go into the building and his office.

From Soyoo

Last year an elderly couple came to Meng Bulag to visit while we were staying with Khanda. They didn't look tough and lean enough to have come on the path we'd traveled. Oh, no, they told us, there is a much easier way. We got maps out and they pointed to Ived and Soyoo. It was just three hours of riding, they told me. Knowing that the ride could be easier made me feel smug. If there were an easier way, I figured, I could come again. Instead of riding horses from Tsagaan Nuur, we could leave from Soyoo, an area closer to the soum of Ulaan Uul, where Yura lives.

So this year, Yura helps us organize the horses and the wranglers by cell phone. Our driver is Davkha, a young relative of Puji. Davkha drives slowly and cautiously. It takes almost as long as driving to Tsagaan Nuur, when it should take three hours less. He is 19 and driving us is one of his first assignments. Our young Mongolian team members (including Khongoroo, Augi, and Bayara) are 19, 21, 23, and 25. Battulga is in his forties and I am in my sixties. We meet the wranglers with the horses at Soyoo and camp there for the night.

In the morning, I off-handedly ask Battulga how long it will take to get to Meng Bulag. I am expecting him to say three hours—four at most.

"Eight and a half hours," he says.

I gasp. "What? You are kidding, right? The whole reason we are here is because it takes three hours."

"No, Sas, that's Ived. We are at Soyoo."

I have Yura's horse. It seems to help that Yura is my age and weight. Hopefully we will both be calm. My healing-school student Ellen gave me some riding lessons this year. With her help, I rode bareback—or maybe I should say I sat bareback on a horse and she led it. "Hold onto the mane," she said. "It won't hurt the horse." She taught me about dominating, about leading the horse by the reins before getting on him. Then he will know who is boss.

Practice. I walk my horse around the area while the wranglers are packing the packhorses. When I mount the horse he seems to follow my instructions better. Battulga is still leading me, though. It starts out a little cloudy, but it's a nice day. When my knees hurt, Battulga lengthens my stirrups. My neck hurts a bit, but I am feeling confident and Battulga is letting me ride by myself. He hangs back and lights a cigarette, then gallops ahead to check on me.

Step by step, I climb a mountain on the horse without Battulga, and when I look back, I feel like strutting, I am so proud. I take one-handed photos; I pick a pink flower that I noticed last year, a lily that only grows at a certain altitude. Oh, I am so relaxed on the horse! I get to appreciate nature—the flowers changing with altitude, the scenery of mountains beyond mountains. Only our little horse train in the immense, pristine land.

It starts to rain, and the rain quickly turns into a blasting downpour with thunder and lightning. The things that have been common and lovely for eight hours—rivers, brooks, ground, mountains, rocks, and trees—turn into scary, roiling, foaming rivers, steep, muddy places where horses' hooves slip, hoof-sucking mud, slick, sheer mountain drop-offs, and slippery, wet rocks. My horse gets stuck in the mud of a riverbank and jumps to the bank on the other side. The reins fly out of my hands. I grab the mane to stay on. Then I lean over and pick up the reins and lead line and keep going. The wranglers are impressed. "Good, Sas," says Battulga, trotting up from behind with his hand out to take the lead line. It may be good, but I can see it makes him nervous enough to resume leading me.

In the past, I have always come from the opposite direction. First we would reach the large Meng Bulag encampment—the one where Dalai and his extended family live—and then travel another hour to Gosta and Khanda's. As we near camp this time, I can feel the angles of the mountains and valleys jogging into the correct pattern, like pieces of a puzzle. Each mountain skyline, each hill, moves into the right position—becoming the place where I spent time last year. And we are here.

Battulga warns me that Gosta has been very sick. He might not be here. We ride up as the sky is darkening and I see a figure in the distance. Immediately, I recognize Gosta in his deel, outside for a pee. I am soggy, wet, and achy, yet I can't stop smiling.

The heavy rain poncho I thought was so perfect doesn't keep my deel dry in these conditions. I pledge to myself that next year we will buy Russian army raincoats. They cover everything. Battulga takes our wet stuff—even my down sleeping bag in its "waterproof" stuff sack is wet through—and hangs it inside the various families' urts to dry. He holds my sleeping bag toward the wood stove, turning it so that all parts will be dry when we are ready for bed. Battulga takes incredibly good care of me.

When I see Khanda, it is like a dream come true, and by the time we get into the urts, Gosta is sitting with us, too. After reindeer milk tea and bread, we set up our tents and go to sleep listening to the grunts of reindeer. We are in the same family camp as last year, but there are three urts here now instead of two. Gosta's adopted son, Baasankhuu, and his wife, Narantuya, are in the middle urts. Last year they were in another West Taiga settlement. Baasankhuu, in his thirties, wears a jacket of military jungle colors and a big smile. On the other side of Baasankhuu's urts is Ganzorig's family's urts.

The next morning, when we start assessments for the Dukha Health Database with Gosta, he tapes a black garbage bag around our new white bathroom scale to keep it clean. He cuts a hole for the gauge. We place it on the dirt floors of the urts. It is a little tricky to find a flat place for the scale. The herders, who are so comfortable walking around outside, up steep hills with pits, and through marshy, uneven ground, and riding reindeer and horses everywhere, are tippy on the scale, like someone who steps into a boat for the first time. It doesn't seem to matter whether herders wear boots or take their boots off; they are still off balance on the scale. They take their deels off for blood pressure checks. Underneath their deels, Dukhas wear western clothes. Khongoroo measures everyone with a cloth centimeter tape from the top of the head to the sole of the boot. She takes pulses. Soon we have a system. Name. Age. Weight. Height. Blood pressure. Pulse. Hemoglobin. We ask each person questions about his or her health, write everything down, offer a candy, and go on to the next. I take blood pressures, which are astoundingly high. One of our goals is to see if the taiga people actually do have high blood pressure, as claimed in a government study. The herders believe that their high blood pressure is related to living at a high altitude. The highest blood pressure we find is 192/130. I tell the woman it is amazing she is walking around. I discover that the men have thick calluses on their fingers from hard work, making it hard to get a drop of blood to test their hemoglobin.

For two weeks everyone is busy. Augi and Baasankhuu play chess. Baasankhuu carves antlers. Gosta answers my questions while Bayara shoots the footage. He also cooks for us in his tent. Khongoroo translates, assists with the database, and washes dishes. Augi plays with the children, gets them to sing on camera, and takes lovely photos of them. Khanda does what she always does: carries water, chops wood, builds the fire, makes food, visits with neighbors, and takes care of Battummur and Gosta. She also tells us her story.

Khanda's Story

Khanda, Khongoroo, and I are sitting in Khanda's urts, drinking cups of steaming milk tea. The fire is crackling in the wood stove. The horses are neighing; someone is cutting wood with a chainsaw outside; and I hear the reindeer herd walking past, snorting. Like women anywhere, we share stories. Khanda, in her blue silk deel and black boots, with her long, straight black hair knotted into a bun, seems willing to speak. I am interested to learn more about the life Khanda leads. She has finished seven grades of school and has chosen to return to the herding life. On the ground beside her are thread, a needle, scissors, and reindeer skin. She is cutting the leather as she begins to speak. Khanda refers to Gosta as "Uncle" throughout the story.

"I had my son at home in November 2002. Uncle and some other men helped with the birth. It was cold. My mother died when she was 68. She was sick for two years and in bed for two months. My son was born four months before my mother died. It was very difficult for me to take care of both of them.

"After the baby was born, a student from the U.S. named Adam came and stayed for 10 days. He let me use his flashlight at night so it wasn't dark. He chipped through the ice for water. When one day he didn't come back for many hours, I left my baby in the urts and went to find him. He was still chipping through the ice, and finally finished when it was dark.

"When my baby, Battummur, was two months old, a person came to adopt him. Mother disagreed. She said, 'Keep your son. He will turn out well.' Now I get to talk with him and enjoy him. I followed my mother's advice. If I had given my son away I would be very sad."

Khanda moves to the stove door. She picks up a small piece of wood and slices it into half-inch shavings with her knife. She places the shavings in the wood stove and lights them. As if thinking back, she sits quietly until the fire takes hold. She places a pan of bread on the stove to cook. Khanda doesn't mention the father of her baby.

"When it was time to move to the winter place, we didn't think we could go, because my mother was so sick, but we ended up laying my mother on a reindeer and moving with her that way.

"Uncle had to go to Tsagaan Nuur because we were out of food. A doctor came from Tsagaan Nuur to give immunizations to the baby and at the same time to check on my mother. She told me that my mother's health was good, and I thought she would be fine. On the way, Uncle met the same doctor. The doctor told him my mother should only be kept comfortable. When the doctor told him his sister's health was not good, Uncle came quickly. The doctor told us different stories.

"That night my mother couldn't speak and her health condition became very bad. She was sicker and couldn't talk. Uncle was going to go alone to get Ganzorig, but I was afraid to stay, so I bundled the baby up and we all went. I was scared—my mother couldn't walk or talk, she was only breathing, so I went to Ganzorig's with Uncle. It was about an hour away."

Khanda picks up her leather sewing. The wind pushes a puff of smoke from the wood stove into the urts. The metal tings as it expands with heat. Through a hole in the stove, I see red and yellow flames dancing.

"It was springtime—we went to Ganzorig's urts and told him

about Mother's health, drank a cup of tea, and came back. When we got back, the reindeer had dispersed and Uncle and Ganzorig had to find them and bring them back. I stayed with my mother and made a batch of tea. I heard my mother say something and leaned closer to hear. She had stopped breathing. I was afraid and took my baby outside the urts to wait for Uncle. We were cold, but I was afraid to go back in. Uncle came two or three hours later and I told him what had happened. In the morning, Uncle and Ganzorig took the body outside the urts and laid it on the ground. After three days, they moved it to the top of the mountain. Then we moved."

Khanda has a soft expression on her face as she uses a leather needle we have provided to attach the pieces of the reindeer skin boots together. She is not in a hurry, yet her hands move nimbly as if they are made to do this work.

"One night soon after this, I was so tired from taking care of my mother and my son, I fell asleep with the candle burning. It fell over. When the fire began burning my baby's bedding, he started to cry. I opened my eyes and saw fire and heard the baby crying. At first, I was trying to stamp the fire out with my hands. Then Uncle woke up, untied the swaddling, unwrapped the baby, pulled the child from the blanket, and threw the swaddling out the door. He asked me why I didn't tell him. I couldn't say. I think I was in shock. I burned my palms because I didn't know how to stop the fire. The baby's first blanket and a cotton sheet were burned and the fire had started to burn the baby's hat. At that time it was hard, with a new baby and the reindeer giving birth. Ganzorig's two children (one boy and one girl) helped a lot.

"Sometimes I miss my mother. I think my mother's death reduced her pain. Staying in bed so long damaged her hips—she had bleeding bedsores. She was in bed six months. I tried using a pillow for her hips but she was very thin. For me, living with my mother was nice, but it was hard to see her health get worse and her body dying.

"My mother was poor, cleaning for rich families when she was a child. She had no food, no clothes. She became blind in one eye from a stick. I am thinking this might be why my mother died so early—she worked very hard as a kid. Her parents came here from

Tyva with reindeer—but most of the animals died along the way. They went to Ulaan Uul with only one reindeer for milking. That was wartime. They got scared from World War II and came to the taiga. My mother was 10 years old when she came from Tyva. It took seven or eight days. Uncle was a baby. Ganzorig was born here. One sister was born here. Their parents came with three children—my mother, her little sister, and Uncle. My mother's father was a shaman. Her grandfather was a shaman. All our ancestors were shamans.

"At the end, Mother went to the Tsagaan Nuur hospital two or three times but it didn't help. She had swelling all over her body. She used a lot of medicines but they didn't help. I think my mother didn't see happiness in life. I don't think I did good things for my mother when I was younger. When she was sick, I helped to clean her up because she couldn't leave her bed. Maybe that was the good thing I did for her."

Ganzorig's youngest son comes into the urts. Khanda pours him some reindeer milk tea, and he reaches behind the kitchen curtain, taking a piece of bread. Soon he leaves and Khanda continues.

"I had three brothers and one sister. My older brother reached 30 years old. He left to collect musk deer antlers and never came back. We found his bones seven years after he went missing. I thought he would come back. It was hard to see the bones. Before we found them, I was waiting for my brother. I thought maybe he was in Tyva, had lost his way. There were a lot of people trying to find him, but no success. A dog went with him when he left, and one month later the dog came back really skinny, with bones and ribs sticking out. The dog died one month later. Maybe the dog was waiting for my brother. We wished we could get a message from the dog. My brother was lost in 1993."

Khanda states this matter-of-factly. It is as if she spent years crying about her brother and there are no more tears left. She doesn't look up, however, as she continues sewing and talking.

"Bayandalai found his bones near the Tyvan border, the Buss River. I rode my horse there to find my brother. After my brother went to Buss I dreamed several times that he was drowning and I could only see his eyes. I told my mother. Then I had the opposite dream. A while after my brother got lost, I was always dreaming about him in his fancy deel, his beautiful face, coming back—always dreaming about him that way. When I saw my brother's remains, his skull, I recognized his teeth. There I saw his saddle, stirrups, and all his stuff. I trust it was my brother. It took seven years before Bayandalai found him—2000. If no one had found the remains, I'd still be waiting for him.

"After that, I stopped thinking that my brother would come. When I told my mother and she agreed with me that he had died, it was hard for her, of course. He was her last son. She had already lost the others. She took care of my brother. She didn't like me as much as she did my brother. She was a very strict woman. Sometimes I think if I had my brother…sometimes when I move, there is so much to do, I could use help from a brother. When I am sick, I wish he were here to help me. Other times, I see brothers and sisters arguing and think maybe it is better to be alone."

Khanda snips the thread, finishing the front seam of the first boot.

"A guy came this past spring. We got married, and then I told him to leave. We got married and divorced in one year. He liked to drink. For two months Battummur liked him and called him Father, and when he didn't come, Battummur cried. Now he's forgetting, says that person is very bad. Doesn't want to see him."

We hear a rumble, like far-off thunder. The ground we are sitting on vibrates. Click, click, clicking of reindeer joints. Diminishing rumble. The reindeer herd of 100 has come and gone.

Khanda takes a deep breath and continues:

"I used to think I wouldn't marry, but you can't tell the future. Now I know I don't need a lazy, bad, drunk person. Once he went to buy flour, tobacco, and tea and didn't come home for one month. I put his stuff together and sent it to his home. He came back and I said, 'No.' I married late, I was used to doing things my way. I can't say if I'm a good person or not, but I didn't like the way he did things. It doesn't matter that I was taking care of my uncle's home and my new home, although it was hard. I can't leave Uncle alone now that his health is not so good. When I looked at Uncle then, he looked tired because of having no woman to help him. I am thinking about Uncle—not only is he a man, but also he is sick. He cannot manage on his own."

Khanda pauses, concentrating on the sewing in her hands. In this nomadic life, there is a division of labor by gender. We in the U.S. fight this—we want each sex to be able to do everything the other does. Here in the taiga the women are in charge of the home and children, along with milking and birthing reindeer. The men herd the animals and take care of them. They cut and stack wood. They hunt and protect the settlements. Doing either job is a lot for one person—even a healthy one. After a brief silence, Khanda begins her story again in a soft, steady voice.

"I hate drinking and drunk people. It changes their character. For me staying alone is the best way. Sometimes that man made me angry. I asked him to help with things and he would just lie down. When I am angry, I get sick. I know bad people, but when I was living with him I told him he could be a good person. I thought he was clever, but.... Here in the taiga, when people divorce, people say if the person is lazy and bad, get divorced. They talk about the person in a bad way.

"The best solution is to do things by myself. Sometimes when others are doing things it looks too slow. I do my work and I don't like to ask people to do it—they can't do it perfectly. My uncle is not lazy—he works hard. When my uncle asked my ex-husband to saw wood, he was always trying to debate with Uncle. It was too hard for him to do and he had all sorts of excuses. My uncle's main goal was for us to be a nice family, but the lazy man thought Uncle was trying to tell him what to do and didn't like it at all.

"You know, there is a new law. When a couple is married, the government gives them 500,000 tugrik ($350). If you are divorced within three years, you have to pay the whole thing back. It has to do with how many months you are married. Now I have to pay. I will. In August I will sell reindeer meat. When you have a wedding, you need a new urts. In the taiga, the covering and wood need to be new. Uncle had his own urts, so after I got married I had to take care of both. Few people came to the wedding in October because in September all the families had moved far away. Four or five families came. My feeling after I got married was so different. I changed, moved to another urts. Living in another urts changed me—it was very boring. I felt like I had moved to another place. If I go far away, I can't live. When I saw a bride crying before, I thought I wouldn't cry, but I did. I knew him four years before we married. He seemed like a good man at first, but after the marriage his character changed and he started drinking. Maybe my way of life was going in a bad way. My mother died, my brother died, I got a bad husband."

We sit quietly. I smell the wet earth and grass, horse manure, wood smoke, lingering cigarette smoke, and the bread baking on the stove. "Will you be a shaman like your ancestors?" I ask.

"I am not preparing to be a shaman. I need a costume first. Someone else needs to make it. I can't do that. I don't know when it might happen. I made Ganzorig's costume, his boots. The *khengereg* (drum) is made by a man. The costume and boots are made by women. I sewed Uncle's costume and boots when I was in seventh grade. On the costume, I sewed a special human bone using reindeer wool. Ganzorig has heart disease. To be a shaman, the person has to be sick. We all have to agree that the person is a shaman. If we don't agree, he will get sicker."

"Ganzorig's oldest daughter has epilepsy. Does it mean she will be a shaman?" I ask.

"Yes. She also has some problem with heart disease, so probably. Sometimes when she is angry, she has epilepsy. We will know it is time for her to become a shaman when Uncle says so.

"I don't want to be a shaman because I don't believe in it. I can tell some fortunes from my dreams. I believe in my dreams. After my dream, if I imagine the whole event, it can be true. If I think of the dream all day, especially bad things, it will happen. I can always dream the bad way. My mother, my brother, always dreaming bad things.

"Baasankhuu had a little baby. I was always dreaming the little baby was trying to fly to the sky. I told Uncle. He said, 'Oh, don't worry, you always dream these stupid things.' Then someone came and told us the baby had died—we were living far away. The baby died at two months of age.

"I don't pray or have a religion. I just follow my life. I can't talk about shamanism. It is hard to talk more about shamanism. I don't believe in it.

"I can talk about my life. For seven years, I didn't ask anything about my brother. It is life so it doesn't matter. Just work. My relatives asked about my brother. All the information was wrong. At first I couldn't believe my dreams. I saw my brother drown in a river. Sometimes I see faces and they change color and die in two years. Battulga's younger sister? I saw her face change. Soon she died.

"Uncle asked, 'Am I dying soon? Please tell me.' Uncle will die in five years. When people are going to die, their spirit is gone and their color is white. Amgalan's son came here and I realized he would die soon. The boy killed himself. Since then I realized that it meant something if faces changed. This winter J. Bat's son lost some teeth fighting and didn't talk much—then he died. I saw the difference in his face. It turned white, then gray. He had been in a fight, so his face was discolored. I told him not to fight—it's bad for you. He had a big alcohol problem. 'You will kill someone or they will kill you if you drink too much,' I told him. He was drunk, maybe in a fight. This winter they found two bodies in the water—his cousin's and his. Dead."

I know J. Bat. He is one of the most welcoming of the East Taiga people. In both the East and the West there are only 210 herders, so the deaths of his son and nephew affect the whole community.

Khanda lifts the pan of bread off the stove, turns the round loaf out of the pan, and returns it to the pan upside down. The top is browned. The smell of sourdough bread baking is especially tantalizing right now. Khanda picks up her sewing and looks sad as she continues.

"Here, if someone is 25, people say they are old and nothing more will happen. They won't fall in love. I am over 30. If a man has a good character, I like him, whether his face is pretty or not. In spring I miss my mother and brother—when things are blooming and blossoming. At other times of year, I don't miss them. Each spring I miss them more."

Her cousin comes into the urts. Khanda flattens the boots she is making under a rug, between the rug and the ground. The ground rumbles—the herd is running past again.

"In August Battummur and I will fly to the Gobi for a competition. A photographer came here one time and now he wants to use Battummur for a photography contest. I have never been on a plane. I wonder how it will be.

"Reindeer are really bothered by bugs. They get in their eyes. They spend so much time trying to get rid of bugs that they don't eat enough. That is why the cold weather is better for them. There are fewer bugs at 6:00 AM, so we let them go to pasture then. In winter, reindeer are able to pasture by themselves because there are no wolves from October until April. The wolves are around the cattle families. Wolves can't walk on thick snow. Reindeer can. They have more power in winter than in summer.

"In winter when we need to move, my hands are frozen. When loading the urts and other things, I can't use gloves. It is our life. We have to do it. When Battummur goes to school in two years, we will stay near Tsagaan Nuur in the winter. I have no relatives there so I will have to stay and look after my son. The reindeer will be fine. In the winter it is easy to pasture them. We can leave them with another family, probably with Baasankhuu. They won't be hungry, they prepare for the winter in the fall pasture.

"For our own food, we prepare cow and horse meat. We use one big animal—one horse or cow is enough. We buy it in the fall. If we have enough money, we buy enough for the whole winter; otherwise, one part at a time. It stays frozen.

"We are alone in the winter. Baasankhuu will hunt. Ganzorig lives in town with his children. We can't go hunting so we stay near the river. Sometimes I try to find squirrels. I can make money selling squirrel skins. In the winter, I stay in the same urts. When I get up, the blanket and everything is ice. The urts is white about three feet up the sides. The top of the urts is white, too. Outside the trees are white. I first boil tea so there is a fire inside. I cut wood without gloves. January is the coldest, but we know how to manage and our reindeer love the cold, so we are happy."

Khanda, finished with her story, continues sewing the boots in silence. I watch her, awed by her story. I am impressed with her strength—with the way all the reindeer herders accept the hardships of their lives so their reindeer can survive.

The entertainment for the evening becomes watching me try to balance on a reindeer. Everyone gathers around. Ganzorig hoists me up. I sit up straight. The reindeer takes a few steps. I don't fall off. A few more steps. I am still on. Ganzorig nods with a smile. Antlers graze my cheek. Ganzorig leads the reindeer and me in a circle. It seems I have finally gotten the knack of balancing on a reindeer! Tomorrow we need to do health checks and continue the health database at another settlement, and I will ride a reindeer like everyone else!

Khanda doesn't usually go with us when we go to a different settlement, but she will go with us today. She ties one reindeer to another. We take off. First Khanda, then Battummur, me, Ganzorig's wife, Erdenchimeg, Khongoroo, Bayara, and last of all, Ganzorig's young daughters, both on one reindeer. Augi is as good a reindeer rider as a horse rider. He gallops to the head of the line, takes some video, and trots back. For me it is very comforting to have our reindeer tied together and know that they will just keep walking—through brooks and over marshy land, past barking dogs and birds warning us not to get near their nests. This is one of my most glorious moments: riding a gentle reindeer, totally calm with no fear, moving across the green expanse of land instead of along the river bank as we have to do with horses. I feel a part of this indigenous life.

When we arrive, Khongoroo and I give the elder, Bayandalai, a first aid kit for the settlement. Khongoroo explains the use of each item in it and points out that she has translated every item into Mongolian. Tsetsegmaa, Bayandalai's wife, tells us how much she appreciates our help. The vitamins have helped the taiga children and the antibiotics we gave her son last year for an ear infection cleared it up. We give out hygiene kits and other community members reiterate their gratitude. While Augi and Bayara walk around outside taking videos, we spend the morning in an urts doing health checks for the database. Augi stops in to tell us that many people from all the West Taiga settlements are here. Today is the day of a Nadaam Festival with wrestling, reindeer races, and reindeer polo.

When we finish, we follow the crowd. Twenty taiga women sit in a line on the side of a hill. Every one of the women is wearing a brightly colored deel and has a long, shiny black ponytail tied with a colorful ribbon. Below them, on flat ground, the festival is about to begin. First the wrestling contests, starting with little children like five-year-old Battummur, trying to get his opponent to step out of a circle on the ground. Then reindeer polo with men and even some strong women riding reindeer fast, competing to get a furry object through the goals at either end of the field. The festival ends with reindeer races and festival food like soda and candy.

We are finished with our Dukha Health Database for the West Taiga, having assessed 89 people. Tomorrow we will go down the mountain to the steppes and then up to the East Taiga.

East Taiga Scholarships

We are on the horses leaving the West Taiga when I suddenly feel it is time to speak to Battulga about something that happened last year. Herders in the East Taiga requested university scholarships for four of their teenagers. During the year, a wonderful, generous, angel woman asked if she could do something special for Mongolians, and I e-mailed her a photo I had taken of the four teenagers who wanted scholarships. She was touched by the four together and drawn to the idea of supporting the education of these children of reindeer herders, who do not live on a money economy. The tuition for each would be $300, so she generously provided the whole amount of $1,200, which I am taking to them now.

Since the largest denomination of Mongolian bills is equal to about $10, and university tuition in Ulaanbaatar can be paid in U.S. dollars, I am riding my horse with 12 one-hundred-dollar bills in my money belt. I plan to give the scholarship money to the students when we get to the East Taiga. The perfect person to discuss this with is Battulga, since he has been to the university and is a Dukha.

He is the only one of us who understands Dukha culture and can tell me how I should give them the funds. I am bursting with the secret that I actually have what they asked for, but I want to make sure we handle this appropriately.

"You can't do that," he says right away. My heart sinks.

"Those girls didn't take the entrance exams in the spring. That was when the two young taiga men drowned, and the whole community was dealing with the tragedy. They couldn't afford the test or the cost of travel to Murun. So, none of them has been accepted into university."

I am filled with apprehension. I have no idea how to negotiate this. Earlier, it seemed so easy. Now I have this money and the expectations of a beautiful donor. I have no idea what I am dealing with. We keep riding, but my interior work now is to change the picture of the parents and girls glowing with happiness and excitement as I present them with the money to…what?

I look back and see Khongoroo on her horse. Bayara is plodding along. Augi rides his horse with abandon, holding the reins in one hand and shooting video with the other. He gallops ahead and circles back. Endless energy. I just can't get how he can ride "extra" like this. Every step is a challenge for me. You won't catch me going over the same land twice.

Khongoroo rides beside Battulga and me. "So, what can we do if there are no students ready to study?" I ask.

"I don't know," says Battulga through Khongoroo. "We'll just have to see."

After a day and night in Tsagaan Nuur, we are on our way to the East Taiga. A filmmaker named Eric joins us. He has extensive equipment, having made films for Fox TV and National Geographic. One horse bucks when the equipment is almost tied on, so we find another horse for the 200-pound load. Then we are on our way. We arrive at the East Taiga summer camp after a five-hour ride. We set up our tents at the top of a small rise overlooking the settlement on the opposite side of a small river.

The community gathers with us so we can get their news, introduce our team, and describe our plans for this visit. When I mention that an anonymous donor has given money for tuition scholarships, faces light up. When I mention that the students need to be accepted into a university to get a scholarship, faces fall. I have never seen Dukha faces express emotion like this. The topic of education is obviously an important one. Our job is to figure out how to resolve this.

I have had some pretty difficult facilitation jobs in the U.S., but I feel inept here. Everything is going through the filters of three cultures: the Dukhas, whose native language is Tyvan and who live here with their reindeer; Khongoroo and Bayara, city Mongolians who have attended university in Ulaanbaatar; and Augi, a city Mongolian who has studied in the U.S. I am the least helpful when it comes to cultural understanding. I only know how education works in the U.S., and, as I am learning, things work very differently in Mongolia.

Battulga bridges the gaps—speaks Mongolian and Tyvan, is a Dukha, and attended university in Ulaanbaatar. He explains that if the students do not go to a university, their degree is useless. Private colleges here don't have the same standards as universities. If they go to a college, they will be no better off than they are now. Battulga also explains that he cannot get involved in a meeting with the Dukhas, because the parents will hold it against him if their children don't get scholarships. He lives in Tsagaan Nuur and still interacts with everyone after we leave.

We have to manage the community meetings without him. This is very awkward. The students tell us they plan to go to college, even though they haven't taken the entrance exams. When Khongoroo asks where the students plan to go to school, one of the young people brings out a printed brochure from an obscure college. Khongoroo reads it to the community. The brochure claims that the school has eight students from the taiga. Khongoroo looks up from reading and asks who those students are. There are none, everyone says. Khongoroo explains that anyone can print anything. It doesn't mean that it is true. She explains that, by extension, the rest of the brochure might be made up, too. Everyone starts speaking. Sharkhuu tells us again how important education is for her children.

At one point, when we suggest that there might not be a scholarship for Saran and Naran, their mother, Pruvie, S. Ganbat's wife, says, "Do you mean to say that my daughters will not be able to go to the university this year?" Then she leaves the circle and begins to angrily chop wood. Khongoroo, always diplomatic, does not translate this to me, but I can see Pruvie's anger as the ax meets the logs.

When we talk about finding a way to split the money so that many can go to school, heads nod in agreement. This seems fair to me. Since Battulga is not with us, though, after we offer this suggestion, we have to go across the river to our tents and report to him. When we tell Battulga, he says that won't work. If they don't have enough money for the whole tuition, they will get to Ulaanbaatar and just spend it. Plus there is the problem of colleges being inferior to universities. So we have to call another meeting and say we changed our minds—not something I have ever had to do while facilitating. It is very tricky and uncomfortable.

That night a storm comes. Our tents are pitched on a rise where the wind has no mercy. It whips the side of the tent into me, bending the fiberglass pole again and again until it snaps. I am alone because Khongoroo is visiting in the other tent. The violent rain lasts so long, I wish for room service and indoor plumbing—or at least a companion.

The next day we meet Pruvie on a path and she apologizes to me. Khongoroo translates, but I don't know why she is apologizing. Khongoroo says Pruvie said angry words to me asking if I meant that her daughters would not be able to go to school. These discussions and strong feelings are definitely not things tourists see when they visit a settlement and not something I have seen before.

We find out that there are two other students who actually took entrance exams the year before last and were accepted into universities. They were unable to attend because they did not have any money to go. Khongoroo suggests that we meet with all the students—the four original girls and the two who have taken the exams already. We gather them into one urts. Then another student from the far camp arrives by horse with her mother. They heard about our possible help for education and left home at 5:00 AM, riding until

1:00 PM to meet with us. "Rough ride," they say, as they drink the welcoming suutai tsai.

Now we have seven interested students. We ask them to write down why they want to get a higher education. We have three questions: "What will your life be like without school? What do you imagine it will be like if you go to school? How will you help your taiga people by going to the university?" They sit and lie around the urts and write their answers. When we collect the papers, we discover that they all think they will be missing a lot without an education.

Batjargal, a 20-year-old male who has been accepted by the Agriculture University, writes: "My life will be very dark without school. Taiga people do not have an education, so they don't know much about law. They can't have their human rights. They are in a very difficult position now. If I study in school I will develop my knowledge and my future will be brighter. I will study as hard as I can. After graduation from my university, I will share my knowledge with my taiga people and help them. I will do my best to develop their life."

M. Solongo, a 19-year-old female who has been accepted at a Music University, writes: "If I do not go to school, my life will be the same as now. We don't have any educated people. It is hard for us. Like my parents. They are herding reindeer with no jobs and missing culture, so I want to study. My life will be dark without school. If we study somewhere we can communicate with other people. We can be good people with good educations. I'll study very hard and after education I will be an educated person. This means we can live very well. After graduation we will work somewhere. Example: I will be a music teacher. After graduation I will come to Tsagaan Nuur soum because the school lacks music teachers, so I will choose this school. My future goal is to study very well and then share my knowledge with the next generation. If people from the taiga study, it will be very helpful for the young generation, who will also study more. I want to be a good person, able to help the taiga people. I really trust myself. I'll do my best for the taiga people and help them a lot."

We really don't know how to make this fair. We will keep talking, hoping something will evolve, but we cannot spend more time on it today. We need to meet with the herders individually to do health checks and to document their vital signs and conditions for the health database. We sit on the ground in Pruvie's urts, and family by family, the herders come for checkups. There is no privacy. While we are assessing each herder, the others sit and wait.

When we finish the health checks, we research shamanism on video. Battulga considers our friend, J. Bat, the father of one of the hopeful students, to be an expert on shamanism. J. Bat agrees to give us an interview if we can do it at a remote place in nature. Battulga, Bayara, Khongoroo, and I follow him for half an hour around granite and quartz rocks covered with lichen, over ground with hillocks, and over a ridge to a quiet, secluded spot overlooking the mountains of Tyva. J. Bat sits on the ground. He is a small man with a mustache and thick glasses, wearing a flat cap. Bayara sets the camera on a tripod. Battulga holds a reflector. Khongoroo and I stand off-camera. As he begins to speak, the only sounds that we can hear along with his voice are wind and birds.

"There are two types of shamans: white and black. Black shamans are for evil and bad intentions, whereas white ones are for good and happiness. In black shamanism, one can, for instance, pay a shaman to do some evil things to someone else. If the shaman is really powerful, what is done can cause mental illness or can even cause death."

On top of a hill to the west I catch movement. I watch while J. Bat speaks. Then I see that it is the children from the settlement playing. Khongoroo is translating.

"When many shamans come near each other, they compete. There are stories in which shamans compete to see who is the most powerful. The most powerful one is the one who has survived in the past, especially in Tyva regions. During the competition, powerful shamans can transform themselves into animal forms like dogs and wolves and go to visit families in the evening. When a shaman does this, it means the transformed shaman would like to capture a good shaman's spirit. Really powerful shamans can transform into ashes and enter the other shaman's bowl while he is drinking milk tea. If that drinking person is a good shaman, that person will know. If it is a bad shaman, that person will drink and die." J. Bat talks as if he is pouring out some great knowledge he has held in for a long time.

"Good shamans have the ability to suck sickness out of someone through a metal straw or a pipe. One example I can tell you about is my uncle, who lived nearby. He could do that. He basically sucked the sickness from relatives and took it into himself. Those who cannot really perform this should not do it because it can actually hurt them."

J. Bat tells us about the requirements for becoming a shaman—sickness, like heart disease or epilepsy. He continues.

"The father of my grandfather argued with a powerful shaman about a work issue because he was an officer. Ever since that time, the shaman comes to us in the form of a bear. That animal form sends bad energy to us. Our family does not have a good shaman against this shaman now, so it is dangerous. I think it is better not to go to the bad shamans. Better to respect them by staying away. Instead make offerings of food, drink, juniper smoke and prayer, to the pure sky, water, and mountain spirits. They will protect us."

When we walk back to camp from the interview, the community is still discussing the educational funding. We believe that the only option is to give the scholarships to Batjargal and Solonge, because they took the entrance exams last year and are already accepted at universities. The tuition has gone up to $450, so the total will be $900. I feel sad that we can't help all the students, but I tell them that if they take the exams next year, maybe we can help them.

"How can we take the exams next year?" a student asks.

"We have no way to pay for the exam," adds another.

"How can we pay for transportation to Murun?"

"We will help with funding for transportation and application fees," I reply, but they say, "We will have forgotten everything by then."

Khongoroo suggests that we could get them study guides in Ulaanbaatar and they could use them during the year. We have $300 left for study guides, transportation, and entrance exam fees. Khongoroo asks the students what exams they want to study for. They say they want to take exams in English, communications, and Mongolian language. We will send study guides on these subjects from Ulaanbaatar.

When we get to Tsagaan Nuur, administrator Buyantogtokh gives us more information about the process of getting money for education. Pruvie and Ganbat's daughter, Saran, wants to be a veterinarian, so she will probably get a government scholarship this year, he explains. The government will help some of the others because there are scholarships for minorities (Dukhas are a minority ethnic group) and for herders' children.

"How can we keep the money safe?" Khongoroo wants to know.

Buyantogtokh says he will be happy to co-sign a new bank account with S. Ganbat, who is a Dukha elder. They will safeguard the money so that it will only be used for this specific purpose.

Making the transition from my vision of handing scholarship money to four students to our final agreement was a complicated, emotional, and challenging experience. I definitely felt out of my element. There were many aspects of the educational system that I had no concept of—entrance exams, the difference between college and university, and who could get a government scholarship. This experience showed me how strongly the community values education and how difficult it is to facilitate across three cultures. Khongoroo, Bayara, Augi, and Battulga, though, made the harmonious resolution of this challenge possible. Having Khongoroo for an assistant was like having an extra brain, heart, and body.

And, amazingly enough, we had no problems with wolves or bears. When we climb on our horses to leave the taiga, we are all in one piece.

Nergui

Back in Tsagaan Nuur, Battulga says there is a very good shaman named Nergui. He says we need to try to interview him and see if he is doing a ritual ceremony while we are here. I give Battulga money for gas so he and a friend can take a motorcycle to visit Nergui and set up a meeting. Battulga comes back some hours later to report, "Tonight he is performing a ritual for his sister's child, who has a health problem."

Nergui is generous in his interview. He says he is interested in speaking with an elder foreigner. He's never met one before. Nergui himself is in his early fifties and has a thick, but short, dark beard and mustache. We speak about religion, his mental illness as a teenager, and how becoming a shaman has allowed him to manage a normal life.

Then it is time for the evening ceremony. Bayara is shooting the action and Khongoroo and I are sitting on a metal frame bed in Nergui's one-room log home. When Nergui is dressed in his ceremonial clothes and the room is full of juniper smoke, and visitors are seated all around the perimeter of the wooden house, the ceremony starts. Battulga attaches a blue khadagh we have brought to Nergui's costume, and he begins to chant and drum. Once in a trance, the shaman makes sounds like a cuckoo bird and a wolf and brings in ongods, or ancestor spirits. Suddenly, Nergui leaps into the air and collapses, landing on our laps. His assistants stand him back up. He continues drumming and chanting.

Still in a trance, he motions for a young man to sit on the floor and pounds the drum over his head. The shaman hands the young man his sacred mouth harp with khadaghs attached. Nergui sits behind him, places his drum on the floor, and darts his head around like a bird to check on the young man as he plays. It is fascinating to watch Nergui and the young man interact in a trance state.

When we drive back to Tsagaan Nuur, it is after midnight. Battulga tells us the young man has come from Erdenet to study with Nergui. In the morning, as we leave for Ulaanbaatar, I realize that this is a perfect story for my film about becoming a shaman. I regret that I didn't get any information about the young man—not even his name.

Yura's Ceremony

Yura's home in Ulaan Uul, is a convenient stop halfway between Tsagaan Nuur and Murun. Ulaan Uul means Red Mountain. When I look at the mountains from Yura's home, I notice a pink tinge, yet Battulga once told me there is one mountain nearby where the rocks are red, and the name comes from this particular mountain. We drive to the family khashaa and the driver hits the horn. Yura comes out with her large black pocketbook over her shoulder and under her arm. She juggles the bag as she unlocks the double metal door for our car. Her house, situated on green steppe land, is made of logs and has soft green window trim. Yura's smile lifts her cheeks so they nearly make her eyes close. She has short, wavy black hair and glasses. Yura is my age and about my size. Whenever I see her I am wearing camping clothes, coming or going from the taiga. She is always dressed up—today with a pearl necklace, pearl earrings, and a freshly laundered top with matching pants. I don't know how she manages this look with no running water or machines to help. She does have a generator powering her television and lights. Sitting on a low stool in the kitchen, Yura chops mutton into tiny pieces, alternately smoking and chopping. Her grandson builds a fire in the tin stove and soon we are eating dinner.

A bit later, when it is dark, preparations for the shaman ceremony begin. Yura's assistant and husband, Gurbazar, is here this time. First, Yura changes her clothes—from her blouse and pants to a green silk deel and a black bowler hat. In all the shaman ceremonies I have seen, the shamans have been younger than we are, so I am wondering if she will have the stamina and energy it takes to perform a ritual ceremony. Also, she is a chain smoker and not an athletic person. The drum, two feet in diameter like Ganzorig's and Nergui's, is heavy. From ceremonies I have seen, I know that ancestor ongods are active and demanding, wildly swinging the drum from side to side and over the shamans' heads.

Incense is lit and all the shaman's accoutrements, the altar, Yura, and all of us (Bayara, Khongoroo, the driver, and I) are smudged with juniper incense. Yura gives offerings of food and drinks to the ongods before she settles herself on her living room floor facing her altar to begin playing her *aman khuur* (mouth harp). When it is time, Gurbazar smoothly takes Yura's green deel off, and he and their grandsons dress her in a leather shaman costume. The costume has khunkhinguur, blue khadaghs, and manjin attached to the back. A fur scarf made of the skins of some little animal surrounds Yura's neck. Her pink plastic sandals are taken off and soft leather boots are placed on her feet. Gurbazar takes off the black bowler hat and ties on a red headdress with eyes, nose, mouth, and ears embroidered in white. Colored cloth strips hang in front of Yura's face.

The reason she needs someone to dress her is that she is already partially in a trance. We have the video camera on, but we will turn it off as soon as her ongods come and the family indicates it is time. The role of Gurbazar and the grandsons is to keep Yura safe, prevent her from crashing into furniture or falling on the floor. They follow her around with their arms outstretched to protect her.

Ongod energy comes in as Yura begins chanting. The khunkhinguur jingle. She begins to dance in addition to drumming and singing. The lights are turned out and the video is dark. Yura sits suddenly and makes whistling and kissing sounds. Her husband makes a sound like "Show, show, show, show." The tempo is up. She is swinging her head from side to side. Laughing. Stands up. Sweeps the drum over her head and around her body. Her grandson gives her a drink of vodka. Kissing sound. "Ha, Ha," laughing loudly. Stands to play the drum and chant. Smokes a pipe her husband gives her. "Ha, ha, ha, ha." She talks to the ongods.

Then she makes sounds like a cuckoo bird. As I watch, I can see there is some other energy in her, allowing Yura to dance, jump up high into the air, swing the heavy drum around, and chant. One ongod knocks her over and her family catches her. For another ongod she drinks milk tea and smokes a cigarette. Six spirits come before the shaman begins to slow down. She sits on the floor and plays her aman khuur, then changes into her green silk deel and bowler hat with her family's help. They put her pink flip-flops back on over her socks. Yura does not come right back. She comes slowly, like one waking from a deep sleep.

Then she is back in her home clothes and we are all climbing into bed. It's late.

The next morning we leave and, after six more hours of driving, we arrive in Murun one day early. We are told that our MIAT flight for tomorrow is canceled. Then we hear that an Aero Mongolia flight is on for tomorrow. It just happens that an Aero Mongolia representative is staying at the same guesthouse we are, so she changes our tickets and we are blessed with a good flight back to Ulaanbaatar.

Imagination

A well-known shaman from Ulaanbaatar kindly invites me to Terelje, a nature spot an hour away from the capital. He is about my age and prosperous in body and worldly possessions. Terelje has a famous rock formation in the shape of a turtle. Nestled in the valley below are rows of tourist gers that you can rent for a night or so.

I say no. Why? It is so generous of him to invite me. I'd get to see beautiful nature and have an opportunity to hang out with a real shaman. The tricky thing is, he doesn't know he is dealing with an experienced visitor to Mongolia.

On reflection, I can imagine how the trip would go. We leave a couple of hours after the planned time. Maybe we have a good car, so it doesn't break down on the bumpy roads. He and his men friends tell me which ger I will sleep in. There might be two gers, or maybe we will all be in one. Or. I drop my toothbrush and night things off on the lanolin-smelling bed. The party begins. Someone opens a bottle of Chinggis Khan vodka. The men tell me to join them. They tell me to drink this. I don't drink. The party goes on most of the night, with slushy and heart-rending toasts, until they can't walk or they pass out or stagger to my bed.

Me? Wide-eyed? Oh, yes, in the past I have had hopes like this: the glory of hanging out with a famous shaman. Getting the best shots for my films. Patiently waiting for a shaman to divulge some secret that he has never told a westerner. Thinking I might fit a question in between the toasts. Placing the bowl of vodka or fermented mare's milk to my lips while Mongolians urge, "Drink it up. All at once. Bottoms up!" Oh, yes, I understand those words.

The next morning? No information. No secrets. The guests, hung over and pale, get up late. I sit on my bed, gazing out the door at the shepherds on their horses who guide their flocks of sheep and goats past our ger. I wait, impatient to get back to the city.

One "no" at the right time saves me from all this. Instead, I stay in Ulaanbaatar, where Khongoroo, Bayara, and I make a trailer for our shaman film from the footage we have taken in the taiga.

Dukha children, like other Mongolian children, love to play basketball. This handmade hoop is in the farthest East Taiga settlement. Often the ball is too flat to bounce and the ground is bumpy and wet, but many animated games are played here anyway.

photo credit: Fred Thodal

Shaman Nergui performs an outside ceremony at "a beautiful place," which is a grove of larch trees near Tsagaan Nuur.

photo credit: Sas Carey

2008

> If thunder and lightning occur, cover your head.
> Hairs are antennae and draw lightning to you,
> especially in this place with so many different
> metals under the ground.
> — KHANDA

A Discussion about Khengereg, Shaman Drum

Khongoroo, Bayara, and Battulga will be my team again this year, so when I first get to Ulaanbaatar, I meet with Battulga and Khongoroo in the playground gazebo outside Munkhjin's apartment. We are planning this year's trip to the taiga, discussing how many horses we will need, how long we will be there, and the current condition of the trails.

Out of the blue, Battulga asks, "Would you like to buy a shaman costume and drum, Sas?"

"Me?" I answer with a jolt and a question. "No." I have learned that if you are a shaman in Mongolia, seven women in your family make a costume for you. And if you are a real shaman in the taiga, your male relatives make the drum for you. If you are a traditional shaman, you had mental problems or epilepsy when you were a teenager. If you are an authentic shaman, your ancestors were shamans. I do not meet these criteria. I am not a shaman. And since I am not a shaman, why would I want a costume? Except...as Battulga knows, I have been seeking to meet and learn from shamans for many years—from the southern border of Mongolia, near China, to the north, near Tyva and Russia—finally finding them in the north. He knows that I want to touch the unknown that they know, get inside the mysteries, and learn how they connect to the ongods. I will never be a shaman, but maybe I would learn more by experiencing my own drum and costume. When he asks me I do get a jolt, just as I do when I have a Quaker leading. Maybe Battulga knows something I don't know—he has gotten us into ritual ceremonies and shaman interviews before. Understanding shamanism, which has been an integral part of the Dukhas' culture for generations, gives me a fuller appreciation of their world. Plus I have a personal appreciation of the practice, as it gives me a chance to deepen my own spiritual healing work.

"I was in front of the post office in Ulaanbaatar the other day and someone was selling a shaman costume and drum. I thought of you. I have the phone number," continues Battulga. I am tempted, because the shamans' costumes are one of the striking aspects of their practice, and the drum…wouldn't my son, who makes drums himself, be interested in seeing the type used by Mongolian shamans? But I will be here for two months, and I don't know what expenses I might incur. I can't buy a shaman costume and drum. A little corner of me is still searching, craving to get closer, wanting to touch the mystery. I already do spiritual healing. Would a costume and drum get me closer?

"No," I repeat. "Why would I want a costume and drum? I'm not a shaman." So Battulga drops the subject.

Robbery

In nursing school I learned that having good proprioceptors means that you are aware of what's happening all around your body. You know where you are in space. If you have good proprioceptors, you know how to keep safe in Mongolia. When someone is too close, you move away. Thanks to fine-tuned proprioceptors, I am proud to say that I never got robbed in the previous nine trips to Mongolia.

It is May and still cold in Ulaanbaatar. I bundle up in layers for my early morning Mongolian language lesson, but two hours later, when I walk to Peace Avenue, the main street, I'm hot. I stuff my sweater into my large black leather pocketbook. When I stop at the First Hospital to meet my teacher, Dr. Boldsaikhan, he has the last four copies of his herb book ready for me to buy. They are large format books and heavy, but I pack them into my bag along with the sweater and Mongolian language book and put my small purse on top. I close the zipper, put the straps over my shoulder, and hold on with my arm sticking out like a chicken wing. It's noon on a Friday and Khongoroo is graduating today from the Health and Sciences University, formerly called the Mongolian Medical University. She has asked me to be her family, since her father and brother are doctors and have to work and her mother is homebound with rheumatoid arthritis.

I cross the street from the First Hospital, walk through the courtyard, and enter the Medical University. I assume the graduation will involve sitting in an audience, with diplomas and speeches I can't understand. Still, I feel honored to be Khongoroo's family. I step into the lobby. Men, women, young people, and grandparents are sitting and standing around, waiting. Waiting is something Mongolians do with great patience. I am not so practiced at it, but I take the cue and lean against a post. I take a seat when someone gets up. The way I know I am in the right place is that each group is holding a bouquet of flowers in a paper cone. Oh, great! Another cultural faux pas on my part—no flowers. What I've brought is a sand dollar I found on the beach in San Francisco. I am hoping it is enough. Mongolia is the largest landlocked country in the world, so something from the ocean is usually a hit.

The Mongolian families are a mixture of city and country folk. The countryside families wear traditional silk deels with black boots. The city-dwelling men are in suits and the women wear wool suits and spike heels. I could be in Paris, except that every single deel is silk brocade. I am the only foreigner in the lobby.

My bag is heavy. My wing of an arm is still holding the zipped bag against my body. Where are they? What's happening? When do we get to go in? Did I get the time wrong? Why did I choose today to get the books? They weigh my shoulder down. I try to call Khongoroo on her cell but there's no answer.

A young woman walks into the lobby and is greeted with a bouquet. She wears a tailor-made silk skin-clinging outfit that would make any Oscar winner jealous. Another young woman comes, then more and more. All their clothes are different, yet gorgeous. I look at the door. Am I at a medical school graduation or a fashion show? I love clothes. I love silk. I love colors. I have never seen such a fashion show—silk deels in green, blue, white, lavender, turquoise. Some wear the traditional boxy design and some are wearing full-cleavage, mini-skirt models and spike heels. Well, we just don't see this in Vermont.

As families exit with their graduates, one minute I am leaning against a post, entranced, and the next I am getting slammed into by young men on all sides. I am familiar with this Mongolian technique. I know before I look that I have been robbed. I step away from the parade and the crowd. My arm is still clutching the bag, but it is half unzipped. When I look, my little purse is gone.

I feel deflated. This is what I get for loving beauty and being off guard. What's in the purse? I find myself taking stock as I step outside and sit on a stone fence. Not my passport; I know better than that. Maybe $200 in cash, to buy supplies for the trip to the taiga. My debit card…now that creates a problem. Not that anyone can use it here, because they would need to have the PIN or show a passport. But how will I get money for the trip without the card?

Before I can dwell on feelings of being violated or wondering how I am going to get money, Khongoroo calls my cell phone. My intrepid assistant, the one who camps in the taiga, uses the nature toilet, rides a horse, and eats sitting on the ground is walking toward me. She is a fashion model. With her curled hair, skin-tight white silk suit, a plunging neckline made just for her, which features ribbons on her legs, and spike heels, Khongoroo smiles and waves her red diploma, which shows she is one of the top eight students out of 650.

Her jaw drops when I tell her I've been robbed. How? What? When? Here? She calls the police, but we both know I will never see the purse again. She is sharp, angry, and ashamed of her countrymen. We don't dwell on the robbery, though. It is time to celebrate her accomplishment with a fine restaurant meal. She's thrilled with the sand dollar when she opens it at Silk Road Restaurant.

After her graduation lunch, I need to figure out how to get

money for the trip to the taiga. We are leaving in five days. I wonder about calling Western Union or arranging a bank transfer, but I need to wait until Monday evening to call my bank, since the time is 12 hours different from Vermont and it is Friday night there. When I call on Monday, I explain that I have been robbed, but I don't want to cancel the card because some of my bills are automatically paid with it and I won't be home for seven weeks to deal with the bills. Mine is a small community bank with personal service, and they promise to watch for any expenditure on my card. I feel comforted.

Still, figuring out how to get the money takes some brainstorming. I have dinner with Shebana, a friend who is a Fulbright scholar from the U.S. Sitting in an Indian restaurant, we discuss various ways to get money. We settle on this plan: I electronically transfer money from my account in the U.S. to her account in the U.S.—that transfer is free—and then she can withdraw it for me. She has cash that she can give me right now, since I am leaving Ulaanbaatar before the transfers will be complete. This way I have money for the taiga and my transferred money will be ready for her before she leaves for the U.S.

In the future, I promise myself, I'll tune in to my proprioceptors and their information about the position of my body, but I have also learned that with the support of friends and bank employees, I can manage even being robbed in Mongolia. The next year, just to be sure, I will bring more American dollars and keep them safely under my clothes until it is time to exchange the money!

Apprentice

Khongoroo's father's good friend is the president of the Mongolian Shaman Association. We try to find the name of the young shaman, Nergui's student from last year, through this connection. We hear his name is Altansukh and that he lives in Erdenet. So Khongoroo, Battulga, Bayara, and I go by way of overnight train to Erdenet to find and interview Altansukh. Then we will drive to Murun. If our movie is to cover "becoming a shaman," then his experience training with Nergui could give us important information.

Puji has arranged for a car and driver to meet us in Erdenet. Unfortunately, Puji forgot to mention that we carry a lot of luggage. The driver, Sukhe, does his best to fit us, along with our luggage, into his small car, but his best is not quite good enough. A traffic policeman spots the car and stops us with his baton, insisting that we pay a 5,000 tugrik fine—about five dollars. Sukhe shrugs his shoulders when he gets back in the car after paying. "He needs to feed his family, like we all do."

After spending a night in Sukhe's apartment, we search through the ger district of the city asking for Altansukh, but have no luck. We go to zakh and sit in the car while Battulga searches for someone who might know where to find Altansukh. He meets a friend who says he knows of a young shaman who fits the description. Battulga's friend jumps into the car with us and directs us to some women selling wood. The shaman's mother usually works here, but not today. We get directions to her home outside of town. Goats and sheep pasture outside the ger where we stop.

We interview the woman, who says yes, she is his mother, but we have his name wrong. Her son's name is Oyunerdene, and he is out of town. Maybe we will bump into him in the taiga.

Battulga's Request

Without Battulga, our work in the taiga would be very different. Except for the year I broke my foot, when he was compromised by alcohol, he never drinks when he is working with our team, and I appreciate it. That is, until the last night in Erdenet. The friend who led us to Oyunerdene's mother also led Battulga to stay out all night drinking. Or maybe Battulga led him. In any case, on the way to the taiga, the car smells strongly of his alcohol breath.

As we four sit together in a Murun restaurant, he brings up his addiction.

"I just can't drink any more. My liver is so bad, I will die if I do." I try to figure out what to say. I think about people in recovery in Vermont. How do they do it?

"In the U.S.," I say, "we believe that if you are an alcoholic, you cannot drink at all." As he listens politely, I think, *what good is it to say that?* Let me think. I do workshops for Recovery Vermont, an organization that supports recovering alcoholics. What would the experts say? Then, as the conversation goes on to other things, I keep thinking about Alcoholics Anonymous and recovery. I think of the belief in Higher Power, but I don't quite know how to translate it into Mongolian culture. Then, as we discuss shamans, I get it. Battulga is shamanist. "Maybe you would like a shaman ceremony dedicated to helping you with your alcohol problem?"

Battulga's face lights up and he nods his head. "Yes."

I can see ideas flood him, as his eyes open wide. "I could get a male shaman called Munkhuu who lives in Tsagaan Nuur. He has the same ongods I have. I could get help. We can find him when we go to the taiga…." I watch the expressions on his face change as he is planning and figuring out how to meet the shaman, even as Bayara, Khongoroo, and I go on to other subjects.

Arriving in the West Taiga

After our usual stay at Nyama and Ganba's, meeting the horses and the guides, and packing the luggage on the horses, we ride for a couple of hours. Our guide is now Lkhagva, whom I call Mr. Lovely, partly because he is tall, dark, and handsome and partly because his name requires some mouth gymnastics for a foreign speaker like me. He is extremely competent with horses and makes sure everything is just right. In charge, he directs us to camp overnight on the way. The wranglers set up their tent a bit away from us, build a fire, and cook meat for dinner. Our team, the same people as last year—Khongoroo, Bayara, and Battulga—set up the tents and boil water on a little gas hot plate for ramen noodles.

During the night it rains, and when I stick my head out of the tent in the morning, the mountain in front of us is covered with new snow. As I climb a five-foot rise behind our wet tents to find a "nature toilet," I discover slushy snow. We are right on the edge of the freeze.

After three and a half more hours of the splat, plop, and swish of mud and water from Battulga's horse to my horse and me, we are nearly there. Despite Battulga's laughing denial that I see some urts ahead of us, we are here early enough this year (June) to find the West Taiga herders in their spring camp, much closer to Tsagaan Nuur. I feel like I have not endured enough hardship to deserve the honor of seeing Gosta, Khanda, and their family group. The way has been muddy, but not steep.

"No, they are not urts, just white rocks," claims Battulga, but I know we are nearing the camp. I see brown and white animals in the distant pasture: reindeer. The taiga is beautiful at this time of year. Cuckoo birds sing, hawks and eagles swoop over us, and the tamarack trees are a soft green haze of new needles. We ride out of the forest into a clearing, where the urts are pitched beside a flowing brook. Ganzorig meets us.

"Welcome," he says. "We thought you were strangers, but, no, it is you—you are like our tall mother, returning to take care of us." Khongoroo explains that the term "tall mother" is from a popular Mongolian movie in which a woman gives everything she has to others—she is not tall, but her heart reaches everywhere. I am touched.

Ganzorig tells us where to set up the tents and as we are doing it, I see Khanda coming out of her urts to gather wood. Each year when I see her for the first time, I feel like I am in a dream in which she has remained since I last saw her. She smiles at me. My eyes crinkle and moisten in greeting and I keep setting up the tent, sniffling.

Friend

In the U.S., blood pressure is considered high if it is 140/90 or over. In our Dukha Health Database, 69 of the 182 children's and adults' blood pressure readings are above this standard. If we consider just the adults over 18 years of age, 67 out of 123 have hypertension. Two children under 18 also have high blood pressure. In the U.S., people would not be walking around with the blood pressure levels that taiga people have. They would be given medication to prevent them from having a stroke. In our database, a 55-year-old woman has a reading of 234/118, a 41-year-old woman has one of 218/140, a 28-year-old man has one of 180/124, and a 64-year-old man's blood pressure is 260/128. Medication requires expense, monitoring, and compliance. It also requires a supply stream for the medication. None of these is available for taiga people.

Nomadicare, our program, focuses on health education. Khongoroo gives a survey, asking about risk factors—salt in their diet, smoking, and chronic alcohol use. We attempt to help the herders link these to high blood pressure, but this is as far as we can go. As for diet change (adding fruits and vegetables), the herders eat what they produce—milk, meat, and flour products. They buy the flour in Tsagaan Nuur. Few are overweight. We have found no diabetes. All taiga people exercise every day doing their daily activities. These factors will not change. But with the prevalence of untreated high blood pressure, we are concerned about the risk of stroke and hypertensive heart disease.

Since we were here last summer, Gosta, at 61, has had a stroke. In our database before his stroke, his blood pressure was 170/120. The effect of his stroke is left-sided weakness. Gosta needs Khanda to help him stand and walk him outside the urts to the "nature toilet," which has been upgraded to accommodate his needs. Now there is a hollowed-out tree trunk two feet in diameter with a soft bearskin around the top for Gosta. When he finishes, the toilet is turned on its side and the dogs clean up.

This year Gosta's nephew, Magsar, has joined the encampment with his wife and their three children—one is a new baby. Magsar delivered the baby. An untrained *bariach* (bone healer), he discovered his gift of helping when a friend had a concussion and Magsar found that the pulses on the two sides of his friend's head were not the same. He massaged the person's head until the pulses were equal. "I found that I was good at it," he tells us, as I hear "cuckoo, cuckoo" in the distance.

Magsar is here to help Gosta. Every day he does range-of-motion exercises and massage on Gosta's left leg. The exercises are the same ones I learned in nursing school, but the presentation is a bit different—the practitioner has a lit cigarette hanging from his lips while he works. The cigarette, with its smoke trailing out the toono, doesn't seem to get in the way.

I am shocked to see that Gosta can still ride a reindeer. Battulga and Magsar help him on, lifting him by his belt as we would while ambulating an unsteady patient in the hospital. They hand him a long stick and he takes off with his nephew leading, balancing himself by holding the stick on the ground with his right hand. It is a remarkable sight for me. The day he rides to another settlement, we also ride there by reindeer to assess the herders, and I slide off my reindeer. This is evidence either that Gosta is magical or that I am a handicapped reindeer rider—or both. Fortunately, it is a warm morning when I fall onto the boggy ground and get wet, because it actually feels refreshing. Gosta never falls.

Since we have visited a number of times, when we visit Gosta, he says, "Okay, I'll talk to her, she's always coming back." We listen for hours and hours, with Khongoroo translating and Bayara videotaping. Sometimes we ask questions that Gosta won't answer; other times he goes on and on, expressing opinions on anything and everything. He is sarcastic, judgmental, and rude, and at the same time he is caring and giving. He always emphasizes the importance of respecting the land and the water.

Important changes are happening because of his stroke. Gosta still smokes, but has stopped drinking. As he says, "Vodka was my friend for 35 years. Now I am finished with it."

The other change, though, affects me deeply. No more being a shaman. "I can't stand up, so I can't do a ceremony. I have done my time. Now I give it over to my brother, Ganzorig." After my initial disappointment—my dream of seeing Gosta do a ceremony will never come true—I come to another realization. Gosta, eldest shaman among the Dukha reindeer herders, is my friend. I haven't watched him perform a ceremony, but I have seen him mime a city woman putting on makeup in front of a mirror until my sides ached from laughing. I have flirted with him and he has flirted back. I have listened to his views on the environment: if someone makes a hole in the ground to extract gold, he needs to fill it back up. I have heard him talk about shamans praying for mountains, rivers, and the sky—how each mountain has its own spirit and how, when one person tried to dig a hole in that mountain, the one Gosta was pointing to with his chin, his hand became paralyzed so he couldn't mine the gold. I have sat in his urts and heard of his life's disappointments—his divorce and his children's deaths. I know his views on climate change: it is getting warmer, there is half the snow there used to be, trees are growing at higher altitudes, and the reindeer are getting smaller because they lose body water; they need humid weather, a wet climate.

"We need to teach children how to do REAL work," says Gosta. "How to take care of animals, how to sew boots, how to make saddle blankets, leather straps, and ropes, how to ride a horse in the right way. Living work. They need to remember the culture and customs." I have heard him say these words. I have lived in his urts. Over the years, I have experienced Gosta. A ceremony lasts a night. A friend is forever.

We Meet Chuluu G. Again

To visit Gosta and Khanda we need to cross a brook and rocky, boggy areas near both banks, but we can see them from our campsite whenever they are outside. When I see Khanda go out for wood, I get a soft feeling, remembering our intense time living together. Low rhododendron bushes with purple flowers are plentiful between us. Rocks jut up. Behind our tents is a high log platform—a safe place for our food. Close to that is a fenced-in area where Khanda and Magsar pen the reindeer at night. Around us on three sides is thin taiga forest.

We ride Gosta's reindeer along a trail, through larch trees with needles just beginning to emerge, to another West Taiga settlement for health checks and the data for the database. The forest is a green haze. Chuluu G. is the first person I see. The canvas of her urts slaps in the wind as we take the scale, stethoscope, and hygiene kits out of the bag. We haven't seen Chuluu G. since she told us her story four years ago, because she has been living close to town where life is a little easier. She has aged. Her upper teeth are gone. Her eyesight is deteriorating. Her hip hurts from lifting ice in the winter. Taiga life is hard on a body. Yet in spite of these ailments, she still sparkles. And she is proud to tell us that shamanism in her family has skipped one generation and has just reappeared. Her 35-year-old son, Khalzan, is now a shaman. When he comes for a health check, he tells what happened. "I became mad. I was running through the forest. Our ancient people came before my eyes."

"How did you become a shaman?"

"I spent a lot of time in the forest. I have a teacher now. To be a good shaman, you need to respect all nature and protect the ancestors' homeland, especially from forest fire. Also you need to protect the rivers and water. I think shamans have to study until they die."

I nod, knowing that I am continuing to learn, too.

"After doing a ritual ceremony, I have to study more and more. I had some kind of mind picture of what shamanism was before, but it is very different. When I was a kid, I saw my grandfather do ritual ceremonies. It looks so different from the outside. From the inside it is so…how can I express it? If people harm nature, only we shamans can feel it. So we have to pass this from one generation to the next. When I am 60, I should be teaching. It is a big responsibility for me. I am one kid, one person who knows…."

I show him some video clips of Nergui's and Ganzorig's ceremonies. He nods his head and says he is doing a ceremony tonight. "Tonight you can visit." I am hesitant to spend time with Khalzan—a little afraid of him—because I have heard that he once acted irrational and angry toward a tourist from Yale. We are exhausted, anyway, and will leave tomorrow, so we decide to go back to our settlement and sleep. I hear Khalzan is a powerful shaman. Maybe I will be braver another time.

Leaving the West Taiga

We came with eleven horses and three wranglers. Because of the cost—$11 per horse per day plus $11 per wrangler to lead each packhorse—we have sent the horses and wranglers back to Tsagaan Nuur. Otherwise we would have had to pay each day while they hung around waiting for us. Horses are too big and heavy anyway—they can't go where reindeer can, and they disturb the ancient moss. We will ride reindeer back.

We have met our goals: to assess the health of the herders and document it, to teach hygiene, and to provide what we can to improve health—all in an effort to help them sustain their culture. First aid and hygiene kits donated by our Nomadicare project have been distributed. The health database for the herders has been updated. Medicine has been supplied. Interviews with shamans are finished. We have presented monetary gifts to Gosta and Ganzorig from the Mongol-American Cultural Association in honor of shamanism. We have huddled in our tents during a snowstorm and seen purple rhododendron flowers covered with snow. Battulga has become a full member of our team, sleeping in Bayara's tent and helping with cooking. I have even flown over the antlers of Magsar's reindeer, not hurting myself, but cracking an antler so it bled.

It is June 14, and the needles are coming out on the tamarack trees. Gosta tells us that when the needles come out, it is time for the herders to migrate to their summer camp. We will leave on the reindeer today so they can be back tomorrow to carry the herders and their belongings on their spring migration.

Gosta is supplying reindeer from his herd for our two-hour ride. We negotiate a price. "Round it off, I want to buy another horse," he says. We pay $100. Battulga has radioed a message to Tsagaan Nuur to ask the driver to meet us a day earlier than we had planned. Now the community is gathered to help pack the reindeer and say farewell. It is a lighthearted gathering, but I am sitting on a log, feeling a bit sad about leaving, when Ganzorig trips over a twig and falls. Everyone breaks into laughter. Taiga people are extremely surefooted, even though the ground here is very uneven. That is, they are surefooted except when they are drunk. We've already had some drama, caused by a visitor sharing three bottles of vodka with three herders the day after we arrived. In fact, those three men have been lying pretty low ever since. There were fights, arguing, and stumbling galore among the three who shared the bottles. Now people keep replaying Ganzorig's sober fall over a twig, the rest responding with giggles or loud laughter, as if they are a television audience with a prompter. The fun is contagious. I am treasuring this moment. Yet I am also conscious of the deep rending that will take place when I leave these people who are so dear to me.

We four get on reindeer. Three reindeer are packed with our camping and camera supplies; when we came we had three horses, who can carry a lot more. We have left vitamins, hygiene kits, and food behind. Ganzorig's 28-year-old daughter, BG, is guiding us and will lead the reindeer back to the taiga. As I sit in my saddle, I notice that clumps of winter fur are falling off the reindeer. I reach forward and take some for a souvenir. It is about an inch long and smells like a clean, wet dog. A light rain begins. I was true to my decision last year to buy them, so Bayara, Khongoroo, and I are wearing Russian army raincoats. The thick, light-green rubber coat, with elastic at the cuffs, drawstrings for the hood, and a length that nearly covers our boots as we ride, is perfect for Siberian and taiga weather—that's what they are made for. We bought them for $15 each at the zakh in Ulaanbaatar. BG and Battulga are wearing silk deels but never complain, although they are getting wet. Through boggy meadows we file, into the wet larch forest. It is a gentle ride with softly falling rain. We slosh through groundwater, around rocks and trees, up mountains, and down the other side until we come to a steep, rutted downhill slope. Battulga and BG dismount. The ground is too slippery and steep for the reindeer, they explain. We need to walk. Our guides take off holding four reins each, reindeer fanning out behind them. Bayara walks with them.

I am wearing -100° F Canadian leather boots lined with sheepskin, great for cold weather. The pronounced heel makes them perfect for riding, but they are not so perfect for walking down a slippery, 45° incline with roots, mud, and rocks. I am a bit challenged because ever since I broke my foot, I have a little trouble on uneven ground. Now I am nearly falling face-first from the boot heels throwing my weight forward. Of course, Khongoroo, my fabulous assistant, is nearby. "Come on, young lady," she says as she grabs my elbow. We walk slowly until the others are out of sight, and then we can't even hear them. We are alone in the cold, wet wilderness, home of numerous bears and wolves. We come to a fork and have no idea which way the others went. Now's the time to use what my son taught me about tracking. We shuffle over to one fork, examine the tracks, and hobble over to the other. Both have wet, muddy tracks.

Oh, great. Now we are two soggy, chilly women looking down a steep hill either way. The rain is noisy on our sturdy raincoats and the hoods nearly cover our faces. We are easy prey for anything. We choose the left fork, just to choose one, and because maybe the tracks are newer or denser. We get partway down the hill where the track turns a corner, and there is a reindeer munching on lichen. Not just any reindeer. A saddled reindeer looking suspiciously like the one Khongoroo has been recently riding.

"What is my reindeer doing here?" asks Khongoroo, as she gathers the reins. I guess that BG and Battulga weren't paying attention and the reins slipped out of their hands. Slowly we pick our steps, moving steadily downhill, Khongoroo holding the reindeer reins with one hand and my elbow with the other. Then we hear someone singing, and it is getting louder. BG appears around the corner, riding toward us. She is missing a reindeer and has come to find it. We walk with her. When we meet up with Battulga, Bayara, and the other reindeer on some flat land, we re-mount and ride the rest of the way to the place where the jeep will meet us. But there's no jeep.

We unload the reindeer and stack our gear under a tarp while we wait. Half an hour goes by. It is pouring rain now. The world smells like wet leaves and grass mixed with sage. My wicking microfiber ski gloves are saturated, but still warm. I have retracted my hands into my raincoat sleeves. I feel like a cozy caterpillar inside a cocoon. I peek out and realize I am hanging out here with eight tiny reindeer, and immediately the poem "'Twas the Night before Christmas" comes out of my mouth. It is a poem my parents read every year on Christmas Eve, and I read it to my children. How could I resist saying it now? "I don't understand a word you are saying," says Khongoroo. It doesn't matter at all. Who ever gets a chance like this with eight tiny reindeer? The rain doesn't stop and the jeep doesn't come.

"Can we ride the reindeer farther?" I ask. We did this last year with horses when our car was missing.

"No, reindeer are good only in the taiga, not on the steppes." Battulga lights a fire and says he will walk to find us a car. We have given BG some red, white, and blue plastic tarp material to wrap around herself. She has taken the deels used to pad the reindeer off the animals and put them on to fight the cold. She ties the plastic on like a shawl with a big knot and looks like the little match girl—only drenched.

An hour goes by. BG decides it is too long to wait, even though the driver was supposed to deliver something to her. She returns the plastic to us, puts the deel back on the reindeer, ties all the reindeer in a line, climbs onto the first one, and takes off through the brush to go back to the taiga. I have layers of clothes under the raincoat: long underwear, nylon pants, fleece jacket, and wool deel. I huddle inside it all, lie down on the tarp covering the gear, and fall asleep. When I wake up, Khongoroo is sleeping on another pile of gear and Bayara is faithfully feeding the fire. I get up and collect some dead brush, walk around a little. Khongoroo gets out the hot plate, heats water, and serves us ramen. It tastes warm and filling. Three hours have gone by.

"Should we set up the tent?" Khongoroo asks.

"Let's wait two more hours, until 5:00," I say.

"Sure, sure."

It is barely above freezing. I am blessing the Russian raincoats and the wicking gloves Munkhjin gave me. No one is talking. We have been together for weeks—in the Gobi, on the train, in jeeps and ferries, on reindeer and horses. We just are. Words are extraneous. Our focus is on the fire. Collect twigs and feed the fire. Our world is distilled to this.

It is five minutes before 5:00 when I feel the ground vibrating. Maybe I am imagining it. Then it gets stronger and I realize I can also hear it. I know it's a car coming for us. We become alert and begin to move the gear up the bank to the dirt track. Battulga jumps out of a Russian jeep. It isn't the one we hired; it is the first car he could find. He walked 18 kilometers (11 miles) in this rain. We will certainly buy him a raincoat at zakh next year. I am thinking that that Russian army raincoat might be the best $15 I ever spent. The driver opens the hood and begins some mechanical work. Battulga had told him to wait and fix it after he picked us up. We listen to Battulga's story and the driver tinkering with the engine as we sit inside the jeep with a roof over our heads and no rain falling on us. When the engine is fixed we move along—running on gas, not legs, riding to Tsagaan Nuur.

Battulga's Shaman Ceremony

When we get to Tsagaan Nuur, Khongoroo overhears Battulga telling his friends that we will provide him with a ceremony. He finds out that Shaman Munkhuu is away, but assures us that there are other shamans with the same ongods. We are on our way to the East Taiga and have just crossed on the Shishgid River ferry when we make a turn off the usual road. Now we are on the worst road I have been on during my nearly 15 years of traveling in Mongolia. We have to get out of the jeep so it can make it up a 45° hill. I can barely even walk up the hill under my own steam, it is so steep. When we get back into the car, we jerk to avoid sharp boulders at the top of the hill before we come to a dirt track down the other side. Now we can see the river again, and small log cabin homes spread out along the flood plain.

We stop at various houses to ask for Omban. Finally, we get a positive response. "Yes, this is his house," says his wife, "but he is out visiting his friend, back that way." She motions with her chin. We drive there and see men sitting in a circle on the ground, smoking and having a conversation. Battulga walks up to a man wearing a brown deel, a thick, tooled leather belt with a silver buckle, and a wrestler's hat of red silk and black velvet with a gold spire. The two men leave the circle and sit on the ground out of hearing distance. Omban means "elder," although he looks middle-aged to me. After about five minutes, Omban stands up, walks to the car with Battulga, and says, "This is a good day for a ceremony."

Back in the jeep, we return with him to his home, where he and his wife begin to prepare for a ceremony. Since we are on our way to the taiga, everything is packed. We have to dig into our bags for offerings of candies and cookies and the ceremonial vodka that the shaman will drink during the ceremony. Omban gives us permission to set up our video cameras, so we dig through the luggage to get to the Pelican case, which holds the cameras.

The interior of Omban's one-room log house reminds me of the inside of a ger. As I step inside the door, the altar is straight ahead of me, on the wall beyond the stove, which is in the center. The articles men need for herding are on the right as I face the door from the inside. The left side of the house is the kitchen area with pots and pans, dishes, and food. There is a single metal frame bed on each side of the room. I set up my camera between the altar and the herding equipment and Bayara sets his up near the door. Omban's wife lights a juniper branch and smudges Omban, his costume, the altar, and the drum. The room becomes close and smoky; with each breath I inhale the scent of Mongolian juniper incense. When everything is ready, Omban's wife helps him out of his everyday deel and hat and into his costume and headdress. Then he lifts his drum and begins to beat. He motions to our guide to sit on the floor and beats the drum right over Battulga's head. ("It feels good," Battulga tells us later.) Omban chants and invites the ancestor spirits to visit and give messages. The chanting and drumming put the shaman into a trance. The juniper incense puts us all into a slightly altered state. Battulga sits humbly on his heels on the floor. Even though he is wearing a baseball cap, he has a peaceful, reverent look on his face. Omban takes a sip of vodka from the silver bowl his wife hands him and passes it to Battulga, who places it on a trunk without drinking from it. Omban's wife sits on a bed with a wooden bucket at her feet. She places a long, flat wooden paddle with nine indentations on it into the bucket, gathering milk in the indented spaces. She blesses the ceremony by casting milk into the air in six directions, which include the earth and the sky. Then she hands Omban his mouth harp. He bows to the ancestors at the altar and sits on the wooden floor to play the mouth harp. He jumps up to dance, chant, and drum, varying the intensity. After an hour, the sound and movement decrease. Omban is back from his trance. His wife takes his hat off and puts his wrestler hat on him. She helps him take his costume off and puts his deel back on. He gestures to his wife and she rolls a red string and plies it to make it thicker. Omban now plays his mouth harp and prays over the red string, chanting:

This man came over here to visit you.
He came over passes and walked seven times.
He brought full offerings with livestock products,
A person who was born in the year of the dragon.

Sky King, please better this person's fortune.
His entire body should be healthy.
Blessings to him and send good fortune into his body.
Don't allow bad things, evil, disasters.

Virtuous mother, old mother, Sky King,
Lighters with one light,
Mirror gold, silk khadagh scarf, Shug, shug.

I have instructed…
Sky King, you who knows everything,
With your power of being Sky King,
A child will live in one hometown with health and wealth.
He will live easily without worries, stress, flood.

The nice fresh juniper will know
This person is the same as your father.
Better take care of him. Shug, shug.

Change his life to prosperity,
King Skies, Mother. Shug, shug.

As you have said that,
I have tied a red thread on his wrist.
For three years, look after your child who was born in the year of the dragon.
He can whisper his wishes three times to the string.

Virtuous beautiful mother, your body cannot be seen,
But you will not forget to look after him.
You have blessed the blood colored string. Shug, shug.

As he finishes, Omban ties the string on Battulga's wrist. "Okay, it is too long. Are there any scissors?" he asks his wife. Omban cuts the extra string and blesses it again with music from the mouth harp. Three times Battulga puts his forehead to the snake-like manjin, attached to the mouth harp.

The two men sit on the floor, smoke a cigarette, and talk.

"If you think of drinking, just look at the red string to remember. If you have a dream of something that you want to happen, just whisper it to the red string. Don't drink anything at all for seven days."

Battulga nods.

When we leave Omban's, we are too late to ride horses all the way to the taiga, so after a couple of hours, our horse guide stops and we set up camp. The next day we ride three hours and arrive at the East Taiga settlement where scholarship student Solongo's sister's wedding is taking place. Battulga tells us we are not going into the settlement until tomorrow, but setting up our tents right here in the horse field.

"Here?" I ask. "Why?"

"Drama," Battulga answers. Vodka is present at all celebrations in Mongolia. We will stay here to avoid the alcohol-induced drama certain to be a result of the wedding of Tuvshin and Taivan. Since we already witnessed "drama" in the West Taiga, and to prevent pressure for him to drink, Battulga helps us dismount here. We will visit the herders tomorrow when things settle down. Seeing the herders is always my reward for the rough ride, like seeing a baby at the end of labor, so I am not too happy. You mean we won't even see the herders today? And I rode all the way up here? I grumble to myself as I put the tent stakes into the ground. Battulga and Bayara are setting up their tent and Khongoroo and I are setting up ours. There is no flat ground, and there is horse dung at all stages of decomposition everywhere. Plus the stake keeps hitting a rock. I am hungry and still shaky from the ride. Why am I doing this again? My riding pants are uncomfortable, and I want to get my boots off as soon as I can go inside the tent to change. Plus, where's the water? Our filter isn't working because the water in the west clogged it. Mostly I am grumpy about not seeing the herders.

Just as I am sinking lower into my bad attitude, a reindeer herder named Mungunshagai comes running from the direction of the settlement with a rifle over his shoulder. I am still trying to pound that stake. Without slowing his pace, he shouts, "Hi, Sas!" and keeps running. It takes me a moment to realize that he not only knows my name but also said hello in English. Right away everything is all right. I remember why I am here. The horseback ride, like labor, is becoming a faint memory. The tent is set up. I change into my Merrell Jungle Mocs and hiking pants.

Soon Mungunshagai returns, heading back toward the settlement.

"Thought I saw an animal to hunt, maybe a wolf," he says, stopping this time. "I was wrong."

Drum Sound

Two days later, after interviewing the Dukhas about their health care, visiting the newly married family with presents, and eating on that special ground—never completely rid of horse manure—it is that time of night when even the horses are quiet. There is only the occasional yip of a dog or wolf. Bayara and Battulga's tent is quiet. Khongoroo is breathing evenly. I can't sleep; my eyes are open, staring into the darkness.

Then I think I hear a sound. Muffled. Boom, boom. Boom, boom. I lift my head. It's quiet. Then boom, boom. Boom, boom. Maybe the shaman Saintsetseg is doing a ceremony? It must be. Or maybe there's a new shaman? The drum continues. After the sound stops for a long time, I fall into a deep sleep.

The next morning J. Bat is visiting us in the horse pasture. "Did Saintsetseg do a ceremony last night?" I ask.

"No."

"Maybe there is a new shaman?"

"No."

"I heard drumming last night."

"Was it in your dreams?"

"No, I was awake."

"Must be the ancestors welcoming you," says J. Bat. "That happens sometimes."

That night Sainstsetseg, a shaman newly graduated from the mouth harp to the drum, performs a ceremony. At the end, she looks at me and says, "Do you have any questions?"

"Yes," I say. That mysterious drumming has me confused. "Should I get a shaman costume?"

Saintsetseg sits quietly, checks with the ancestors who are still around. Then she answers in Tyvan, her brother J. Bat translates into Mongolian, and Khongoroo translates into English.

"Yes, but if it has black on it, cut it off. It will absorb negativity."

"What about a drum?"

"A drum is no problem."

"Hey, Battulga," I say the next morning as we sit on the ground eating instant oatmeal, "Saintsetseg says I should get that costume and drum."

"Oh, that? I threw away the phone number before we left Ulaanbaatar."

"Oh, okay," I say, practicing the Buddhist tenet of non-attachment. This, of all things, is not to be forced.

Baby Reindeer

While here at the settlement, we check on the students and discover that they were able to use the study guides and the funds for transportation to take the entrance exams. They have been accepted at universities this fall. There will be nine students, including two who just graduated from eighth grade (the final year before university). The government is giving scholarships to the new students. Saran, who is studying to be a veterinarian, got a government scholarship two years ago, so she will continue. Batjargal, supported by our angel donor, has finished two years in Materials Science at the Agriculture University. Solongo did not finish this year because she lost interest in the music school and let her grades fall, and we cut her funding. She plans to start at the Teacher's College this year, but we will not support her because she used some of the tuition money for other things and ran out before the second semester.

As I could see last year, a scholarship to study at a university in Ulaanbaatar is one of the most important gifts someone could give a reindeer herding family. So while we are here at the East Taiga encampment where Batjargal and Solongo live, their parents honor me. They show up first to greet us and are first in line for health checks for the database. Then together the families invite Khongoroo, Bayara, and me to Solongo's family's urts for dinner. As we walk there, Khongoroo tells me that they have a present for me, but it is a secret. I feel a little sheepish, knowing that we gave Solongo tough love by cutting her scholarship. When we get there, I apologize to her mother, saying, "I am sorry it worked out that way."

"Oh, no," interjects her mother, Munkhuu. "It is completely my fault. I told her if she loaned us the money so her sister could study English, we would find some for the second semester. My mistake. I couldn't come up with the money. I am only grateful that you gave my daughter a chance to live in the city, to experience a life different from ours here, and to get some education. It was a big gift."

The dinner is one of my favorite taiga meals—rice and reindeer milk—very creamy and delicious. I appreciate that I can digest reindeer milk, even though I cannot digest other kinds of milk. After dinner we talk, but there is a lot of whispering in Mongolian that is not translated. Then we leave the urts. No present. We walk through the area where the reindeer are tethered. We walk right up to a baby reindeer. "This is your present," announces Solongo, pointing to a soft baby. "His name is Sas, born on April 20. Just two months old." I get down on my knees to hug the gentle being. So soft and smooth. It is a moment I will never forget—kneeling down to meet my reindeer. What an honor! Solongo's mother, Munkhuu, will care for Sas, and I will see him every time I visit. Having a reindeer named after you is a legacy in the taiga, one that lasts the whole life of the reindeer—18 to 20 years. Maybe some year I will even ride him. We'll see.

Shaman Nergui

After sleeping one night in a ger at Khogorog, where we return the horses, Shaman Nergui is supposed to meet us and do a ceremony outside at a sacred power place nearby.

We made this plan when we were in Tsagaan Nuur. We showed Nergui clips of the ceremony we videotaped last year—the one he did with his apprentice, Oyunerdene. When Nergui saw the ceremony on video, he realized that the ongods had given him a message to meet again at a certain time of day to finish the ceremony. Nergui said we needed to do this and he needed money to prepare. As luck would have it, we had funds to honor those practicing the shaman tradition. When I presented the gift to Nergui, Battulga stipulated that this would be all he would get. My mistake was to give him the money before we left for the taiga.

The Russian jeep comes a few hours late and drives us to a "beautiful place" where the ceremony will be held. A "beautiful place" is a power spot, where a shamanic session is charged with more energy and success. The driver says he is late because Nergui has already started drinking and didn't have his ceremonial accoutrements ready. Vodka is what he has bought with the money. When we arrive, blue and white khadaghs, along with yellow and green ribbons, flutter from a grove of larch trees with needles the yellow-green of springtime. Beside the grove at the edge of the far-reaching steppes, Nergui and some male relatives are sitting on the ground in a circle. He pensively smokes, taking long pauses between inhales. Two women are tending a fire. The khengereg is warming by the flames. Bottles of vodka stand open beside the sacred paraphernalia.

Nergui says it is fine to videotape the entire ceremony. Bayara sets up one camera on the east and I set up another to the southwest. After a while, Nergui is ceremonially dressed in his shaman clothes and headdress and handed his drum. He begins chanting an invitation to the ongods. His wife gives milk offerings to the six directions. Some of his ongods are upbeat. At a certain point, we are asked to hang new ribbons from the trees.

An ongod takes over Nergui's body for a time, making him drum, chant, and move faster or more slowly. Then another ongod takes over and Nergui's actions change. Suddenly, one ongod gives him such a jolt that his drum flies out of his hands, he flies into the air with his arms straight out from his sides, and his relatives catch him before he lands on his back. His wife picks the drum up and coerces him to bend his arms and opens his hands so he can hold the drum again, and he continues.

Nergui sits, hands the drum off, takes his aman khuur out of its wooden horse case, and calls other spirits with it. There are three instructions for me. I need to gather three stones from a brook we drive through. I need to give a present to a herder on a horse. And Nergui and I have to tie a blue khadagh beside a river. After the messages, Nergui stands and drums some more, obviously taking on new ongods, then motions Battulga to kneel on the ground, take his hat off, and lower his head. Nergui "beats" him with manjin—cloth, snake-shaped, padded whips. Nergui calls his assistants and does the same to them. Then the frenzy of the drum and the dance decrease and the costume is changed.

We sit together, eat hard candy, and drink tea.

Now the question is, how are we going to get all these people back to Tsagaan Nuur when we have only one Russian jeep? Do I want to pay for two trips or can we all squeeze in?

This is Mongolia; we can all squeeze in. Khongoroo shares the front bucket seat with me. Mongolians have a way to do this: one sits all the way back and one sits forward on the edge of the seat. As we cross the first brook, we stop. "Don't forget those three stones, Sas," says Khongoroo. I walk to the bed of the brook and return with the stones, which everyone has to hold and study. Nergui is sitting in the middle of the back seat, perched on the front. His face is close to mine and I can smell the vodka on his breath. He begins singing bawdy songs. A teenaged boy is riding his horse by the side of the road, watching his sheep, and we stop. Nergui steps out and rolls his arm in a circle, signaling for the boy to come. Without a word, I present the herder with a bag of candies and cookies.

When we get to the Shishgid River, the one I swam across on a much warmer day, we have to wait for the ferry. Nergui motions to me that we need to tie a khadagh on the cable. He does an incantation for both of us that our work will be successful, and in a joint moment of peace, we tie it. It just so happens that our wranglers, who have been riding from Khogorog while we have been at the ceremony, are ahead of us, so we have to wait for them to cross and for the ferry to come back for us. I don't notice that when they load up, Battulga joins them and gallops off toward Tsagaan Nuur on a horse.

Nergui walks his friends down a little rise, where they sit in a circle and finish another bottle of vodka before the ferry returns. Now Bayara, Khongoroo, and I are crowded into the Russian jeep with three very drunk men—without Battulga. When we get to Tsagaan Nuur, Nergui and the other men determinedly stagger into our bedroom at the guesthouse. Nergui sits on the floor beside my bed and asks for more money. I say no and he says he won't leave until I give it to him. He says I have to give him the videotape if I won't give him money. This goes on for half an hour, with increasing anger. I am feeling jittery and scared.

Khongoroo somehow moves them into the dining room and answers all of their frantic requests in a calm voice. Bayara leaves. Finally, Battulga arrives and talks with Nergui, reminding him that we have already given him money. "Give him a tape, Sas. Even a blank tape is fine. Just give him one. His young nephew told him Americans are rich, and convinced him to ask for more." I label a tape and hand it over and he finally leaves. When he comes back the next day, more sober, and asks us to show his wife the clips from last year, we give him a real copy of the outside ceremony he performed yesterday.

This seemed to be the year of male shamans arguing, creating drama, and giving me butterflies in my stomach, yet I respect and am grateful to them for opening to the energy of the ongods and sharing their ceremonies with us.

Drum

A few days later, when we are in Murun to catch a plane back to Ulaanbaatar, Battulga says, "Hey, Sas, I found a drum from Tsagaan Nuur, a khengereg."

"I can't buy it," I say right away. I don't have much money left. I shouldn't buy a drum.

"Well, I'm going to check it out," says Battulga. "Maybe it's not the real thing."

When he leaves, I lie on my bed in the guesthouse and keep repeating to myself, "I will not buy the drum. I will not buy the drum. I will not buy the drum." I feel drawn to it. Maybe it is a leading to get it. I feel my heart beating. I feel excited. I feel desire—this would not be a good quality if I were Buddhist. Yet I feel drawn toward touching a drum, holding it, taking it with me, learning from it as a way to understand the mysteries, embrace them, get inside them as much as possible. I want to know the ways others connect with the spirit.

Khongoroo's cell rings. She translates. "Battulga says the drum is perfect. Three-year-old female deerskin with a wild sheep tail for the beater. The real thing. You aren't buying it, right?"

"Right," I gulp. Having researched shaman equipment over these years, I know everything is right about this drum—the three-year-old female deerskin it is made from, the wild sheep tail beater. Battulga knows it, too.

I use my cheap phone card to call my friend Eleanor in Vermont, who has studied shamanism and is a mentor to me. We have seen three shaman ceremonies on this trip and I want to describe them to her. When I finish telling her about the ceremonies, I say, "Oh, and there's a shaman's drum I could buy, but I'm not getting it."

"Don't feel guilty if you don't get it, but feel guilty if you don't get it." I know she is purposely giving me a riddle. *Okay*, I think, *I will look at it*. Khongoroo calls Battulga's friend, and he appears with the drum in an orange reinforced plastic bag.

"Hit it," he says when he unties the bag. I pick up the drum with shaking hands. It has a raw, earthy smell. I tap—boom, boom. Boom, boom. It vibrates into my heart.

"No," he says, "I mean smack it."

Thunder. The deep, resonant sound shakes my heart, my soul, the room, waking the very walls—and the drum. I know it is mine.

I put the drum back into its bag and place it carefully on an empty bed. We go to bed early because we have a morning flight to Ulaanbaatar. I lie on my side, then roll over, trying to sleep, but I can't. The drum is still vibrating. Even though I do spiritual work, I am also very practical. I have never given an inanimate object live characteristics. But the drum is putting out a powerful energy. I get up and move it onto the windowsill, away from me. Still I can't sleep. At 1:00 in the morning, when it is 1:00 in the afternoon in Vermont, I call Eleanor.

"I bought it."

"Oh, yes?"

"But we can't sleep."

"Oh, no. Did you feed it? It needs tobacco. Any sage there? Talk to it."

Doing a ritual for a drum is new to me, but so is a shaman's drum. Bayara donates tobacco from a cigarette. Khongoroo donates incense that Saintsetseg gave her. We light the incense and circle it around the drum three times. I say, "Please go back to sleep. Please be calm so I can take you to Vermont."

We sleep, but this is only the beginning of the drum making its presence known.

A Bad Day in Mongolia

A reindeer, a khengereg, friends, health care, shaman ceremonies! I am feeling grateful for dear friends, honors, and gifts. Buddhists talk about impermanence, which makes it important to notice these blessings when they happen. Buddhists also use the word "suffering" for the state of human life. Tummurbaatar, a Buddhist lama and yogi friend I met in 1995, once showed me a book in English that translated "suffering" into "annoyances or frustrations." As a westerner, I find the word "suffering" difficult to comprehend, but I am very familiar with the others.

Khongoroo, Bayara, and I are going to fly to Ulaanbaatar on the last leg of our journey. In the morning we cram our luggage into a small car—the only taxi available at this early hour—and drive to the airport. The Murun Airport gates are closed and we have to transport the luggage piece by piece across the empty parking lot, to the entryway, up the steps, and into the airport. We are the first ones to arrive, and check our luggage as soon as the Mongolian Airlines (MIAT) people arrive. With all our camping and filming equipment, we have to pay $100 overweight. The drum doesn't have a case, so we can't check it, and it is too big to carry on. Fortunately, Battulga will stay in Murun a little longer. He says he can keep the drum with him, have a case made, and bring it to Ulaanbaatar when he comes in a week or two. I am disappointed that we can't take the drum, but it is okay because Battulga will take care of it.

Khongoroo tells me the plane isn't here and no one knows when it will come. It still has to fly from the capital. It is already 8:30 AM and the plane hasn't left Ulaanbaatar. The flight was scheduled to leave here 10:00 AM. I project a definite attitude toward Khongoroo for not telling me this before putting all our stuff on the other side of the window in off-limits airport-land. I want to get back to Ulaanbaatar. I'm tired of the countryside and could use a shower and some veggies—tired of noodles, with or without mutton, being the main choices. Bayara leaves our Sony PD 150 video camera sitting naked on a windowsill in the airport. I wonder why it is not in its case or in his hand—it could so easily be stolen. I give Khongoroo the silent treatment, with scowls and faces, but she is in her usual balanced calm, listening to her iPod. ("I know you," she says later.) I make a list of what I hate about Mongolia:

- Waiting
- Not honoring the individual person
- Not informed when changes occur
- A locked gate at the airport so you can't drive in with your stuff so you have to lug it a long distance
- No space respect, using cell phones all the time and anywhere
- Speak Mongolian, a code I can't crack
- Television blaring
- Boarding house changes prices after we have an agreement. (Paid for two empty beds last night because we didn't want

anyone else in our room, but do they give us the three-bed room? No.)
- The food sucks and I am tired of eating sweet stuff to feel good.
- Six weeks is good. Two months is too long.
- I am ready to go home—my mother fell again and is having a hard time.
- No one says "bless you" when you sneeze.

I feel better after I show Khongoroo the list and she smiles. Then I sneeze and she says, "Bless you." It is hard to have an attitude with her around.

The Mongolians drift away from the airport. "Flight at 1:00," says the flashing red digital sign. No flight. "Flight at 4:00." Flight cancelled. It's 7:00 PM and the flight is scheduled for 8:00. Then it's 8:00 and no one except two Mongolians and the three of us are left in the airport. One of the two Mongolians says to an agent, "Look, there's a foreigner here. She needs to be taken care of."

The MIAT agent speaks to Khongoroo and takes us in his van back to the Murun Hotel to treat us to dinner. The hotel is next door to the guesthouse we checked out of this morning. While driving, he checks his cell phone every few minutes to see if we are flying tonight or not and talks to his wife, who sits beside him.

"What happened?" I ask. "We confirmed the flight yesterday."

"The plane for this flight has reached its kilometer limit for the month and can't fly any more."

"Didn't they know that yesterday when we confirmed the flight?" I am polite now. At least there is someone listening.

"Right," he says. "You'd think so. This is Mongolia, after all." This puts an end to any confusion.

We go back to the guesthouse. He will pay for our night here. Our toothbrushes and toiletries are all in airport-land. We expected we would be in Ulaanbaatar at 11:00 this morning, so everything is checked.

"I will call you when I find out about the plane," he says.

"What about all the other people?" I ask.

"I will pick them up," he says.

It is past midnight and we three are stretched out on our beds, waiting for a call on Khongoroo's cell phone, when we hear a shout from below our balcony.

"Okay, we're going," says Khongoroo, translating the shouted message. We climb back into the MIAT rep's van. His wife is still in the front. We turn toward the airport. Then we detour though alleys and fences. He gets out of the van, pounds on khashaa and house doors, and wakes passengers staying with relatives. The passengers squeeze into his van with us. At the airport, the waiting room is magically filling. Security is quick. The plane is here. As we take our seats, I sneeze. "Bless you," says Khongoroo, and we both laugh.

Ulaanbaatar: Four Days in July

We are back from the taiga in time for election week in Ulaanbaatar—the fifth election since the Soviets left. My cell phone rings to the tune "I Don't Have a Wooden Heart." I always know it's my phone because I am constantly asking myself, "Why am I here again?" And then the answer comes from my cell phone, "I don't have a wooden heart." I care. Sitting with my Mongolian language teacher in a cold, sparsely furnished classroom with a desk between us, I practice the words *tom mundur* (huge hailstones) so that I can talk about my experience in the taiga. Two weeks ago we were camping out when hail the size of large marbles pelted our tent. On the phone, Munkhjin says, "Sorry to bother you, Sas, but be careful if you come into the center of the city today. There may be a riot. The Democrats are angry—they believe that the Mongolian People's Republic Party (MPRP, the former Communist party) is not the legal winner. It might get dangerous." Munkhjin works for the Ministry of Culture and Education, right in the center of Ulaanbaatar, so she knows what is going on.

I think back over the modern history of Mongolia. I have never heard of a riot here. Mongolia was a socialist country closely aligned with the Soviet Union from 1920 to 1990. During that time, the Soviets built hospitals and schools in the rural areas and Soviet block apartment buildings in Ulaanbaatar, and collectivized nomads. They killed thousands of Buddhists monks and destroyed their monasteries. At the same time, they punished shamans by destroying their costumes and drums. Close to the time the Berlin Wall collapsed, there were peaceful demonstrations in Sukhbaatar Square, the central square of Ulaanbaatar. The Soviets left abruptly. The country became a parliamentary democracy and held its first election in 1992.

I pause before returning to my lesson. Two days ago I went with Munkhjin when she voted. The election seemed organized and calm, as all four previous elections have been. As I watched, voters took passes and identification cards to the polling place, where guards checked them at the door and marked the cuticle of the voters' left index fingers with black ink on the way out.

On Monday's news, a report said that 74 percent of the population had voted. The news also said that in our district, Bayanzurkh, someone broke into the ballot boxes and ripped all the ballots up. I saw pictures of the vandalism on television. Now there are accusations of people destroying ballots and the MPRP not being the legal winners. I would feel self-righteous about corruption here if I could forget the two recent U.S. presidential elections.

In the classroom, I close the phone, decide not to go into the city, and go on with my lesson. When I get home to Munkhjin's family's apartment, which is not in the center, the television is blaring the news. In Sukhbaatar Square, dissenters are throwing rocks at the MPRP building. The MPRP has been in power since 1921, except for four years, 1996 to 2000, when the Democrats led. The MPRP was not only the most powerful party, but also the only party allowed until 1990. In keeping with its status, the MPRP headquarters is no small building: it is a cornerstone of the square. Four stories high and made of stone, it is one of the most prominent buildings, along with the Parliament Building and the Central Palace of Culture. Watching the angry mob makes me nervous. I know people are capable of all kinds of violence. The head of the government is sitting at his desk inside the building, calmly reassuring the citizens, but when the camera switches to outside, there are sounds of angry voices and breaking glass. The crowd is throwing rocks at the building, smashing windows. Police in riot gear huddle together in a corner of the square. Basically, as I see it, no one is doing anything about the situation. I feel a little relieved when I remember that Mongolian city dwellers do not have guns.

Tonight I have plans for dinner with a friend named Wayne, a redhead from the western U.S., whom I met in the taiga. We will meet a few blocks away from Sukhbaatar Square. I stand on the side of the road near Munkhjin's house and stick my index and middle fingers out sideways to get a taxi. When one stops, I direct him to the restaurant. The closer I get to the center of the city, the more police in military garb are guarding the street corners. I feel hyper-alert, but the restaurant is not right in the center, so I breathe to relax. Soon Wayne appears and tells me there were no taxis from his hotel, so he walked from the center, where the MPRP building is now on fire. We have dinner outside at a Mexican restaurant; the owner and head chef comes out to visit with us. We discuss the Mongolian countryside, even as we hear sirens in the distance. After our food and conversation, Wayne suggests that we go to Le Bistro Français for a glass of wine. As we sit on the porch and order, a car with a megaphone goes by announcing something. In a moment, the waiter is closing the panels on the porch.

"What?" we ask. He sticks out his pointer finger, making a gun. I call Munkhjin. "Is there a curfew?" I ask.

"No," she says, "I haven't heard of it, but you should come home. It is not safe out there." We leave without drinks, Wayne flags down a taxi for me, and I go straight home with no problems bigger than jitters in my belly.

The next morning things have changed, though. We hear that the fire not only burned the inside of the MPRP building, but also damaged the Central Palace of Culture, where the traditional orchestra keeps its instruments. Many artifacts have been damaged and vandalized. It is rumored that three people have died. A four-day state of emergency with a curfew is announced. Everyone must be home by 10:00 PM and no one can go out before 8:00 in the morning. There is a ban on selling alcohol. In the U.S., not selling alcohol would not necessarily amount to a ban, since many homes have liquor cabinets or beer in the fridge. In Mongolia, where the cultural rule says, "You buy a bottle, you drink it. You open a bottle, you finish it," homes do not have stores of alcohol.

Normally, vodka bottles, from the cheap stuff to expensive brands in gilded boxes, cover shelves on both sides of one aisle in the local grocery store. But today, when I stop at the store for bread and yogurt, I see the clerks placing the vodka bottles into milk crates. I watch as they put tape over the tops and carry them out back to the storeroom. Soon the shelves are vacant except for the top shelf, which holds empty vodka boxes.

As part of the state of emergency, all of the television stations are off the air—except the state station, Mongol TV. In the evening, the program is…what would you show if your country were in a state of emergency? Their choice is a sappy old romance movie showing gers, countryside Mongolians in deels, and nature, with plenty of traditional songs about Eej, or Mother. This is to remind everyone that, after all, they love their country and these MPRP people will make it the best for them, even if they didn't win…or did they? Munkhjin tells us that people have been killed. But there are no reports on this. In fact, there is no news at all.

It is evening—I am in bed. It's too quiet. As I lie here, trying to sleep, I remember a story Mats, a Swedish friend, once told me. When the dam in his hometown, Mockfjärd, was shut down and the townspeople couldn't hear any water flowing, no one could sleep. It's that kind of quiet tonight. I live on the third floor, above a karaoke bar, and I can't sleep without the usual sound of drunks singing off-key until 3:00 or 4:00 in the morning. I toss and turn, finally sleep, and wake up just before 8:00 AM to silence. Usually, at 6:30 AM a country person is yelling, "Suu avarai. Suu avarai." "Milk for sale. Milk for sale." Customers run from their apartments with containers to get fresh milk. At 8:04 a voice comes through my window: "Suu avarai." Then I hear a car, and then two, and gradually the normal sounds of traffic resume. For four days, there is no alcohol. It is very quiet everywhere. Bars, and even restaurants, are closed. The boisterous Ulaanbaatar nightlife has come to a stop.

On the fourth day of the curfew, the U.S. Embassy holds its annual Fourth of July party. I used to go to make connections for work in Mongolia. Today I want to feel some American culture and see my friend Khaliuna, who works at the embassy. There are hundreds of people under a red, white, and blue tent and food stations offering hot dogs, potato salad, soda, bottled water, and cake. How am I going to find Khaliuna? She was the translator for my movie *Gobi Women's Song* and is now the assistant to the head of the military at the U.S. Embassy. I look forward to seeing her. She is one of my Mongolian daughters, who share their ups and downs with me. When I get to the party, I don't see her, but there is an honor guard, with three U.S. military men holding the flags. I figure that they should know where she is. First I ask, "Are you allowed to talk?" They look so official and serious.

"Yes," they say.

"Have you seen Khaliuna?" I ask.

"No, but if we see her, we will tell her someone is looking for her."

I make connections with friends: Susanna, who goes to school in Montana, and Millie, who is from Ethiopia and the U.S. and who cooked for me even before she opened the famous Millie's Café, where all the expatriates eat. Then I hear, "Sas!" Khaliuna clicks toward me in her spike heels and tight little outfit. She has worn heels for so long she can't walk in flat shoes any more. In fact, I remember hiking with her the year I lived with her family—Khaliuna hiked in heels. There is a handsome American man with her. She draws me over and tells him I am the one who took her to the Gobi. She says that before we went to the Gobi, when she was 19, she had never been there and had never seen a birth. "It was amazing!"

Then she says, "I need a glass of wine."

"How can you get any, when there's a ban on alcohol?" I ask.

"Oh, the colonel, the head of the U.S. military here, has alcohol at his house. Right there." She points to a home in this upscale neighborhood. Of course there are liquor cabinets. They are Americans. When we arrive, Marines and Army soldiers, drinking in the yard, swarm around Khaliuna, beautiful young Mongolian that she is. She is happy to throw them a comment once in a while, but she wants to hear all about my trips to the taiga and the Gobi. "How are the Gobi women, anyway?" she asks. She wishes she could see them again. "And Altijin is seven? We saw her born! I just can't believe it."

"Did you have a hot dog?" the head U.S. military man in Mongolia asks me when she introduces us.

"She's a vegetarian," says Khaliuna.

"Well, come right this way," he says, and leads me to his modern, two-door metal refrigerator in his wood-paneled kitchen, complete with inlaid table and Oriental rugs. He opens some storage containers to give me authentic grated carrot salad with raisins and walnuts and the perfect dressing, coleslaw with pineapple, and a green salad with cilantro. My eyes light up, just looking at the food. Carrying a full plate, I walk past the dishwasher as we talk with the country Peace Corps director and U.S. soldiers. I am in culture shock, having just come from the taiga—where women's hands swirl dishes in a pan of cold water to wash them, where we sit on reindeer skins to eat, not at an inlaid kitchen table, where the kitchen is a line of pans behind a curtain in an urts, not a wood-paneled room, and where the food comes from animals, unlike gourmet American vegetarian food. When I put the first forkful into my mouth, though, it tastes just right.

The soldiers and Khaliuna are just as happy with the alcohol as I am with the food. After a few beers, a young Latino Marine dramatically declares a crush on Khaliuna and she begins a game of "come here, go away," declaring to me as we are leaving that she could never go out with him. She is in charge of all these men—it is not allowed. Just before we are out of voice range, though, he calls out, "Khaliuna, I didn't even know you knew who I was." While he goes off to dream land, we go home. It is the last night of the early curfew; tomorrow the state of emergency will end. City life will be back to normal—noisy, alcoholic karaoke, 56 television channels, and full grocery shelves. For tonight, I get a little quiet—and I relish it.

Grocery Shopping in Ulaanbaatar

In 1994, when I first came to Ulaanbaatar, there were no supermarkets. Dairy products and meat from the countryside were hawked on the street; bread, candy, and vodka were sold at kiosks. These were the choices. Over the years I have been coming here, I have witnessed enormous changes. Now there are supermarkets in the center of the city and small neighborhood stores in the districts. They carry processed and packaged food from many parts of the world.

This morning I wake up from my dreams in English into a Mongolian world. An intercom radio on the wall near the door (left from Communist times, I imagine) greets me as I step from my bedroom into the hall. A bit later, when I step out of my apartment door, lock both locks, and head down the stairs, I need to join the language. "*Sain baina uu?*" ("*Hello, how are you?*") I say in greeting as I pass an elderly woman in a deel. "*Sain baitsgaana uu,*" I say to a couple as I meet them on the sidewalk. I walk under the urine-smelling underpass, take a right, and climb the stairs to the neighborhood store. Today I want some cheese, eggs, yogurt, tomatoes, and black bread. There are lockers with an attendant ready to store my bags, but I am fine—I just have my empty shopping bag and change purse. I grab a blue plastic shopping basket from the pile and head to the produce department, which is a quarter of the size of the meat department. Mongolians love their meat. I think of a restaurant window I saw yesterday that said, "Meat for Mongols. Grass for animals." I am happy that our neighborhood grocery displays and sells vegetables and fruits. In Murun, in the countryside, we craved veggies on our way back from the taiga, but there were only a few wizened potatoes and five small onions in a large, but sparsely stocked "supermarket."

I put a seedless cucumber, carrots, scallions, tomatoes, and potatoes in my basket. I don't know how to ask someone ahead of time to come help, so the produce person comes running and takes everything out of the basket. He puts one item at a time into a thin plastic bag, whether I want bags or not, puts a bag on the scale, writes a price on a small tag, and puts it back into the basket. What I would love is to be able to make small talk with the man. I would love to tell him I don't want so many bags. They split; they barely make it home with me. Or maybe I could tell him I have been here for two months already. Or ask if he lives in the area—anything, really, to make a connection. But I just walk away with my flimsy bags and their protruding veggies. I carefully pile six eggs into another bag. There are no egg cartons. I place the bag of eggs on top of the veggies.

Meat is not sold in sterile packages as it is in a U.S. supermarket, where a customer might forget that it comes from an animal. There is a whole, skinned sheep in the freezer, wooly tail and all. I go past this section to find cheese. The white products, as Mongolians call dairy, fill two walls. I am looking for some aged cheese. Let's see, there is fresh Mongolian cheese in plastic wrap, and processed cheese in foil. I saw Edam cheese here last week. There is butter, fresh from the countryside, margarine, Russian butter packaged in foil, cream, and *aaruul*—dried cheese curds. There is bulk yogurt that you can scoop out into your own container, or Mongolian yogurt in a soft plastic container you can squeeze out into your mouth, and then there is Russian yogurt packaged in four small plastic containers attached with a foil top, with pictures of peach, strawberry, kiwi, and pear on the top. I get a package of the Russian kind; I can relate to the pictures. I can't find Edam cheese. I know *byaslag* is the word for cheese. I point to the cooler and ask the clerk, "Edam byaslag?" She picks up some processed cheese wedges in a cardboard box. "This?" Organic health food snob that I am, I can't suppress a smirk. I often take this stuff to the countryside. I like the kind with mushroom best, but today I want the real thing and I scour those cases. Where did it go? No luck. I want to explain it was here a week ago or ask if there will be a delivery soon. Instead, I pick up a little loaf of black bread that I know is delicious and go to the candy aisle. Candies, vodka, and beauty products are the traditional gifts for Mongolians. I don't buy vodka, even though I am probably considered rude and culturally inappropriate. To be completely truthful, I have to admit that I did buy it once for my teacher. He knows how long I have been coming and that I should know the traditions by now. He also likes his vodka. I don't know what other people think about me not giving the proper gift. I try to choose healthy presents, but candies—yes, I'll get some for presents or for guests, even though children here have bad teeth because adults are always giving them candy. There are Russian candies, Mongolian candies, Chinese candies, and Polish candies. A box of chocolates is proper for the lady of the house. I walk past the vodka aisle to the checkout. There is a line. Of the two registers, only one is working. My food comes to 6,150 tugrik, about $5, and I count out the money, slowing down the line because I still have to look at the bills. Then I walk down the steep, uneven steps. "Uneven steps" in Mongolia means that in the same staircase any given riser can be eight inches or four inches or twelve inches high. I wonder if this is to keep everyone totally present and in the moment. It is impossible to go down steps without paying attention. I safely make it to the sidewalk and take my food home.

    I know the store. I know the money. I know some of the words. I even generally know all the names of food products in Mongolian. Still, there is a certain bottled-up feeling that comes of not being able to shoot the breeze, make a joke, comment on some small thing. There is a frustration about living in Mongolia that is cumulative. I realize what a relief, a release it is to speak my own language. Even when a child recognizes me as a foreigner on my walk home and says "hello," it is like a momentary window of bright light in a gray world. A comment given and received is not a small event. A moment of language understood fills a need for belonging. When I think of being home in Vermont, I feel overwhelmed with gratitude that language there flows from me and into me. Knowing this feeling of isolation makes me think about how many people in the U.S. and around the world face this every day. I am determined to learn to speak Mongolian before I come back next year.

Eyebrows

Mongolian women are beautiful, even older ones my age. There is barely a gray hair among the women in Ulaanbaatar. Their faces are often a lovely moon shape and the city women wear makeup, eyebrow pencil, and lipstick—at least, this is what I think until I get to know the women and see that Munkhjin's mother gets ready for work in a jiffy. I know she has her secret ways, because she does not laboriously stand in front of the mirror preparing, yet she looks perfect. One day I ask Munkhjin how they look so great.

"Well, they dye their hair."

"What about makeup?"

"They get their eyebrows tattooed."

For a year after this conversation, when I am back in Vermont, each time I brush my teeth I check my eyebrows. I have gray hair and I wear no makeup. The last time I wore lipstick on a regular basis was when I was in high school. My eyebrows definitely are beginning to match my hair, turning white one strand at a time. I start to look at faces as canvases. Eyebrows, I notice, define the face shape the way walls define a building. Women in their sixties—that is, my friends—are beginning to lose the walls of their faces.

I have been to the Gobi and the taiga and will go home soon, but not until I do one more thing—Munkhjin and her cousin Sodoo promise to find me a beauty salon that tattoos eyebrows. We walk down Peace Avenue, the main street, but don't find any such salon. We go to the Third District, the shopping district, and find the upscale Ulaanbaatar Salon. The hairdressers nod when we ask if they offer tattoos here and point with their eyes and chin to the back of the beauty parlor. A glass booth with a sink, a shelf, and a chair is the tattoo area.

"There are two choices," explains a young woman whose straight black hair has obviously just been washed. "There's the solid eyebrow or the individual lines, where you can still have your own eyebrows. It looks more natural but costs more." Then she mentions that she only has black ink. Of course, that color works for everyone who has black hair, which is every Mongolian. I think of Quakers in the old days in their bonnets and gray clothes, of the Quaker tenet of simplicity. I think of how important it is to be natural and how I want to keep my own eyebrows. And how I want my face to remain defined into my older years.

"I'll take the individual lines," I say.

Munkhjin and Sodoo, who was once a beautician, are sitting just outside of the door where I can see them. I sit back in the chair as if I am at the dentist's office. First, the woman plucks hairs from my eyebrows and draws lines where she will add the tattoo. Then she gives me a mirror. Munkhjin and Sodoo come in and lean close to have a good look. We all agree it is fine. Then what feels like bee stings begins. I think this is just another lesson in torture and patience to add to horse rides, climbing hills, jeep rides, and waiting for planes.

Finally, the needle stops. Munkhjin and Sodoo nod their approval. I pay $45. Munkhjin goes to the pharmacy to get a tiny vial of some medicinal gel I need to put on twice a day.

The black color of my eyebrows is pronounced for a few days. The area is a little swollen and then it is back to normal—actually better than normal, since I now have a smooth eyebrow line. When I get home, no one notices. Even when I tell my daughter, Jasmine, a beauty queen, she looks closely and says she can't tell. When I tell my parents and lean toward them so they can see, my Mom says she can't tell. My Dad says, "God made you the way you are supposed to be. I don't approve of this." At my age, it is nice to have a Dad who cares. But personally, I am happy with the way my eyebrows look.

The Drum Comes Home

Battulga stays in the province center until he gets his foreign passport, as he has a standing invitation for an international reindeer herder conference, which he believes he can attend now that he is sober. Two weeks after we left him, he comes to the capitol bearing the shaman drum in a square pine box, heavy enough to be a coffin. I can't lift it. I can't keep it in my room in Ulaanbaatar because I learn that Buddhism and shamanism can't occupy the same room and there are Buddhist gods here. Battulga lugs it up the four flights of stairs to Khongoroo's apartment. We open the box. Whoosh! The drum energy pours out—strong, pulsating. We feed it tobacco and burn incense. We also order an instrument case lined in velvet with a handle—one I can carry to the U.S.

Battulga doesn't tell us right away, but he has had his own adventures with the drum. "That drum is strong, Sas. The older man I was staying with never slept for the 10 days it was at his place. Then I had a hard time finding a ride to Ulaanbaatar. I finally found one and put the box in the back of the van. The assistant driver was drunk and lifted the box. 'What's this?' he asked. 'Khengereg,' I answered. The drunken man dropped the box on the ground like a hot potato. I couldn't let someone insult the khengereg, so I kicked him as he was leaning over. My foot knocked out his two front teeth. So I carried the box with me to the police station to report what I had done. The police asked if the man was drunk. I nodded. 'Then no problem,' said the police, 'he deserved it.'"

Well, obviously, this is not Vermont and Battulga is not a pacifist. The drum is alive and sacred—and people interact with it. I will have to be respectful of it. Then I start thinking about what that episode would look like in Vermont and how much those teeth would cost, plus lawsuits. Here it is like being in the Wild West.

With the drum in Ulaanbaatar, we now need to think about getting it out of Mongolia and transporting it to Vermont, as I am leaving in a week. I have had "artifacts" confiscated at the airport, with fines, before. This year looks like it could be especially difficult, because the riots destroyed a wing of the Central Palace of Culture along with the MPRP building, a few days ago. The tally is that 1,000 ancient instruments, costumes, and art objects were stolen, broken, or destroyed.

It's not a good week to take artifacts out of the country. We call customs and ask if we can take a khengereg out. "No, of course not," they tell us. I call Munkhjin at work; she will know what to do. "Hey, Munkhjin, could you find out if there is any legal way for us to take the drum out of Mongolia?" I ask. And sure enough, there is. First, take a picture from the front and another angle. Second, write in Mongolian what you will use it for and that you collect Mongolian artifacts. Third, tell where you got it and that it is new.

While we are waiting to hear from the Ministry of Education and Culture, Khongoroo and I reminisce about the taiga. "That day it rained and we sat around the fire was our best day, wasn't it? Like a meditation. No need to say anything. Just gather wood and feed the fire," she says. Yes, out in nature, peaceful in the pouring rain, providing wood for the fire, and tired from the trip. Relaxed. On that day our team had reached the level of family where you don't have to do anything or say anything—you can just be.

Two days before I leave, I get the stamped permission to take the drum. The drum goes into the checked luggage on the plane. Even there, I can feel the vibration of that drum's energy as I cross the Pacific. At U.S. customs, there is a question on the immigration form asking if you have any animal products.

"Yes," I mark the square.

"What do you have?" asks the immigration officer.

"A drum."

"Go through the red line."

The drum goes through the x-ray with everything else and out the other side, and now the khengereg and I are on the last lap of the trip, from Chicago to Burlington, to our final home in Vermont. I guess it feels well taken care of, because it is peaceful. I know it still has much to teach me.

Battulga Travels

When Battulga returns from the international reindeer herder conference in China, I speak to him by Skype from Vermont. "You can't believe the beautiful land I saw, just like our taiga. It was a wonderful conference. I finally got to go! Thank you so much for caring about me and giving me that shaman ceremony. It is because I have been sober that I have been able to organize everything and now have had this beautiful experience."

All year I feel good thinking of Battulga sober.

The next summer, when we provide health care at the farthest East Taiga settlement, a woman named P. Ganbat thrusts a photo album into my hands. "Our trip to Norway," she says, nodding at the page. I didn't realize Battulga had also gone to Norway, but there he is, one of four representatives of the herders at a conference with Sami reindeer herders. "They herd, but they also live a modern life," says Battulga, who has come to sit beside me. "They live in town and ride their snowmobiles out to herd the reindeer. It is amazing to see that life, so like ours in Mongolia, yet very modern." Even though Battulga's red string is gone, the ceremony obviously affected him profoundly. I hope the shaman ceremony will continue to help him stay healthy and sober.

The Drum in Vermont

Eleanor, who gave me the riddle about getting the drum, invites me to take the drum to her house for a little ceremony to welcome it. I am in awe of it and don't have any idea what to do with it now that I have it. She has some women friends visiting, and each one gives an idea of what she perceives that the drum needs: flowers, incense, tobacco. Someone says my grandsons should be the first ones to play it. The drum is peaceful. I have no problem sleeping. My grandsons are the first to make sounds on this side of the Pacific.

A few weeks after the drum welcoming, a client calls and asks for a healing, and I think it would be powerful to use the drum as part of his session. He lies on the massage table and I beat the drum, holding it in front of me as I stand over him. My arm gets tired. I sit down and beat the drum sitting down. It is so heavy. I beat it as long as I can, letting the rhythm and healing come through it. My arm hurts. I stop.

The client says his healing is amazing and leaves, but I can't move the next day. I can't twist my torso. It hurts to get into and out of my car. But still, I drive to my massage therapist's home. I hurt so much I can't wait for her to get to her office and meet her there.

"How much does the drum weigh?" she asks me when I am lying on the table, groaning.

"About 25 pounds," I say, sure that only something that heavy could cause this much pain, but when I get home I weigh the drum. When I see the number, it makes me laugh. Four pounds. How could I be so far off? And what made my side hurt so much? I decide to wait for a leading to use the drum again. Then maybe it won't feel like it weighs 25 pounds. The experience changes my view of shaman ceremonies. The way they swing their drums around for three or four hours, they must be getting help from somewhere.

Technology for Shamans

Even though we went all the way to Erdenet to meet Nergui's young apprentice, I get back to the U.S. without ever catching up with him. As I begin to edit my shaman film, I realize I have a number of important questions for Oyunerdene. How did you become a shaman? How old were you? What was it like to have epilepsy? Did it go away when you started practicing? Why didn't you have your own aman khuur when you were with Nergui? Do you have a costume and a drum? What changes when you become a shaman?

Khongoroo tells me by e-mail from her graduate school, Taiwan University, that she will call Oyunerdene and ask him these questions when she is in Mongolia on winter vacation. As soon as she arrives in Ulaanbaatar, she calls him and after a couple of days she lets me know that he has offered to go to Ulaanbaatar (an eight-hour trip) to be videotaped. Bayara will use my Sony PD 150 camera, which is still there. Khongoroo will translate and they will call me by Skype so I can direct the shoot. Sometimes technology can do the most magical things.

For the shoot, Oyunerdene and his wife, Bayara, and Khongoroo are all at Khongoroo's house. The camera is working. The tape is in. It is 7:00 AM here and 8:00 PM there. Windows are light in my room, dark in hers. But Bayara can't find a microphone. I forgot that I brought it back to the U.S. with me. I hesitate, but can't miss this opportunity to get answers when everyone is together. So Khongoroo asks the questions. Even though Oyunerdene is a fuzzy green on my computer screen, I set my other camera up and tape the fuzzy interview from Skype. I feel gratitude all day. Even if that is all I get on Oyunerdene, at least we have his voice and the answers to the questions.

Bayara says he will find a microphone. Khongoroo arranges a session for tomorrow at 12:00 noon there, which is 11:00 PM here. I don't really believe that everyone will show up again. I work on letting go of the attachment to the idea of getting excellent footage. I try to keep myself awake. 11:00. 11:30. I write a message to

Bayara. "Just a minute, Sas," he writes back. I am starting to get a headache from being overtired. I have been up since our early morning session. Then, at midnight, everyone is back together, this time at Bayara's home. It is light there and dark in the U.S. Oyunerdene has his costume and drum, Bayara has the camera, tripod, and microphone, and Khongoroo is at the computer with a headset. I lie on my bed with my laptop, exhausted. Then magic happens. The questions, the translations, the shots are easily recorded on tape. We have all the information we need. At 1:30 AM here, when the interview is finished, Oyunerdene puts on his costume, lifts his drum, and begins to call his ongods. I can feel the energy flowing through Skype, through 12 time zones, from halfway around the world, and I jolt.

Reindeer transport wood from the taiga forest to be used for heat and cooking in the urts. The soft wood from the larch trees burns fast.

photo credit: Sas Carey

Elder Punsil stirs reindeer milk tea over the wood stove in her urts at Orton, the East Taiga's farthest settlement.

photo credit: Fred Thodal

2009

> The connections we make in the course of a life—
> maybe that's what heaven is.
> — Fred Rogers

Preparations

Now I have this down. I know how to do this trip and I know where I start. Before I hear anything about funding, I walk into Middlebury's Ben Franklin 5 and 10 Cent Store and buy a Mead composition notebook with a black and white marbled cover for $1.99. Once I have bought it, I know I am committed to going on a trip to Mongolia in the summer. When I get home, I scan two or three monthly pages of my Day Timer calendar and glue them into the middle pages of the notebook. To choose the dates, I consider several things: When will my grandsons be at camp? What will the weather be like? How do the dates fit around Naadam Festival, July 11–14? In pencil I jot down a day to depart and a day to return. I mark down when I will go to each part of Mongolia and how long I will be there. Although there are still many mitigating factors, details, and unforeseen events, generally the trip happens the way I first write it the day I buy the Mead notebook. Only then do I start the fundraising—the rest follows. The money comes. The plane tickets come. The team forms. The supplies appear and I pack.

This year The Shelley & Donald Rubin Foundation will support my work for the fourth year. Knowing this, I feel calmer about raising funds for the rest of the budget. For the first seven years of my work in Mongolia, before the Rubin Foundation's help, I wondered each time if I would be able to go—where the money would come from. Each year the Mongol-American Cultural Association, my Quaker Meeting Friends, and other friends donated to make it possible. My budget was always minimal, yet I was able to accomplish the work. Since The Shelley & Donald Rubin Foundation started helping, I feel relieved to know that basic costs are covered before I start asking individuals for donations. It is touching to have generous donors believe in the work we are doing. During this process I am always grateful to the Quaker concept of "leadings," in which the way forward opens. Otherwise, I would doubt that the process could happen this way. Each year, though, it is still like a miracle. I make a plan, put everything I can into making it happen, and watch all the pieces come together.

The marbled notebook marks the beginning of the trip. By the end of the trip, it is full of clinical notes, feelings, lists, expenses, and details of the experience. By the end of the trip, duct tape may be what holds it together.

For June and July this year, before we go to Mongolia, Khongoroo visits Vermont, tasting life in my world and learning about fundraising, planning, and packing for the taiga program. Her favorite part of being here, though, is picking cherries from our neighbor's tree. There are no cherry trees in Mongolia and she marvels at the abundance.

When we arrive in Ulaanbaatar, Khongoroo has two cultural observations. She bends down to pick up a scrap of paper in a parking lot, saying, "I wonder what I dropped. Oh, I just came from a clean country to this dirty one—this is just litter." The second is, "My brother is so much bigger—his face is so wide." I don't mention that that's how all Mongolian faces are, but I remember that one year, after staying for three months and seeing only Mongolian faces, I was shocked when I looked in the mirror and saw the shape of my face, my gray hair and blue eyes. For some reason, I thought I had grown to look like everyone else!

The End of the Line

Our 2009 team includes Khongoroo, Bayara, Battulga, and Fred Thodal, a young man from Middlebury who is volunteering to take photos and videos with his high definition camera. By the time we reach Tsagaan Nuur, it feels good to stop. Tourists from Italy, Korea, Austria, France, Germany, and the U.S. pass through here on their way to the taiga. All of us have endured three days of pounding, clattering, and swerving over Mongolian roads in a car. Even though there is no electricity or running water and there are no bathrooms, it seems luxurious after being on the road. The beds in Nyama and Ganba's guesthouse are made of birch logs and boards covered with a couple of layers of padding. Sleeping here is more comfortable than sleeping on the floor or the ground, plus there are sheets and duvets. This means I can spread out a bit—my sleeping bag is a mummy style and while it is really warm, I feel constrained sleeping in it. Artist Ganba has created a unique space with bark for wallpaper. The wood stove is going even though it is August; the weather is already chilly here. Tsagaan Nuur, the lake, stretches beyond the log houses. The blue sky and puffy clouds are reflected in its water.

Yet, there is something different this year: people on cell phones. Technology is reaching here, the small soum near Siberia and the Russian border in northern Mongolia. Last summer the only way to make a phone call was to go to the post office, hand the clerk a paper with the number, and let her dial it. She'd hand you the receiver if the call went through. If it was raining, it wouldn't go through. Life is changing, even here. Now two cell towers, so new that they reflect the sunlight, are powered by 50 shiny solar panels flanking the post office.

Cell phones take a bit of getting used to here, where water is carried by hand and the small amount of electricity used to run a black and white television is sporadic, depending on the sunshine. Where do you put your cell phone while you squat over a wide slot between the floorboards of an outhouse to relieve yourself, as it rains on you through one-inch gaps in the roof and the wind blows through the cracks in the walls?

Cooking here is done over low wood stoves, as it is in the taiga, with large set-in pans similar to woks that are used mostly for boiling food rather than sautéing. Each onion, potato, or piece of mutton is cut by hand into tiny pieces so it will cook faster. Still, cooking takes hours. The cutting board is often on the floor, and the women squat or lean over the stove. Now all this is done while talking on the cell phone.

Nyama never stops working—there are no time-saving devices. She washes sheets by hand with water Ganba carries from the lake. The cooking and heating stoves constantly need wood. This is the taiga, so there are forests, but they are a distance away. Soft larch is the only wood that grows here and it burns fast.

Food is local except for rice and flour. Nyama and Ganba catch whitefish, the kind they have given us in the past, with a net. It is the best fish I've ever eaten—canned in glass jars over the wood stove, smoked outside in a stovepipe, fried on its own, made into soup, or breaded into *khuushur* (pancakes). Whitefish is so delicious I don't have a favorite way for it to be served. But it must be cooked or processed quickly. There is no refrigeration, so it has to be eaten right away, too, as I learned in the taiga. Because of the fish, being in Tsagaan Nuur is always a relief for me. Generally, there is not much fresh food besides the fish, except for meat and dairy brought by herders. Mongolians eat a lot of meat, mostly mutton, and being a vegetarian is challenging. In the morning a sheep is tethered in front of the restaurant; at noon mutton is served. When I open a closet door, I see the rest of the sheep hanging there. Soup, khuushur, and other mutton specialties appear for the next couple of days.

Into this small town at the end of the line and over steep, rutty roads thick with mud and the roots of trees, ELECTRICITY is coming next month! I can only imagine what changes this will make for the people of Tsagaan Nuur. Already there are cardboard boxes with washing machines, refrigerators, and even rice steamers waiting to be unpacked and used. With a population of 1,470, a school dormitory with 110 children and 446 students in grades K-11, there are bound to be changes for everyone. For one thing, the students will not need candles for studying any more.

Getting electricity to Tsagaan Nuur is a momentous task. In Mongolia, where remote countryside soums often get promises without results, we see actual electric poles being placed and wires being strung. Erdenbat, Minister of Electricity and Power, proposed this project and found the money to complete it. Since the coal plant that will produce the electricity for Khovsgol Province is in Erdenet, 150 miles away, getting the electricity here is incredibly arduous. One-ton concrete poles are being set into the ground with gigantic yellow machinery. Since there is permafrost four feet under the ground, each pole is set seven feet deep. We notice on our way here that most of the poles are already set—all except for the ones at the 7,000-foot mountain pass of the Thirteen Ovoos. There the ground is still frozen and the river is still covered with ice. Here in Tsagaan Nuur, we watch a truck with a giant auger dig new holes and place the heavy poles into them. Next month, for 12,000 tugrik, or $8.40, Tsagaan Nuur families will be able to unpack their new appliances and plug them in. Tsagaan Nuur is the end of the line.

East Taiga

Our friend Fred, who is helping take photos and videos, needed a tent. "No problem," we told him, "we can get one at zakh." In the tent section, we pointed to one that looked adequate and the seller ran to a storage place, returning with a tent like ours but with a new, improved rubber-backed fly to go over the tent and keep the rain out. Ours has a nylon fly. When we saw Fred's, we decided a rubber-backed one was an improvement that would make our tent perfect. The salesperson pointed to a tent just like ours and said the fly was made to fit that tent. Khongoroo was a savvy buyer. She asked the salesperson to set up Fred's tent to make sure all the parts were included. Everything worked just fine.

"Okay," we said, "We'll take a fly for ours, too." Later, when I packed, I left the old fly in my apartment and took the new one—without trying it on the tent.

When we met in Tsagaan Nuur this year, Battulga suggested that we go to both East Taiga settlements this year. We are on our way now. It is mid-August and there has been excessive rain already, causing deep mud on the already hard-to-climb horse trails. We will see the furthest East Taiga Dukhas for the first time in three years and get their statistics for the health database. The last time we saw them was when they were in their spring settlement, when Tsend was sick. New scenery awaits us at their summer encampment of Orton, which we have not seen before. We hear there is even a waterfall, something unusual in Mongolia. Since the conditions are more challenging than normal and the West Taiga settlements are farther apart than usual, we won't go there. Our plan is to meet with many of them when the herders bring their children into Tsagaan Nuur on September 1 for school.

I have been waiting to be on my way since the last trip—having prepared all year to come again to these taiga people I hold so close in my heart. Our car gets to Khogorog later than we planned. As soon as the wranglers get all our packs tied onto the horses, there is a downpour, so we wait inside a little building. Then we are able to ride only four hours before we set up camp and stay overnight.

Coming here to the closest East Taiga settlement, we have fifteen horses, five packhorses, five wranglers leading the packhorses, and five of us: Khongoroo, Bayara, Fred, and Battulga, who is leading me on my horse. Our horse guides convince us that we need to stop and camp overnight because it is too late to go farther. It is cold and wet, the riding is hard, and if we keep going we won't make it before dark. The wranglers and guides unload all the gear. We set up our tent as we always have before, but the fly doesn't quite fit like the other fly we had. In the middle of the night there is a downpour and Khongoroo finds herself in a cold puddle. She takes her wet self and sleeping bag and moves into Bayara's tent between Bayara and Battulga. I feel abandoned, but my side of the tent is fairly dry, so I go back to sleep.

In the morning, after four hours of tense, muddy riding, we see the white triangles of the urts in the distance, but still have an hour of riding before we reach them. There is one last river to cross and Battulga's horse shies from it for some reason. Then Khongoroo's horse has gotten it in his head to take off at a gallop, so the last moments of the ride are not particularly calm.

Arriving at a settlement is always emotional for me, like coming home. As we dismount, our Dukha friends surround us with smiles of welcome, open hearts, and gentle greetings. Seeing the taiga people in person makes me fight back tears; at the same time, my heart races. Then I am back to normal, watching a tourist group prepare to leave, the herders taking advantage of the moment by displaying their antler carving souvenirs on a cloth on the ground to see if there are any buyers.

When we arrive at the closest East Taiga camp, our wranglers, knowing the problem we had with our tent last night, set it up so it will be dry for tonight. First they stand the tent up and then add a layer of red, white, and blue woven plastic, the kind grain bags are made of. Mr. Lovely tucks the plastic under the tent floor to make sure it will be dry, then adds the rubberized fly. It should work.

My father taught me how to camp from the time I was a little girl. I know the principles of proper tent camping: 1) The fly can't touch the tent. 2) Never touch the inside of the tent when it's raining. 3) Everything has its place and needs to be shipshape, like on a boat. 4) An arc is stable in the wind. 5) The material must be stretched and taut. 6) Separate lines hold the fly and the tent. But I also know the protocol in Mongolia: outside the ger or urts, men are in charge. As a woman, I am not "allowed" to make a change in the arrangement of layers, even though the red, white, and blue plastic hangs down over the screen door, making the entrance miniscule. Even though the window on the fly is crooked and there is no way to close it. Even though the weight of the plastic and fly are collapsing the poles so they are concave instead of convex. The space inside is like a tunnel. I know we are in trouble.

Health Care

The next morning we gather with the community in the urts of S. Ganbat and Pruvie to explain the goals for our visit. But first, they tell us which families are in which urts and give a brief report of the important news of any births or deaths. There have been two births. I love to scan the radiant faces of the herders above their brightly colored deels. Side conversations in Tyvan and Mongolian caress my ears. We sit in a circle on the ground inside the urts. The earth smells rich, the fire crackles, and the reindeer milk tea is warm and smooth. I speak and Khongoroo translates.

"We would like to continue with the health database," I begin. "If you have had any changes in your health, please come. We especially want to look at the tonsils of the children and see everyone with high blood pressure. We would like to weigh and measure all children and check everyone with high blood pressure, and we invite everyone to have his or her blood pressure taken. If you haven't met with us before, we especially would like to see you. In other words, please come for a checkup. Our goal is to harmonize all types of health care so that you are as healthy and resilient as possible. The results we get from the database guide us in what help we bring every year."

Pruvie says, "Yes, you can do the checkups right here in our urts."

"Thank you, Pruvie. We would like to help you figure out how to get daily vitamin C in your diet by using what you have in your environment. Vitamins come through your reindeer milk, and when the reindeer stop lactating you could boil pine needles or use dried cranberry leaves or rose hips."

Gerlee says, "We notice that the children have fewer coughs and colds now that they are taking vitamin C every day. And we have used up last year's supply."

"We have brought sunscreen for each family. If you use this every day it will keep your face and hands soft, unwrinkled, and light, in addition to preventing skin cancer."

Solongo looks at Batjargal and says, "Light? Okay, that's great. Then maybe we won't look like countryside people when we are in Ulaanbaatar."

"In the past we found 100 Dukha people with high blood pressure," I continue. "This may be related to the altitude, but it still can cause problems. If you have high blood pressure we will give you a daily low dose of aspirin to prevent heart attacks and give you a health survey to help you look at risk factors and causes of high blood pressure. We have enough aspirin for each at-risk person for the year, thanks to an American pharmacist."

"Will that help pain, too?" asks Tsendelii, who has already had a stroke.

"Probably. Of course, I will offer energy healing as usual. You are welcome to come to be treated for your pain. As in the past, we brought floss, toothbrushes, and toothpaste. Do you know that brushing your teeth at night is better than doing it in the morning, because your food can work on your teeth all night to cause cavities? Flossing reaches the surfaces between your teeth to prevent cavities there. We will be checking your teeth this year. And we brought a video to show you about cavities and what foods are good for your teeth. Have you used up the floss we brought last year?"

The children nod, "Yes."

"In 2003, when I met with the men here and asked what help you would like, you told me you would like help to stop cigarette smoking and drinking. These are not only addictions and very hard to stop, but also have deep cultural roots. It is hard for a person outside your culture to help with these, but this year you can tell me individually if you would like help. I could offer a shaman ceremony or other help."

Silence.

"All families will receive hygiene kits."

The parents nod.

"This is Fred, who has come from my town in America. He will be taking pictures and has brought an extra camera for you to use. Tourists are taking your pictures all the time. This is a chance for you to show us what is important to you. It could be your family, your reindeer, friends, nature, whatever you would like others to know about your life. You can take as many pictures as you want and take them of anything you want to show. We will bring copies next year. When the batteries run out, come to us for charged batteries. We will start with the elders, Gombo and Tsendelii, and every three hours, you can pass the camera to another family."

Now everyone talks at once. Their faces are bright. As soon as I hand the camera to Gombo and demonstrate how to use it, young people surround him, showing him what to do. Our horse guide, Mr. Lovely, sticks his cigarette in his mouth and sits beside Gombo. I can see him showing Gombo how to press the button to see the pictures.

The women in their colorful deels and the men in their high black boots tell us about their year, and then most leave so we can begin the health checkups. First the elders come with their families. Khurelgaldan and Sharkhuu wait for us to start. Now their youngest son, Batjargal, is in his third year at the university. He is studying Material Sciences and doing well. They act grateful by staying with us, having the first checkups, and inviting us to come to their home when we finish the work.

Khongoroo weighs Sharkhuu on the bathroom scale. She reports 77 kilograms and I write it in the database. There is no privacy here. Others sit around, tend the fire, listen, talk to each other, and make jokes as they wait their turns. Gombo and the camera have left. Khongoroo measured Sharkhuu's height two years ago, so we skip it for now. This is not a quality-controlled situation. We are using a cloth tape measure, measuring from the top of the heel of the boots or the bottom of the feet if the patient is wearing flip-flops.

Unless it is unbearably hot, which it seldom is at 7,000 feet in this part of the world, the herders wear western clothes with Mongolian deels over their clothes. If it is hot, they wear western clothes and no deel. To remove her deel, Sharhuu unwinds the three-yard-long belt, which is useful to bind the center of the body for bumpy horse rides. She unhooks the seven buttons made of cloth knots from their loops and slides the cloth off her shoulders. Then she rolls up the right sleeve of her blouse so I can take her blood pressure and Khongoroo her pulse. This year we aren't doing finger sticks for hemoglobin—she had the test two years ago. Khongoroo interviews Sharkhuu with a survey of risk factors for high blood pressure and teaches her about salt intake, alcohol use, and foods. We would like to check for protein in urine for the first time, and have urine dipsticks to measure it. I ask Sharkhuu for a urine specimen. We haven't really thought this through, though. I realize we didn't bring cups. Plus, since there are no bathrooms, I'm not sure what will happen.

When I take a break half an hour later and step outside the urts, Sharkhuu's upper body appears from the brush in the "nature toilet area." She waves her hand at me. I wait as she brings a metal tuna fish can with the jagged top still attached—full to the brim with urine. I carefully take it from her, trying not to spill it on my hand, wondering where I can set it down so I can get the dipstick, wondering how I will dispose of the urine and the jagged-topped can after I have tested it. I don't have gloves on. The conditions here are very different from those in the hospital where I worked.

So much for quality control and sanitation in taiga health care. Improvisation and flexibility are the keys here. I test the urine, use antibacterial soap, and don't offer the test to anyone else while I am here. A new lab technician in the Tsagaan Nuur soum hospital is excited when I give her the dipsticks. Even though there are slot toilets in outhouses in the soum center, I believe she will have a safer and more controlled environment in which to perform this test.

Khongoroo's father, a traditional Mongolian medicine doctor, has supported us since I somehow convinced him I could protect his daughter from wolves and bears. For the third year, he has broken down the bulk vitamin C crystals into individual yearly doses at his traditional medicine plant and packaged them in small plastic bags for us to bring here.

This year, he loans us his otoscope. My plan is to check the children's tonsils, as the hospital statistics say that 60 percent of the children have tonsillitis. I don't know exactly what they mean. If tonsillitis has the same definition as it does in the U.S., I don't understand how 60 percent can have it. So I check each taiga child and adult, and discover that only 17 percent have red or enlarged tonsils. The rest appear to be normal.

We have randomly checked teeth in the past. However, this time, as I look into mouths to check for tonsillitis, I see many cavities and decayed and missing teeth. One 14-year-old has a hole through the side of his gum, caused by a decayed tooth. It is my mental picture of his mouth that inspires me to do a bigger dental project next year.

This East Taiga settlement, the closest of the six to Tsagaan Nuur, is the one most visited by tourists. The culturally appropriate present for children is candy, and nearly all of the children here have dental problems. Many adults here also have missing and decayed teeth. When we later check the far settlement, the children's teeth are better, and the West Taiga children's teeth are also better. Using only observation, it looks like the Dukhas in the settlement with the most tourists have the most dental problems.

We expected some dental problems—but not to the extent that we found them. Khongoroo has posters from the Mongolian Dental

Association to distribute to the Tsagaan Nuur schoolrooms, the government building, and other places. There are three different large posters, two feet by three feet, with different messages—the parts of a healthy tooth, diseased teeth, and the prevention of cavities. Khongoroo also found a cartoon rap video in which a child learns that eating the right foods and brushing his teeth will prevent cavities. The children ask to see the video again and again. Research shows that tooth decay and gum disease are serious problems that are linked to heart attacks and other risks. We are committed to trying to help the herders more in the area of dental health the next time we come. And, as a team that has been guilty of giving the culturally appropriate gift of candy ourselves, we will avoid that in the future. We will also work on getting the word out to all tour operators and tourists that this is not an appropriate gift, since there is such widespread tooth decay.

Tent

I try to be nonchalant when I walk from one urts to another. I pretend I don't see our tent sagging. I smirk if I do let my eyes wander to it. It looks like it belongs in a poem my mother read to me when I was young: "There was a crooked man and he walked a crooked mile, he found a crooked sixpence against a crooked stile. He bought a crooked cat, which caught a crooked mouse. And they all lived together in a little crooked house."

Fred is a techie with the ability to visualize solutions. Already the zipper on his tent has broken, so he's not thrilled with our acquisitions. I show him the collapsed interior of mine. He and I thread an old pole, the one broken in a storm two years ago, through some loops down the middle of the inside of the tent. Now there is enough space to sleep.

The second night it rains and Khongoroo's side gets all wet again. She leaves for the men's tent. After a few days, when I look at the tent, I don't smirk any more. I feel embarrassed—just glad my Dad can't see it. But I keep sleeping in it. Khongoroo alternates between Bayara's and ours. Ours is cold, since it isn't tight any more. Getting in and out with the plastic hanging down is a challenge, especially when I'm half asleep and need to make a trip outside.

Before we leave, I get to visit my namesake, Sas Reindeer. His brown and white fur is still soft. His eyes are surrounded by black, like a raccoon's, but it's not a round pattern; the pattern matches the shape of his eyes. He has grown to adult size and has sprouted antlers. When we do a little bonding—Sas and I are hanging out together—he yawns. Munkhuu says that when a reindeer yawns, it is a sign that he is happy. She also tells me, "Sas will become a man this fall. Maybe you can ride him next year." Maybe. I can't stop smiling whenever I think of having my own reindeer namesake living in the taiga.

We pack the tent again and ride the horses over mountains, one of which is snow-covered and so steep that we have to get off our horses and walk. Finally, we arrive at the second camp. It is one of the most beautiful places I've seen yet. The snow-capped mountains of Russia lie on one side, and the settlement is in a bowl, with a variety of mountains of different colors and textures around it. One has larch trees, another is stark rock, and another is covered with autumn blueberry and rhododendron bushes of soft orange and yellow heather hues, with stalks of bright red rhubarb blasting out between.

The settlement includes six urts, six families. We set up the tents, but I'm both tired from the horse ride and tired of being cold. I choose to spend a night with one of the two families who offer floor space in their urts. I snuggle into my sleeping bag; the woman of the family covers me with quilts. I am cozy, dry, and warm from the stove. I am also a little tense, trying not to make any noise or disturb these people I don't know well. This is the summer settlement we haven't visited as much, since it is so far away. The last time I visited them was four years ago. They remember me, though, because Nomadicare helped their daughter with expenses for books and supplies for her university education. When I wake up in the morning, the fire is going and I am handed reindeer milk tea along with fresh sourdough bread. Cozy. But the next night I'm back in the crooked tent, where I stay until we leave.

The ride back to Tsagaan Nuur takes nine hours. We go slowly, because I'm still scared riding up the steep, muddy mountains. Then when it's flat and we trot, I feel like my back is breaking.

Yet, after three hours, when Battulga asks if I want to stop for the night, I say, "No."

After five hours Battulga stops and says, "Do you want to stay here for the night?"

All I can think of is that I can't stand another night in that tent. "No, let's go," I say.

After seven hours, Mr. Lovely and Battulga say, "Sas, should we set up camp?"

"No," I say.

"Okay," says Mr. Lovely. "This is your last chance to stop. If you are sure you want to keep riding, we will ride ahead now."

"Yes, I'm sure," I say. *No way am I sleeping in that tent.* Mr. Lovely gallops ahead with his son and friend and the packhorses. On those packhorses are the food, stove, tents, and sleeping bags. There is no choice now. We have to ride all the way. My mind wonders. *Am I being stupid? Maybe everyone hurts like I do. Maybe the others want to stop.* They are all ahead of me or behind me, out of conversational distance. *Just because I can't deal with another night in the tent, does that justify causing more pain for the team?*

During the nine hours of riding through mud and over roots and sloshing through rivers, my mind watches its thoughts. Every sensation is magnified. My butt hurts. My arm hurts from holding the reins taut. My legs are stiff. My back aches. I just want a drink of water. I say nothing and keep sloshing behind Battulga. I try to let my thoughts go. The sun is setting. I'm blinded and notice that I'm not thinking about being thirsty—I'm just thinking *I need to get the sun out of my eyes.* As soon as we get over a rise and the sun isn't piercing me, I'm back to remembering I am thirsty. My lips are dry. Then, Battulga turns and offers me my water bottle. I take a few sips. I don't want to have enough to make me feel sick, but it is lovely, that feeling of water in my mouth. Now my mind is remembering my back hurts and wondering how much longer and thinking I'm hungry.

I see a fence. My mind says, *I'll give anything if this is our destina-*

tion—Khogorog. It is another thought I try to let go. We come to a river. Battulga's horse refuses to go. Battulga turns him around and heads in at a shallower fording place. Then we are closer to the fence and I see a field, log houses, fences, and a ger. It IS Khogorog! I could never be more grateful. Tonight we will sleep in a building!

Shaman Costume

Back in Ulaanbaatar, Khongoroo points to a sign pasted to a city wall. It says, "Shaman kits made to order. Phone 91818846." Shaman kits? It is that common? She says it is probably not the real thing. I notice there is a lot of discussion using the word "real" in relationship to shamans and all pertaining to them. "Why don't we go talk to Sukhbat, my father's friend?" she suggests. "He is the president of the Mongolian Shaman Association." From my interviews in the taiga, I know there is some question about what makes an authentic shaman. Taiga shamans like Gosta ask what a Ph.D. in shamanism means. Can you study it and become a shaman? What does the Mongolian Shaman Association do? I am paying attention to this throughout the interview we eventually get with Sukhbat.

"Are you a shaman?" he asks after I buy an aman khuur from the Association.

"No," I answer.

"Why not?"

"It's not my culture. I am of European ancestry."

"There are shamans all over the world. I know Swedish, French, Spanish shamans. It is the most basic religion, the first religion."

"Well, I have a drum… ."

"Listen. There is a woman in Ulaanbaatar who makes shaman costumes. She is a shaman herself." He writes her number on a slip of paper. On the way out of his office, Khongoroo dials the number. "What is your shaman tradition?" the shaman wants to know. I have no idea what to answer.

"I am familiar with shamans in the taiga. My ancestors are European." Is that the answer?

When she quotes a price, it is too high and I say, "No. Never mind."

Soon she calls back. Do I need everything? I don't know what everything is. I don't need a drum. I need the costume and a headdress. A headdress will be more, she says, and quotes half of the original price. She invites us over the following day so she can measure me.

The next day we take a taxi to an outlying district of Ulaanbaatar and phone her when we get there. After we stand on the street for 20 minutes, a small woman with a deeply lined face and a cigarette in her hand motions. We follow her to a store where there are piles of dark material on tables. I don't see anything that looks like a shaman costume. Fred is told to wait, with his camera, with the piles of material. She leads Khongoroo and me into the back, past a washing machine and into a small, dark hallway. It takes a minute for my eyes to adjust. Above a bed is an altar and beside it a shaman costume, hanging with the headdress looped over the deel. "Don't touch it!" she warns us before we even get close.

I look at her thin, drawn face and the cigarette in her hand. This is not a healthy person—neither healthy nor happy. I need to be careful. I have contradictory thoughts. This one could do an evil spell—I know it…not that I am afraid of a spell…I know how to hold her in the Light.

"Now, what kind of costume do you want? Oh, you're a beginner. You need a blank costume. The ongods will tell you what you need when you call them. Blue. Blue is a good color. Go to the ongods humbly. Take off your rings and earrings. You need pants. Green is good. A shirt. White. To go under the blue deel. Yes. Do you want a headdress?" I nod. "That will be more," she repeats.

We return to her material store and she sits at a sewing machine with the cigarette dangling from her lips. She pulls out some manjin.

"You will need manjin. You can't do a ceremony without a whip."

"I don't want black and red."

"How about blue and red and white? You need red."

"Okay."

"This is more. Do you need a horse case for your aman khuur?"

"Yes."

"I will see if I can find the man who carves them. But maybe it will be hard to find him tonight." It is Monday. We are leaving Wednesday night for the U.S., so I ask her if she can get it done by tomorrow, since we have to leave.

"Yes, of course." Mongolians love last-minute challenges.

Tuesday afternoon we take a taxi to her shop. The items are neatly folded beside her sewing machine. A royal blue deel, a white shirt, dark green pants, and, most amazing and beautiful of all, a headdress with an embroidered face on it!

She follows my eyes. "That's your face!" When I look, I see not wide Asian eyes, but my own western ones. "Maybe you could give a little extra gift for that? It took a long time."

I try everything on. The deel is the most comfortable one I have had yet. The pants have an elastic top and slide on easily. But the white shirt is too small.

"Oh, you look a lot smaller than you are! Okay, I will make one, let's see, two sizes bigger. I can get it done by tomorrow."

The next morning we go to pick up the costume. She must have stayed up all night sewing. The shirt is done and it fits perfectly now. We run out of time, so we won't get the carved horse case for the aman khuur. A costume needs boots, too, so it looks like I will be back again next year.

My new costume came with me on the plane across the Pacific and the North Pole with no problems and is now in Vermont, resting inside my drum. It is soft and perfect—and blank. Waiting for instructions.

Three West Taiga cousins ride to their urts on a reindeer during a midsummer snowstorm.
photo credit: Sas Carey

2010

> If they are to survive as a culture, the nomads desperately need effective heath care close to their homes.
>
> — Jane Goodall

Gold Mines and Reindeer Boots

This year our team includes an American doctor, Lucy McKeon, MD, and a dentist, Tania Rohany, DDS, with their interpreters—Mongolian nurse Naraa and dentist Ariuna—plus my assistant, Khongoroo, and her new boyfriend, Joost, from the Netherlands, who is our cameraman, and our trusty guide, Battulga. We have Puji and his younger brother Davkha for our drivers—two cars this year. As soon as we arrive in Tsagaan Nuur, Tania sets up her dental office in the soum hospital and patients start coming for tooth extractions. Battulga told the herders ahead of time that she would give free service. In three days, she pulls 200 teeth, runs out of anesthetic, and returns to the U.S. The rest of the team rides to the East Taiga. Lucy will do health assessments and this year's health database.

Taiga Gold

Mining is becoming a huge industry all over Mongolia. The Canadian and Brazilian mining company Oyu Tolgoi will create virtual cities underground in the Gobi Desert to remove gold and other metals. Other years, Dukha herders have served as guides to local gold mines. This year for the first time, though, I feel it is possible that the reindeer herding life might become unsustainable because of mining.

In the past, herders of the West Taiga criticized the herders of the close East Taiga camp of 11 families for not moving far enough to provide cool weather and rich pasture for their reindeer. I heard them say that this group stays too close to Tsagaan Nuur so they can benefit from tourists. The West Taiga herders were proud that they took the best care of their reindeer—that theirs were healthier because they took them to higher altitudes to meet their needs.

During this year, West Taiga's Baasankhuu, Gosta's adopted son, found gold while herding his reindeer in the Meng Bulag pastureland that has been used for generations. And gold has changed everything for the West Taiga reindeer herders. Miners panning for gold, like those of the California Gold Rush, descended upon the area, so the reindeer herders pushed farther and farther from their usual settlement area and from each other. Ten deaths occurred between December and July. One West Taiga herder family has moved to Tsagaan Nuur, built a house, and bought a car with gold money. Another has given up herding—again, gold money. Some are rich in money now—others are not. There is a gold divide.

When we arrive in Tsagaan Nuur, Battulga says we will not go to the West Taiga again this year. The settlements are too far from each other and not easy to reach because Meng Bulag is full of miners, border patrol officers, security guards, and vendors of many services. It sounds like the raw nature I saw during the years I made the long horseback ride up there and camped beside Gosta and Khanda is gone.

Closest East Taiga Settlement and New Ceremony

In the East Taiga closest settlement, extreme taiga weather has come. The rain pounds like a waterfall, full force on my new three-season tent. The wind is blowing. It is hailing, thundering, and lightening. I am dry, eating jelly candies. After the storm, Joost decides to videotape Sas Reindeer to see exactly what he does during a day. I glance toward them from time to time as Sas eats lichen, walks through brush, drinks at the river, lies in the brush, and wanders through the fields with the herd. Khongoroo makes pasta for lunch in a blue Mickey Mouse tent she brought from Taiwan. The front is open. We now have our food in blue plastic barrels, which keep it dry and are animal-proof. She sits on the ground cooking on a gas hot plate, which can boil water in a couple of minutes. Lucy, with Naraa interpreting, is meeting with each herder for a health checkup and to add to the database. She sits on a tarp on the ground. Whoever wants to stay and watch can do it. Some questions are not possible to ask with an audience. She skips those. The taiga children wander where they will—playing with water, stones, logs, and grass and tossing a soft basketball through a metal hoop on a pole.

Batjargal, our scholarship student, says a motorcycle fell on his ankle just before he rode his horse to the taiga. I do energy healing on him and he falls asleep. Lucy immobilizes his ankle. The next time I visit, the splint is off and an herbal treatment—leaves of *Rhodiola rosae* or Golden root, to reduce pain—encircles the damaged area.

Khongoroo and I walk to the other side of the settlement through the river. I am wearing my Bogs boots, which are dry and warm. Perfect. Clearing my throat to be polite, I lift the flap of an urts to visit. Tunga, wife of Ulzii, has a one-year-old baby who is playing with sticks and dirt on the floor. Tunga pours reindeer milk into her cooking pan and stirs it, making cheese. Naran sits close by nursing her swaddled baby. I treasure these moments inside with the women. Khongoroo translates, holds the baby, and asks my questions. Tunga boils the milk until there is no liquid left, only thick curds. We sit to watch this process. She feeds wood into the stove to make the milk boil faster. A neighbor girl comes for a visit and leaves. A young man lifts the door, looks in, drops the door, and leaves. Still the milk boils. Tunga asks if we want a taste at this point and fills a bowl with the hot, uneven-textured curd for each of us. Delicious. When the cheese is thick, with no visible liquid, Tunga pours it into material like a plastic grain bag, puts a board over it, and sets a heavy rock on top. I see that any remaining liquid is pressed out of the curd. Khongoroo and I wander back to our tents and sit with the others on a tarp. She and I, the elite, have chairs with backrests on the ground.

Later in the afternoon, I visit Munkhuu, herder of Sas Reindeer. I have no translator, just intuition and feelings and laughter to go on. Sharkhuu is sitting on the ground working the hand wheel of a sewing machine. I don't know what she is making with the black material she is sewing together. The women are talking. Naran visits here with her baby, too. I understand enough to feel part of the merriment. I wonder how many funny stories they have from watching tourists and visitors. I feel peaceful. Munkhuu cuts rawhide to make string. Usually you can't go into an urts without the hostess making milk tea for you. We don't even need tea right now. We can just be.

Some tourists tell me there will be a ceremony tonight. Since the book and movie, *The Horse Boy*, by Rupert Isaacson, came out, tourists make the journey to the taiga so that Dukha shamans will heal their autistic family members. I met such a family today. They are from Italy—parents, sisters, and a brother with autism. They invite me to the ceremony. But I don't know who will do it. I have met, interviewed, and videotaped most of the shamans from both the East and West Taiga. Maybe Saintsetseg will do it? She's the only one I know in this settlement. Then I hear that S. Ganbat, the father of two students we helped and a friend of mine, is a new shaman and will perform the ceremony. He studied with Ganzorig. S. Ganbat, with his wide smile and warm eyes, has always been kind to my team and me. His family once gave me a sacred rock, which I keep below my computer screens. We often use his urts for health assessments. Some years ago, I asked if it was okay to document the Dukha lifestyle on video. He answered, "Yes, please take video, document our lives. We want people to know who we are."

Lucy and Naraa have never seen a ceremony. It is a good opportunity for them. So, as darkness falls, we walk through the river between the two parts of the settlement to S. Ganbat's urts. I sit on the bed. The drum skin is still wet and gives out a dull thud as family members test it, place it near the fire, test it, take the cover off the stove and hold the drum over it, and test it again until the sound becomes crisper.

I feel a little impatient, comparing this to Ganzorig's adult children spinning the drum quickly over the fire to dry it. I feel the newness. Why did S. Ganbat become a shaman? I wonder, as we wait quietly for the ceremony to begin. Maybe Pruvie, his wife, suggested it. Maybe they need the tourist money. I am wondering if I should trust her, since she blamed me for not giving her daughters scholarships that year, even though they couldn't go to a university because they hadn't taken the required entrance exams. (In the end, they did get scholarships from the Mongolian government to study at a university in Ulaanbaatar. We helped with travel expenses, books, and clothing. Now Naran will take the next year off to take care of her new baby.)

Joost is shooting video and Naraa, Lucy, and Khongoroo are huddled together, sitting on the floor. The air is getting thicker with the smoke from a juniper branch waved under the drum, costume, headdress, and boots. When dressed in his shaman costume, S. Ganbat begins a vaguely familiar chant—very gentle—calling the ongods with what feels like little authority. They don't seem to be coming. The camera is turned off. I am tired. I lie on the bed behind our team members, who are leaning against it. It will be a long night. Just as I am thinking I don't need to see this, I go into my own dream. I feel the energy of the taiga come to life inside me. It reaches outside the settlement.

They visit me
Sit on my branches
Become crows, eagles, and owls
During ceremonies and dreams
Flutter and swoop

Scent of drum
Deer flying
Journey of great connection
To all things

They meet here
Touch into life's stream
Share truth of healing
My sacred limbs hold answers

Generations of ancestors
Tie their common souls

Questioner and answerer
In my high boughs
Tree

I open my eyes and watch the family who is sponsoring the ceremony. They seem engaged, but I can't tell for sure in the darkness. Then the energy of an animal fills me.

Gnawing hunger
Bone against bone
Ribs empty and skin rolling hunger
Driven to the kill
Driven to survive

THE DOGS
Can't get through their commotion
Gnawing hunger
Emptiness
I'll risk those dogs

Plow through them
Grab some meat
Too many dogs
Just my own blood for the try

Light morning coming
I'm still hungry
Back to brush-covered den
Back to watchful sleep

No blood of reindeer
No bones to chew
No fresh flesh to fill my skin sliding ribs
Not until tonight
When hope rises again
Wolf

So that's what they feel like! I am definitely in my own world, not riveted to the ceremony, as in the past. I sense the ending of the ceremony coming, but taiga vibrations are still demanding my attention.

> Running
> Gleaming
> Hard
> Smooth
> Strong
> Fluid of life
> River
> I am the center place of knowing
> You can't grasp me when I am running
> Only when chunks of me form on top
> Even then I have a soft underbelly
> Where you can drink
>
> *Water*

Flowing…Pruvie is standing in front of me, calling, "Sas, Sas, Sas. The ongods are calling you." I stumble up onto my bare feet and go to sit on the ground in front of the shaman. I spread my deel out. I know the protocol. The shaman throws the wild sheep drumbeater into my deel. Pruvie prompts the response in my ear, "Tuguu." I repeat it. She pulls me up. I go back to sit on the bed. The ceremony is finishing, but the riddles still call me.

> I am
> Solid strong
> I point to the sky
> Hold white in crevices
> Without me, no water flows
> Lichen covered granite and quartz
> I catch snow rain hail sleet clouds sun
> Earth forces push up sky forces push down
> Not even wind can move me—only dreams can
>
> *Mountain*

Through the smoky incense and the haze of my dreams, I see the shaman call the person with autism, for whom the ceremony is being held. My eyes close again.

> Spongy lichen of white and red and green
> I feed your reindeer who feed you
> Life can't go on without me
> I am the very ground, the *gazar*—land earth dirt
>
> Without me there is no you
> Wet dry frozen soft mud
> I am the face, the skin of the planet
> The place that feeds you and everyone
>
> Who feeds me?
> Rain, sun, dung
> Gentle footprints of creatures
>
> I was here long before you
> And will be here when you leave
> Pay attention to where your foot falls
> I am holding you
>
> *Earth*

I hear a roar of voices and receive a final message.

> Gruff deep heavy strong
> Black furry heavy footed
> I guard your souls
>
> *Bear*

Now the experience is my own. Visited without a costume, without a drum. Visited by energy, back where I started this trip to learn about Asian concepts of energy. The honor of being singled out by ongods. Given the inner feeling of the taiga and its inhabitants. Coming full circle.

Ganbat and Ganbat's Story

The farthest East Taiga settlement is considered one of the most sustainable settlements for its seven families because it is the least influenced by tourism. This is due to its long distance and difficult horseback ride from Tsagaan Nuur. When we reach it, our first order of business is photos—the ones the herders took of their families last year with the camera we provided. Twenty pounds of photos, in fact—2,000 of them. Sitting on a tarp in the center of the encampment, I distribute them. It is lovely to see the faces, the recognition, and the joy of holding photos that they took themselves of their lives. It makes the extra weight in the luggage Lucy and I carried worth it.

Some things are different for me. I don't feel well, can't eat, keep coughing, don't have any energy to move around. I try to get up but gravity wins. My stomach aches. My head aches. A blister on my coccyx, from the saddle I rode on to get here, has broken. Lying on the ground in my tent, I hear the thud of someone chopping wood. Then the thud of footsteps. I hear Lucy having a quiet conversation while doing a health check. Click, click from fast reindeer. Hooves hit the ground like hammers on nails. A man coughing from his cigarette habit, heavy thud when he walks. A child, light, skimming the earth. Children together fast and light. My new tent has ventilation and even a plastic window. I can see the sky. Today I watch the sun shift positions. Sleep.

Even though I am out of commission, my team is accomplishing what needs to be done. Joost is taking videos. Khongoroo is meeting people. Lucy and Naraa are doing health checks for the database. Nomadicare's work is getting done without me. I wish I felt better, but it is good to know the work goes on. It gives me hope for the future if at some point I can't do this any more.

When I feel better a couple of days later, Khongoroo and I visit the two Ganbats' urts. On the way the wind sucks my breath away, it is so strong. Last year the married couple, N. Ganbat and P. Ganbat, were building a log house. The log walls were finished and the peak log was up, ready for the roof. This year it is gone. We are relaxing in their urts when I ask what happened to the log house. They give each other a shy look.

"Gold mining."

"What?"

"In December we decided to go to Meng Bulag to look for gold. We went by reindeer, really the only way to get there at that time of year. It was a long ride and very cold. We stayed for two months. The ground was frozen so we built a fire and melted the ice under three feet of snow. Then we put the soil into sacks and carried them to the river. We wore felt boots under waders and stood in the river. In December there were 10 ninja miners. In January there were 100. Now there are 3,000.

"The trip depleted the reindeer so much that they couldn't carry logs for the fire as they do every summer. They aren't as strong this year. So we decided to give them a break and use the house logs for firewood."

"Did you find any gold?" Again I see the couple exchange a shy glance.

"Yes. The biggest chunk anyone found was 2 kilograms and 300 grams (nearly five pounds). One kilogram brings $4,000." I don't know who it was that found a piece of gold worth $10,000, but it makes me question whether the effort of bringing hygiene kits to people with these resources is worthwhile.

"I guess you will be giving *me* vitamins and a hygiene kit next year," I say. They laugh.

Reindeer Boots and Khiimor

Battulga says I can get a shaman case for my aman khuur in the East Taiga far east settlement. Shaman accessories come to me one step at a time. When I bought the aman khuur from the Shaman Association, I did not have time to have a case carved for it. The case I need is a wooden carved horse, which will become animated. "Animated" in relationship to shamanism means that the object goes through a ceremony and "becomes alive." *Khiimor* (made up of the words for wind and horse) is the word for our own personal energy. Wind in this connotation is similar to the word *chi*, energy.

Battulga says that Orchirbat is the best one to carve a case for my aman khuur.

Orchirbat is a tall, slender, shy reindeer herder of 49 who is married to Monkhtsetseg, daughter of the famous shaman Tsend and granddaughter of Soyan, the shaman who lived to be 100. Orchirbat and Monkhtsetseg have two young daughters and a son. Last year they were living in an urts; this year they have a log house. The inside of the log house is set up just like an urts: the door faces south, a wood stove sits in the middle, and there are log platform beds on the sides. The door is canvas, too, but, unlike an urts, the log house has a window space that opens to the outside.

Orchirbat agrees to make me a case, and word comes to me in my tent when he is about to start it. Do I want to watch? Of course. I clear my throat to announce my presence, lift the door flap, and walk in. Orchirbat is sitting on the floor with a four-by-six-by-one-inch block of wood, marking the shape of a horse with a pencil. As I watch, he slowly carves with tools provided by Dan. Bit by bit, he digs into the soft larch. His children come in giggling with their friends and ask me questions in Mongolian, and I try to answer them back in Mongolian. They want to know how to say the alphabet in English, then words—house, friend, stove, father, mother, and land. They giggle some more as they try each one. I want them to sit beside me forever.

A day later, Orchibat is finished with a proud-looking horse. It has an indentation on its back that is the shape of my aman khuur and a smooth base just the right size for holding. When I carry it back to my tent, Mr. Lovely asks if I have a khadagh, and he ties it onto the base, wrapping the scarf around the horse. He tells me we will need to stop at Shaman Davaajav's on the way back to Tsagaan Nuur to get the aman khuur animated.

Battulga says, "Sas, you still need boots to complete your shaman costume. The best person to make them is in this settlement—Orchibat's wife, Munkhtsetseg." The children walk me over to the log house again to get fitted for boots. A day later, they are ready—made of reindeer skin, lined with white cotton. They have leather fringes around the tops and some fringes on the sides—for khunkhinguur, or jingle cones, to be attached. They smell like a taiga home—reindeer skin mixed with tangy reindeer milk, earth, and medicinal plants.

Shaman Davaajav

Re-entry. First the luxury of sitting in a car seat, even with billions of flies and sweltering heat. Then driving in a car—it moves without any effort on my part. And I am now connected by cell phone. We get out of the hot van at Davaajav's wooden home, on the way from Khogorog to Tsagaan Nuur. We see a padlock on the door and know no one is inside. Our driver walks around in back and appears with Davaajav, shirtless and with big round glasses on. Embarrassed that we caught him like this, he explains that today is the day for shearing his sheep. He just finished, so if we give him a minute, he would love to see us.

We met Davaajav last year when he did a ceremony for a friend. This year we are returning with photos of him and his family—and requesting help with animating the mouth harp and wooden horse case. When he is ready, I meet with Davaajav to ask if he will animate or endow the khiimor, aman khuur, and reindeer boots with hallowed life to make them sacred. There is not a long ceremony or even a change of clothes from the brown deel he has put on. I sit facing him on the floor. Davaajav asks Khongoroo if we are fooling around or if I truly want it animated. Truly, she says. The shaman ties a string on my aman khuur and to the string ties a blue khadagh, throwing it over his shoulder and asking if he can play the instrument. I nod.

"If you are doing a treatment, use your lips, like this. If you are calling an ongod, put it against your teeth." He prays over it, then softly plays it. He blows into my crown chakra at the top of my head. It feels like a soft blast of energy. Then he hands the aman khuur to me.

"About the reindeer boots—they need khunkhinguur. I can make them for you. Do you have khunkhinguur on your costume? You will need some there, too. Let's see, I think I will have time to make them tomorrow and the next day. Why don't you come back the next day?" Khunkhinguur will jingle each time they are moved. This means they are alive.

When we return to Davaajav in two days, the khunkhinguur are finished. Now I have every item a taiga shaman uses for a ceremony—costume, drum, beater, mirror, manjin, headdress, boots, juniper incense, and even some things I don't have names for. Only...I am not a shaman. Through the process of getting shaman paraphernalia, I learn to honor the properties of each one—how they, like all of nature, are alive. While I will never be a shaman, my goal is to understand as fully as possible so I can share the knowledge with others. Shamanism represents a kind of mysticism, a connection to the unknown, that makes me want to get inside it. This is not a new feeling for me. I always embrace life's mysteries. Connecting with the ancestors, using the drum, energy flowing into the shaman—what do these feel like? What happens? I wonder. My leading has brought me this far.

"Could I be your student?" I ask Davaajav. It is a risky question. There is a big chance he will say no.

"Will you be back next year?"

"Yes," I say, believing I will. He agrees. I hand him an offering, for it is a great honor to be allowed to be his student. I am very grateful.

Only once so far have I put on my shaman costume and headdress and beat the drum. When I did, I began to feel the pulse of another dimension. I don't yet know what I am to learn from that dimension. I am waiting for a leading to tell me when to put the costume on again and to lead me to do what needs to be done. The drum is quiet now.

Update on Taiga Friends

The harsh life of the Dukhas takes its toll on the people. In 2010, Chuluu G.'s 14-year-old grandson froze to death in a blizzard while herding the reindeer. The same year, J. Bat died of alcohol-related issues during the Lunar New Year celebration. So sad.

Taiga news is not all bad, though. I have a photo of eight taiga students in front of the Chinggis Khan (Genghis Khan) statue at the Parliament Building in Ulaanbaatar. (One is missing.) In the fall of 2008, when the nine students began studying in Ulaanbaatar, we were able to give a small stipend to each one for books and clothes. After four years of our scholarships, Batjargal graduates from the Agriculture University in Materials Science. He will work in the mining sector, hopefully speaking up for indigenous people whenever he can. Solongo still attends the Teachers' College and plans to be a teacher. Naran is taking time out with her baby—born in the spring of 2010. Some students are still in school as I write this, including one in medical school. The students have not requested financial support for the past two years, so I assume the government is helping them.

Gosta, known for having one of the biggest reindeer herds, has given up herding. There are many reasons—one being, of course, that he had a stroke and has left-sided weakness, but still, last year he was managing. Now he lives in Tsagaan Nuur. The big change is that his niece, Khanda, has married a man who lives in Ulaanbaatar and has moved to the city with her son, Battummur. Having an opportunity to speak to her on a cell phone after living with her in her urts seems like science fiction, but that's what happens this year.

"Is your husband a good man?" I ask Khanda on the phone.

"He's a man, Sas."

"Is he a *good* man?"

"He doesn't drink, isn't lazy. Yes. He's a person."

"Oh, okay then."

"Thanks for caring about me. I really appreciate it. I am okay now."

One small coincidence: In early 2010 I presented at Lawrence Library's One World Library Project in Bristol, Vermont. I began by showing slides of our trip to the taiga, the Thirteen Ovoos. A young man in the audience said, "That looks familiar." I kept going. Then when I showed a slide of Khanda and Gosta, he said, "I stayed with them." It still didn't fully register. Afterwards, he asked me questions about them and told me he had been holding these questions for seven years. I was in my speaker mode and it did not occur to me until I was driving home that this was Adam, the American in Khanda's story, the one who chiseled through ice for a day and loaned her his flashlight when she was a new mother. I got back in touch with him and he wrote a letter for me to take to the family on my next trip. Khongoroo translated it and we delivered it via Khanda's new brother-in-law. I didn't see Khanda in person in 2010, but did have conversations with her by cell phone.

Future Needs

I heard there was a newspaper article saying that there are 1,000 new shamans in Mongolia. I am thinking about this phenomenon. For 20 short years, shamanism has been allowed. Does this mean that people are trying shamanism to make a living? Or are all these shamans needed and being spiritually asked to serve Mongolia to protect its land, water, herds, and people? No one knows how big a threat mining will be to nomadic life, including the reindeer herders' already endangered lifestyle. Losing a way of life, similar to losing an endangered species of animal on the planet, diminishes the richness of our world's diversity—and it is hard, if not impossible, to get it back. Time will tell exactly what benefits and tolls the mines will bring to Mongolia and the nomads living here. Time will also tell what role the shamans have in protecting the land.

Sometimes 300 tourists visit the 210 Dukhas in one summer. This is harmful to the Dukha's fragile lifestyle and the reason I waited to go there until I could help them in some way. Through this account and the videos that will be made from our clips, I hope to share their lifestyle with many people who will, I hope, choose not to visit the Dukhas, in order to respect and protect their lifestyle. By increasing awareness, we can all help save endangered lifestyles. Diversity enriches our planet. May we find ways to keep it alive.

Dr. McKeon's recommendation after her work in the taiga is to focus our attention on bolstering the Tsagaan Nuur soum hospital and pharmacy, where the herders get health care and medicine all year long. Nomadicare works to harmonize traditional and modern medicine for the cultural survival of Mongolia's nomads. Our goal is to implement training in traditional Mongolian medicine and Western laboratory diagnostic skills for soum doctors to increase the options for assessment and treatment of nomads. By improving and harmonizing western, traditional Mongolian, and even folk medicine, we can help nomadic herders get access to quality health care close to home. With our training and supplies, Tsagaan Nuur soum hospital and others like it will have broader options for health care, giving nomadic herders the opportunity to continue their unique and at-risk lifestyle. We are refining a model over many years of research that will fill the gap Dr. Lucy McKeon noticed. Then it can be replicated throughout Mongolia and the world.

Alcoholism, cigarette smoking, and high blood pressure continue to plague the Dukha people. A shaman ceremony helped once; maybe it can again. We are still attempting to find culturally appropriate ways to address these complex challenges. Dr. McKeon created a flyer on how to quit smoking, which we donated to Tsagaan Nuur hospital and now have on hand for other soum doctors.

I keep studying Mongolian, but I don't think I will ever be proficient. I do know enough to understand if my words are being translated the way I mean them and to get the sense of what someone wants to tell me. I have a translator for details. I don't know exactly how the pieces of my relationship with Mongolia will come together in the future, but I am certain that the relationship still has a long time to go.

Coming Home to Abundance in Vermont

First the familiar faces of the taiga people recede behind me. In Ulaanbaatar I do a double take. Is that Khanda or Battummur? No. When I board the plane to Beijing, Mongolian faces are mixed in with Chinese and western ones. And when I board the plane to Chicago, I can't see a single Mongolian face, although there are still a few Asian ones. When I walk to my seat on the plane to Vermont, I feel sad—all I see are Caucasian faces. I know I won't see another Mongolian face for a long time.

My friends Jon and Ann meet me at the Burlington Airport and drive me to their house, where I have left my car. I can't put my finger on it, but there is something off about the drive, as if I am still in the plane, or the road is made of soft playground material. Then

I get it—the road feels smooth and even, like riding on a cloud.

When I get to my house, I don't know what to do with all the space—even though I have a small house for an American and even though some years ago, after living with Khanda for two weeks, I turned my two upstairs rooms into an apartment. The space is just too much for one person. I don't need it. And stuff? I have been living out of two duffle bags for the past few months. What do I need all this stuff for? I am inspired to get rid of clothing, household items, and papers—anything I am not using.

My first impulse when I brush my teeth is to use the clean water from my water bottle. Then I remember I can get it from the faucet. Having clean water is a luxury. Having clean water from a faucet is more wonderful. Having hot running water—beyond belief. Heat comes from the furnace in the basement—I don't have to cut, chop, and carry wood. Electricity seldom goes out. Phone service is available everywhere, as is Internet service. Sending an e-mail takes a second, not an hour. The riotous color of fresh organic vegetables and fruit greet me at the Middlebury Natural Foods Co-op and the farmers' market. I need to take it slowly to change my diet so radically, even though I want to taste everything: corn on the cob, peaches, and red tomatoes. Friends speak my language. Quaker Meeting is peaceful. It takes three people with arms outstretched to reach around the trunk of the willow tree in my backyard. In Mongolia, it would be a sacred tree, and people would come from afar to bless it. I send it blessings.

No more Mongolian faces appear, except in photos on the walls in my home. My daughter points to them and says to a friend, "My mother's relatives." I hold the taiga and reindeer herders in my heart and when spring comes, I feel them calling me to return.

Appendix

Glossary

ail
Family group living in one settlement

aimag
Province and capital city of a province, composed of soums

aman khuur
Mouth harp

animate
See enliven

bagh
Smallest-level administrative division, section of a soum

bagh emch
Doctor for a bagh

bariach
Bonesetter or healer

baruun
West or right

chud
Short, little (distance)

deel
Mongolian traditional robe fastened with cloth knot buttons or silver buttons and loops on the right side. It is made of silk, wool, cotton, or skin with the fur inside, depending on the season. Silk or wool deels can be any bright color for women, and are often navy, black, brown, or maroon for men. Fur can be lamb's wool, sheepskin, or fur from other animals. A double layer in front is perfect for riding a horse because one side can wrap around each leg for warmth and protection. When a cummerbund, usually orange or yellow, is added, the top half forms a large pocket. A deel is useful for a herder since binoculars, baby goats, cheese, or dried meat can be easily slid in and out of the pocket, even while riding a horse. On a cold day, a parent can tuck a baby inside.

Dukha
Tyvan. Tyva is an autonomous republic north of Mongolia (see Tyva).

emch
Doctor

enliven
To make a shaman costume, paraphernalia, and drum "come alive" for use in a ceremony

folk medicine
Indigenous medicine used in the countryside by nomadic herders who do not have access to other health care. They have learned which plants with medicinal qualities grow in their area.

Folk remedies come from direct experience and include shamanic healing.

ger
round, felt tent of Mongolian nomads (yurt)

guanz
Café, often in a ger

khadagh
Prayer scarf, a long, narrow, specially made band of silk or other material for presentation on formal occasions as a gift or mark of esteem, used for welcoming and honoring people and places

khashaa
Fence around a yard or home area in a soum center or city, with a ger and/or small wooden buildings and an outhouse. Also the name for the home area inside the fence.

khengereg
Shaman's drum

khunkhinguur
Jingle cones or metal soundmakers that enliven shaman clothing and drums

manjin
Tubes of cloth one half inch to one inch in diameter, stuffed with sheep's wool, which are like snakes or whips and are part of a shaman's costume. They may hang from the costume or be connected to an aman khuur (see above).

Mongolian medicine
See traditional Mongolian medicine

naadam
Festival, usually including three sports: horseracing, archery, and wrestling

ongod
Spirit, ancestor spirit or the individual's spirit guide, mountain spirit, water spirit, land spirit, or all of the above. Ongods give guidance to shamans during a ritual or ceremony. The purpose of a ceremony is to connect with the ongods so that they can guide living people.

ovoo
Sacred cairn made of a pile of stones and other objects, usually at the top of a mountain

Sain baina uu?
Hello; literally, how are you? (Sain=good, baina=is or are, uu=question)

shaman
One who contacts ongods or spirit ancestors to restore balance to people, livestock, and land

steppe
Grassland or prairie

soum
County; also refers to county center; composed of baghs

suu
Milk

taiga
Boggy high altitude forest, area in the north of Mongolia, near Siberia

toono
The toono for a ger is a wooden top ring with eight spokes. The

roof rafters attach to the outside of this ring. The center space between the spokes is open to the sky and lets the light in. Dukhas also call the place where the poles meet that is open to the sky a toono.

traditional medicine
(see folk medicine)

Tsaatan
Reindeer people, a term used by Mongolians, but the herders themselves prefer reindeer herders, taiga people, or Dukhas

traditional Mongolian medicine (also called Mongolian traditional medicine or Mongolian medicine)
A Buddhist system of medicine similar to Tibetan medicine, which came to Mongolia in the sixteenth century and changed to include the use of medicinal plants that grow in Mongolia

tugrik or tugrig
Mongolian money; the U.S. dollar to tugrik exchange rate is different every year.

tuguu
Response an individual gives to shaman's ongods during ceremony

Tyva
Autonomous Republic of Russia

Tyvan
Person from the country of Tyva

urts
Tyvan word for Siberian tipi, reindeer herders' homes made with tall poles and covered with canvas. Formerly covered with birch bark or leather. Distinguished from the American Indian plains tipi by the absence of smoke flaps.

zakh
Black market

zuun
East or left

Names of Contacts

The many names in this book are indicative of my numerous connections there. Mongolians usually go by one name. If they need more, they go by their father's first name or his first initial. In the list below I use one name unless there is more than one person with the same name, then I use the father's (or mother's in some cases) first initial.

Altansukh (m) the name we were given for a shaman's apprentice, but his real name turned out to be Oyunerdene

Altjin (f) baby born in the movie *Gobi Women's Song*

Amgalan (m) West Taiga man

Augi (m) assistant cameraman, great horseback rider, and excellent translator

BG (f) daughter of Ganzorig

Baasankhuu (m) adopted son of Gosta whose wife is Narantuya

Badma (f) translator in 2004

J. Bat (m) friend and excellent carver in East Taiga

Batbayar Sumkhuu (Bayara) (m) sensitive video cameraman from Ulaanbaatar

Batjargal (m) university student from the taiga who received scholarships from our program, graduating in 2011

Battulga (m) Dukha guide who led my horse and arranged shaman meetings, 2003–2010

Battummur (m) son of Khanda

Bayandalai (m) and **Tsetsegmaa** (f) elders of one of the West Taiga settlements

Binde (f) translator in 2004

Boldsaikhan (m) my traditional Mongolian medicine teacher, a doctor in Ulaanbaatar

Buyantogtokh (m) bagh chief, government official in charge of the area of the county where the taiga people live

Byara (m) veterinarian who lives in Tsagaan Nuur

Chinggis Khan Genghis Khan

Chuluu G. (f) and **Sanjim** (m) elder couple, leaders of one West Taiga settlement

Dalai (m), **Bolortsetseg** (f), and **Saran** (daughter) young family in West Taiga. Dalai is the son of elder Ulzii and became our horse guide during a July snow in 2006.

Dan Plumley (m) director of Totem Peoples Project and excursion leader of the 2003 and 2004 trips to the taiga

Davaa (f) interpreter in 2006, sister of Zula

Davaajav Shaman (m) shaman in steppe area between the East Taiga and Tsagaan Nuur

Davaajav G. (m) and **Gantuya** (f), **Mama** (daughter), and **Batbayar D.** (son) family of the East Taiga who hosted our team in 2006

Davkha (m) younger relative of Big Puji and Little Puji, driver in 2007 and 2010

Enkhe (m) Mongolian director of the American Center for Mongolian Studies in Ulaanbaatar

Eric Chaikin (m) American filmmaker who traveled to the East Taiga in 2006

Erdenbat (m) Mongolian Minister of Electric and Power

Fred Thodal (m) computer expert and photographer/videographer who traveled to the East Taiga in 2009

Ganaa (f) friend in Murun

Ganba (m) and **Nyama** (f) couple, owners with **Anukha** (f) of guesthouse in Tsagaan Nuur

N. Ganbat (m) and **P. Ganbat** (f) couple with six children who live in the farthest settlement of the East Taiga

S. Ganbat (m) and **Pruvie** (f) couple who live in East Taiga closest settlement, invited us to conduct health database assessments in their home

Ganzorig (m) shaman and younger brother of Gosta; lives in Gosta's settlement in the West Taiga, married to **Erdenchimeg** (f)

Gerelt (f) East Taiga mother of five children

Gombo (m) and **Tsendelii** (f) older couple in East Taiga

Gosta (m) shaman in the West Taiga; "Uncle" to Khanda, with (or near) whose family we lived in 2006, 2007, 2008

Joost (m) cameraman in 2010, when he was engaged to Khongoroo. They are married now.

Khaliuna (f) young woman in Ulaanbaatar who translated for me when I made a movie in South Gobi in 2001

Khalzan (m) shaman, son of Chuluu G. and Sanjim

Khanda (f) our host in 2006, 2007, 2008

Khongoroo (f) assistant and translator 2007–2010

Lkhagva (m) horse owner and guide, also known as "Mr. Lovely"

Lucy McKeon (f) doctor on our team in 2010

Magsar (m) a bariach (bone healer), nephew of Gosta

Mende (m) cameraman in 2003, 2004, 2006

Mungunshagai (m) East Taiga man, exquisite carver

Munkhjin (f) dear friend who attended college in my town and invited me to live in her apartment in Ulaanbaatar for three visits

Munkhuu (f) East Taiga mother of Solongo, who has Sas reindeer

Nansalmaa (f) Mongolian state veterinarian who works closely with the reindeer of the taiga and the Totem Peoples Project

Naraa (f) translator for Dr. McKeon in 2010

Naran (f) and **Saran** (f) daughters of Pruvie and S. Ganbat who attend university

Nergui (m) shaman who lives in steppe land near Tsagaan Nuur

Olzii (f) elder of one of the West Taiga settlements

Omban Munkhuu (m) steppe shaman who lives on the way to the East Taiga

Orchirbat (m) and **Munkhtsetseg** (f) couple; he is an excellent carver and she an excellent seamstress, daughter of Tsend

Oyunbadam (f) teacher of Tyvan language in Tsagaan Nuur School

Puji (Big) (m) driver 2003, 2004

Puji (Little) (m) driver 2006, 2008, 2009, 2010

Punsil (f) elder of the East Taiga farthest settlement

Sainbayar (f) East Taiga student who had appendicitis

Saintsetseg (f) shaman in training

Sanjaa (m) nephew of Soyan

Sharkhuu (f) and **Khurelgaldan** (m) parents of student Batjargal; Sharkhuu is an excellent singer

Sodoo (f) cousin of Munkhjin

Solongo (f) young East Taiga woman to whom we gave a university scholarship

Soyan (f) West Taiga shaman who lived to be 100 years old

Tsend (f) shaman of the East Taiga, daughter of Soyan

Tsermaa (f) wife of Dan Plumley, interpreter in 2003 and 2004

Tsetsegmaa (f) West Taiga herder

Tsogkhuu (m) host to our team in 2003 and 2004 in the East Taiga

Tsogoo (m) driver in Tsagaan Nuur

Tsogtsaikhan (m) friend of the taiga, Taiga Nature NGO director; lives in Ulaanbaatar

Tummurtsogt (m) Khatgal resident working at the Khovsgol Museum

Tuvshin (f) and **Taivan** (m) young married couple of the East Taiga

Ulzii (m) and **Tunga** (f) and **Enkhbayar** (daughter) new family in the West Taiga

Yura (f) and **Gurbazar** (m) couple in Ulaan Uul steppe land; she is a shaman and he is a friend of the taiga people.

Zorig (m) and **Otgonbayar** (f) kind hosts in 2004

Zula (f) translator in 2003

Issues That Affect the Cultural Survival of the Dukhas

(As told to Dan Plumley of Totem Peoples Preservation Project by the Dukhas in 2002)

- Health and success of reindeer herd
- Native rights and Mongolian law that preserves identity
- Education and youth, including a Tyvan language course at school
- Transportation and remoteness
- Equitable opportunities for economic advancement and jobs
- Medical needs and access to modern and traditional medicine
- Self-representation

Reasons for Alcohol Abuse in Mongolia

(As told to me by Sean Armstrong, BSN, MPH, and printed in *Asian Pacific Journal of Public Health*, July 2010)

1. History of a colonial approach (primarily via China) that exploited alcohol and fostered a culture of misuse
2. A very weak set of policies that allows access to alcohol as easy as that in any country in the world
3. A very poor understanding of alcohol abuse and prevention (no involvement of public health in management)
4. Potential genetic background that makes alcohol an especially effective drug for Mongolians
5. A very strong stigma against "alcoholics"

Websites

Support

If you would like to help support the Dukhas, you can donate to Nomadicare or the Totem Peoples Project. Both are under the umbrella of Ecologia.

Ecologia's Virtual Foundation is a unique philanthropy program that supports grassroots initiatives around the world. Nomadicare and the Totem Peoples Project are both non-profit programs under the fiscal care of Ecologia.

Ecologia's Virtual Foundation: www.virtualfoundation.org and www.ecologia.org

Nomadicare: www.nomadicare.org
Nomadicare works to harmonize modern and traditional medicine for the health and cultural survival of Mongolia's nomads.

Totem Peoples Project: www.totempeoples.org
The Totem Peoples Project is an international non-profit initiative dedicated to supporting the sustainability of indigenous nomadic cultures, their totem livestock, and their ecological habitats in eastern Siberia and Mongolia.

Travel

If you would like to visit Mongolia, I recommend two excellent expedition companies that have been working in Mongolia for decades:

Boojum Expeditions: www.boojum.com
Nomadic Expeditions: www.nomadicexpeditions.com

Bibliography

Print

Armstrong, Sean and Byamba Tsogtbaatar. "The Dual Nature of Alcohol Use and Abuse in Mongolia: Reflections Through Policy." *Asian Pacific Journal of Public Health*, July 2010.

Avery, Martha. *Women of Mongolia*. Boulder: Asian Art and Archaeology, 1996.

Baabgai, Ch. and B. Boldsaikhan, Монголын Уламжлалт Анагаах Ухаан [Mongolian traditional medicine] (in Mongolian). Ulaanbaatar: State Publishing House, 1990.

Basilov, Vladimir N. (ed.). *Nomads of Eurasia* (trans. by Mary Fleming Zirin). Los Angeles: Natural History Museum of Los

Angeles County of Sciences of the USSR, 1989.

Clark, Barry. *The Quintessence Tantras of Tibetan Medicine.* Ithaca: Snow Lion Publications, 1995.

Donahoe, Brian. "'Hey, You! Get Offa My Taiga!': Comparing the Sense of Property Rights Among the Tofa and Tozhu-Tyva." Max Planck Institute for Social Anthropology, Working Paper #38, 2002.

Endicott, Elizabeth. *Pages from the Past: The 1910 Moscow Trade Expedition to Mongolia.* Norwalk, CT: EastBridge, 2007.

———. "The Persistence of Pastoral Nomadism," in Ts. Ishdorzh (ed.), *Essays on Mongol Studies.* Ulaanbaatar: Olon Ulsyn Mongol Sudlalyn Khovloo, 2005.

———. "The Mongols and China: Cultural Contacts and the Changing Nature of Pastoral Nomadism (Twelfth to Early Twentieth Centuries)," in Reuven Amitai and Michael Biran (eds), *Mongols, Turks, and Others: Eurasian Nomads and the Sedentary World.* Leiden: Brill, 2005.

Fardelmann, Charlotte Lyman. *Nudged by the Spirit: Stories of Responding to the Still, Small Voice of God.* Wallingford, PA: Pendle Hill Publications, 2001.

Geniesse, Jane Fletcher. *Passionate Nomad: The Life of Freya Stark.* New York: Modern Library, 2001.

Isaacson, Rupert. *The Horse Boy.* New York: Little, Brown & Co., 2009.

Kahn, Paul (adaptation). *The Secret History of the Mongols: The Origin of Chingis Khan.* Boston: Cheng & Tsui Company, 1998.

Lawless, Jill. Wild East: *Travels in New Mongolia.* Toronto: ECW Press, 2000.

Metternich, Hillary Roe. *Mongolian Folktales.* Boulder: Avery Press, 1996.

Mortenson, Greg and David Oliver Relin. *Three Cups of Tea: One Man's Mission to Promote Peace...One School at a Time.* New York: Penguin Group, 2006.

Parfionovitch, Yuri, Fernand Meyer, and Gyurme Dorje. *Tibetan Medical Paintings: Illustrations to the Blue Beryl Treatise of Sangye Gyamtso (1653–1705)*. New York: Harry N. Abrams, 1992.

Sarangerel. *Riding Windhorses: A Journey into the Heart of Mongolian Shamanism*. Rochester, VT: Destiny Books, 2000.

Tracz, Virlana, Sayan Zhambalov, and Wanda Phipps. *Shanar: Dedication Ritual of a Buryat Shaman in Siberia as conducted by Bayir Rinchinov*. New York: Parabola Books, 2002.

Tschinag, Galsan. *The Blue Sky*. Minneapolis: Milkweed Editions, 2006.

Vitebsky, Piers. *The Reindeer People: Living with Animals and Spirits in Siberia*. New York: Houghton Mifflin Company, 2005.

Waugh, Louisa. *Hearing Birds Fly*. London: Abacus, 2003.

Wulsin, Janet Elliot. *Vanished Kingdoms*. New York: Aperture Foundation Inc., 2005.

Film

Cave of the Yellow Dog. Byambasuren Davaa, director. Tartan Video, 2005.

Gobi Women's Song. Sas Carey, director. LET Pictures, 2006.

The Horse Boy. Michael O. Scott, director. Zeitgeist Films, 2009.

Kiran over Mongolia. Joseph Spaid, director. Bulk Films, 2005.

Steppe Herbs, Mare's Milk and Jelly Jars: A Journey to Mongolian Medicine. Sas Carey, director. LET Pictures, 1996.

Taiga Heart Song. Sas Carey, director. LET Pictures, 2007.

The Weeping Camel. Byambasuren Davaa and Luigi Falorni, directors. ThinkFilm, Inc., 2003.

Acknowledgments

Thank you. Euan Bear encouraged me with gentle feedback on my early writing. Bette Moffett suggested that I join Marjory Cady's writing group in the basement of the Ilsley Library in 1997. Marjory and the writers there listened to my stories about Mongolia every week for many years.

Eleanor Ott read 500 pages of my stories and told me I had something here—and let me read the reindeer herder stories out loud to her when we got snowed in at her house for three days. Donald Gibson, a literary agent, gave me confidence that the stories could actually become a book. Jean Arrowsmith, Cheryl Mitchell, Deborah Diemand, David Weinstock, and my daughter, Jasmine Carey, read early drafts, corrected grammar, and pointed out unclear sections. Deborah suggested that the second half of my story, which became this book about the reindeer herders, had "more of a narrative arc" than the stories of my earlier experiences in Mongolia; these will become my next book.

Elizabeth Endicott, Saruul Erdene, and Narantsetseg Tseveendulam checked the Glossary. The first time I thought the book might be approaching completion, Bob Granner and Lou Megyesi gave suggestions, asked questions, and made comments. Louise Watson edited and Winslow Colwell created the design and transformed the manuscript into a book. I am extremely grateful to all of you!

Thanks to everyone who has donated to my work in Mongolia and to Nomadicare, including The Shelley & Donald Rubin Foundation, the Mongol-American Cultural Association, the Vermont Community Foundation, Neat Repeats, Quakers, especially Middlebury Friends Meeting, and many, many generous individuals. Without you there would be no stories.

About the Author

Sas Carey is a registered nurse, healer, educator, writer, and filmmaker. Following her first trip to Mongolia in 1994, she founded and now directs the Life Energy Healing School, which trains students in the art of energy healing, and Nomadicare (nomadicare.org), which provides improved health care options for Mongolia's nomadic herders. Her work has been supported by The Shelley & Donald Rubin Foundation, the Vermont Council on the Arts, the National Endowment for the Arts, the Vermont Community Foundation, and the Mongol-American Cultural Association, as well as individual donors.

Sas is the director of three movies about Mongolia: *Gobi Women's Song*, *Taiga Heart Song*, and *Steppe Herbs, Mare's Milk and Jelly Jars: A Journey to Mongolian Medicine*. These films have screened in Mongolia and the United States at libraries, universities, and museums. Sas has worked as a health education consultant for the Mongolian office of the United Nations Development Programme. A Quaker, she lives in a brick cottage beside an immense willow tree in Vermont and, when not in Mongolia, spends her spare time swimming, kayaking, knitting, and visiting with her children and twin grandsons.

Sas Carey in Ulaanbaatar, Mongolia in 2012.

photo credit: Jonah Kessel

CPSIA information can be obtained at www.ICGtesting.com
Printed in the USA
BVOW041901261112

306505BV00002B/8/P